doing it different

doing it different

LESSONS FOR THE IMAGINATIVE MANAGER

DAVID CLUTTERBUCK
with **SUE KERNAGHAN**

and research by Des Dearlove and Steve Coomber

ORION
BUSINESS
BOOKS

First published in Great Britain in 1999 by
Orion Business
An imprint of The Orion Publishing Group Ltd
Orion House, 5 Upper St Martin's Lane, London WC2H 9EA

A CIP catalogue record for this book is available from the British Library.

ISBN 0-75281-380-3

Typeset by Deltatype Ltd, Birkenhead, Merseyside
Printed and bound in Great Britain by
Creative Print & Design, Ebbw Vale, Wales

Contents

Introduction

This is a book of multiple contradictions. It is about organisations which – according to the prevailing wisdom of the day – couldn't and shouldn't work, yet which frequently outperform their competitors. It is a book that celebrates the value of doing things differently, of *being* different. Yet it seeks to identify the common factors behind how these companies create and sustain their differences. It holds the promise that your business, too, could succeed by taking a radical approach that makes it stand out as truly different. Yet if our message is widely received and understood, and the world is flooded with businesses that have genuine personality and which stand out as different, would being different be such a competitive edge? If the normal, staid boring organisation most people work for suddenly became the abnormal minority, would that become a new secret of success?

Fortunately, the experience of the companies in this book suggest that few companies ever achieve the depth of idiosyncrasy, apparently unjustifiable self-belief and sheer wackiness that characterises the company that is truly different. When others attempt to copy, they almost invariably fail – as a major international airline reportedly did when it persuaded cabin crew to adopt a Southwest Airlines-style humour in the aisles: the experiment apparently went down like a lead balloon, because it was *out of character*. And character is what all the companies in this book have. They do not conform because they see no reason to do so, and because it is more important to them to be themselves than to copy someone else. Their difference is a matter of substance and belief, not simply a matter of style.

The probability, then, is that reading this book, while it may entertain you, will do you absolutely no good at all. Unless, that is, you:

- have a strong belief about how a company *should* be run, and which runs contrary to what people around you say

- are prepared to do it your way no matter what they say and no matter what obstacles get in the way
- perceive profit as a by-product, not an end in itself
- recognise that, whatever the exterior you show to the world, deep down you are pretty wacky yourself
- are prepared to merge your identity with your creation and accept the consequences.

Whether you read on as a voyeur, or as the potential creator of another unique, character-ful business, you'll see these themes echoed time and again.

Our exploration of the world's wackiest companies begins with an overview of the strange phenomenon of the wacky company. Making profit, almost in spite of itself, it thrives against odds and often against logic. The success criteria that drive other businesses, such as market share or growth, aren't very important to these companies – they have their own criteria for measuring success and are not particularly concerned what the rest of the world thinks. The lessons we draw from their experience are:

- If it's worth doing, it's worth doing differently.
- Profit isn't the goal; it's a by-product.
- The worst markets are often the most fertile ground to build a business.

Where does the difference come from? In Chapter 2 we see that, in every case, it comes from a radically different philosophy, espoused by the founders and subsequently by those that join them. These companies are without exception values driven. The lessons include:

- A philosophy is what creates differentiating values.
- A philosophy is hard to copy (so competitors take much longer to catch up).
- Employees and values are more important than customers and systems.

Chapter 3 looks at the structure of wacky companies and

concludes that structure is a by-product of philosophy. The organisation shapes we observe include the amoeba, the blueberry pancake, the boundariless, the chemical soup, the star, the virtual and the collapsed sphere. They have in common greater flexibility, empowerability and general feistiness than the traditional pyramid organisation, however many or few layers they have. Our key lessons are:

- Structure follows philosophy.
- Flexibility and initiative are more important than systems or rules.
- Keep it simple, keep it small, cut the crap.
- There's no limit to the organisational shapes you can choose from.

Chapter 4 shows that being different gives companies and their employees more of a licence to have fun. If you are expected to be a bit odd, why not be a lot odd? Wacky companies and their leaders spend a great deal of time thinking about how to make employees want to come to work and how to make customers want to do business with them. Fun is a critical element in both cases. It helps lighten up the environment, stimulate creativity and it's worth a great deal in terms of advertising spend. Some lessons are:

- People are a lot more likely to commit to your business if they expect to have fun — and that applies to both customers and employees.
- Fun starts at the top — boring leaders create boring environments.
- Craziness makes more and better headlines than sanity. Why pay for promotions and advertising when you can get it for free?
- Fun works better when you work at it. The more effort people put into having fun, the more they and the company get out if it.

Our fifth chapter explores the opposite side of wacky companies. Beneath the flexible, humorous exterior is a hard underside. These businesses are run on discipline at the core. The difference is that the philosophy and values provide such a strong framework of control that managers spend very little time motivating or coercing people to do things and are free to concentrate on the disciplines that matter. Wacky companies typically have a better handle on costs and margins than their systems-driven, traditional competitors. They typically have lower debt, higher quality, higher productivity and lower costs than the competition. Among the lessons we learned are:

- Enforcement is everybody's business (not just managers').
- It's better to discipline your customers than your employees.
- Never, never be beholden to a bank.

Wacky companies are invariably the creation of wacky leaders, who we look at in Chapter 6. In almost all cases, these people are the misfits of the business world. They include very few business school graduates and those who did come from the business world used their experience there as a guide to what not to do in their own organisations. They have a tremendous amount of self-belief and a capacity to infect others with their values. Their style of leadership is both inclusive and enabling, being based on a mixture of intuitive wisdom and personal beliefs/values, as opposed to received wisdom and corporate vision and values. They are, in short, as wacky or wackier than the companies they lead.

While this is a great strength for the organisation, it is also a potential weakness. Many wacky leaders find it very hard to know when to hand over the reins. Studying wacky leaders teaches us:

- Differentiating values are learned outside the business world – and certainly not at business school.
- The main value of benchmarking against competitors is to learn how not to do things.
- Be a role model for inspiring values – never ask any employee to do anything you're not prepared to do yourself.
- Letting go is the hardest bit – the true test of how well the values have marinated into the organisation.

The impact of wacky leadership is more often than not a culture of pride in the organisation, as we see in Chapter 7. Employees are proud to identify with the organisation's values, proud to be part of a success story, from being part of a bold experiment. They respond, in particular, to a mixture of ownership, respect, responsibility, trust, sense of belonging, security, information and the freedom to be themselves. From this, we learn that:

- Pride is what makes employees go the extra mile.
- Pride comes from feeling valued.
- Pride comes from *sharing* values – when the company, the employees and the customers all espouse the same beliefs about what counts.
- Track record is less important in hiring decisions than values fit.

Pride helps build the self-confidence to take steps into the unknown. We call it 'walking round corners backwards' (Chapter 8). Wacky companies innovate successfully in areas other companies have learned to avoid – somehow their innocence and naiveté is a powerful tool. They do things differently because no one has told them they can't. They have a remarkable combination of high self-belief and high optimistic curiosity that sweeps obstacles aside. And they encourage people to think outside the box by creating dynamic, stimulating physical environments. Among the lessons we have drawn are:

- Many of the most useful innovations occur because people didn't know it couldn't be done.
- Different principles generate different approaches.
- A spirit of adventure combined with clarity of values is what stimulates original solutions.
- Who can innovate in an unstimulating environment?

Establishing a radically different company is in some ways the easy bit. Maintaining the difference is much more difficult. This is the subject of Chapter 9. There is always a pressure – especially from outside – to conform, to 'professionalise', to rejoin the 'real' world.

New management, over-rapid growth, international expansion and hard times all carry the potential to blunt the edge of difference, reducing deeply held philosophies to ciphers.

And at some point, the difference will diminish, as society's values change to bring them more in line with those of the wacky company. The great wacky companies of their time – Cadbury, Levi's and others – have played their part in changing society and have largely been absorbed into the background of normality. (Yet, in most cases, even after many decades, there is often something about these companies that sets them apart as a place to work in.)

Maturing is inevitable, but the experience of wacky companies suggests that:

- Professional managers always want to 'cure' the wacky company – they recognise no sanity but their own.
- Rapid growth attracts professional managers, so it pays to find ways of keeping them out.
- Accept gracefully that society and the business community will eventually catch up; be flattered by it.
- It's easier for competitors to catch up if you allow your principles to be diluted. Wacky company leaders spend a great deal of their time fighting 'normalisation'.

In the last chapter we address the issue of how to create a seriously different company. It's a lot easier to start from scratch, but traditional companies can be changed. (Almost invariably, a lot of people will leave, one way or another, because they cannot align themselves with the new values.) The starting point, in both cases, is to really care; to care enough about the way business is conducted to insist on doing it your way. It's also important to ensure that the differences you have in mind are sufficiently numerous and deep-rooted to affect people at both the intellectual and gut level – genuine fundamental beliefs rather than marketing gimmicks. Then all that's needed are boundless energy, an indomitable spirit, a thick skin impervious to taunts and disbelief, a strong sense of fun, and a reasonable dose of good luck. And a willingness to become the living embodiment of the values you want others to follow.

In the end, of course, there is no simple formula to follow. The companies that you'll read about in this book have established their own differences in their own ways. Where they have come up with the same idea, it is usually independently. One thing they certainly don't have is any shortage of ideas! Where they adapt from elsewhere, they do so with their own unique spin and character. We refer to them frequently as wacky, because that is how they are so often described. But as Chapter 1 explains, there's method in their madness.

It pays to be different

'Every time we've done the right thing, it's ended up making us more money.' (Patagonia founder, Yvon Chouinard)[1]

'Remember, nobody loves you, or your money, more than Southwest Airlines.' (Southwest Airlines in-flight announcement)

In a depressed area of northern Italy, 700 people lived and worked in complete secrecy, in a labyrinth of temples buried 40 metres inside a mountain. The group, calling themselves the Damanhurian community, excavated their five-storey, five-chamber underground home with hammers and pick axes, and carried out their work there for 15 years before coming to the attention of the Italian tax authorities in 1992.

The Damanhurians paid up — they could afford it. Between studying and worshipping, the community runs about 40 successful businesses. These include a gourmet food exporter that sells to such top retailers as London's food emporium Fortnum & Mason, a fabric company that makes goods for Europe's leading fashion houses, and a glass works said to be one of the busiest and most profitable in Italy.

The Damanhurians are an extreme example of what fascinates us about wacky companies. It's not just their bizarre behaviour (there's no shortage of that in this world). Rather, it's the way that, even when operating underground like troglodytes, they so often seem to come out on top.

The more odd-ball companies we study, the more we see this pattern. Companies that delight in overturning accepted procedures, that challenge beliefs that other companies with longer pedigrees cherish deeply, appear, remarkably, to win — time and time again.

The stranger the company, it seems, the greater its ability to beat the odds. And they beat the odds not just in good times, but also in industries and under economic conditions that no sensible organisation would expect to thrive in.

These companies – or, more precisely, the people running them – succeed in the face of tough economic conditions, declining markets, unscrupulous competitors and their own inexperience.

Are they even trying?

What makes these organisations especially galling to competitors, who work on business school principles, with all the paraphernalia of strategic planning, business systems and organisation charts, is the way some of these companies grow fast and rake in the profits while looking as if they're not even trying. Some make fortunes with seemingly minimal effort and have little to say for themselves but 'oops'.

For example, Steve Outtrim, an unemployed, 22-year-old New Zealander living in Melbourne, posted a note on the Internet in June 1995 asking if anyone would like to try a little Web page tool he'd designed. Outtrim never intended to launch a commercial product but, within a year, found himself in charge of a staff of 22 people, with sales of five million Australian dollars and a pre-tax profit of A\$1.5 million. By 1997, Sausage Software was a public company trading on the Australian Stock Exchange, and Outtrim was sitting on a personal wealth of about \$90 million.[2]

Outtrim didn't much mind about the money, but Yvon Chouinard, the founder of the \$159 million US outdoor gear manufacturer Patagonia, goes even further. He reportedly can't stand the sight of the stuff. Steve Peterson, a former Patagonia financial manager said that Chouinard once likened financial dealing to 'getting doo-doo on your hand', and has often expressed disdain for material goods, money and even customers.[3]

The Vancouver, Canada based Mountain Equipment Co-op (MEC) isn't exactly disdainful of money: it's just not allowed to make any. Launched in the late seventies by a group of university students wanting access to affordable outdoor equipment, MEC is organised as a co-operative, so any profits must be distributed to its members (who are also customers). MEC doesn't advertise, and it gives away any money it doesn't reinvest, but somehow – with annual sales of 115 million Canadian dollars and locations in most major cities –

MEC seems to be making more money than its profit-oriented competitors. In fact, they look to the co-op as a market leader, and scramble to secure retail sites within the MEC orbit.

The secret to profit, suggests MEC president William Gibson, is to not think about it too much: 'If you focus on providing service, you will make a profit. If you focus on making a profit, you'll go out of business.'[4]

A lot of wacky companies are unlikely, even accidental, successes.

In 1985, Canadian musician Nicholas Graham retired from the San Francisco punk rock circuit to design silly underwear. Claiming he chose the business because he 'needed some underwear', Graham had minimal garment industry or business experience and was completely unconcerned about details like demographics and target marketing. He aimed his wacko designs at anyone with enough of a sense of humour to wear them. Sales, after just three years in business, hit $2 million and, according to Graham, have increased by 70 per cent every year since.[5]

WOW Toys founder Ednan-Laperouse has no formal business training, has never written a business plan, and never intends to. He started his three million pound toy company with a blank sketch pad and an 80p plastic template for drawing circles. He and his team of young art school graduates saw the direction that toy marketing was headed and chose precisely the opposite route. Where the big toy makers marketed directly to children with hi-tech gadgets and media tie-ins like Teletubbies, WOW made toys that parents would actually like their children to have. 'We aim our educational toys at parents, not the child,' he says. 'They want their children to have worthwhile toys to help their development. Parents do not actually want their children to buy Power Rangers or Tamagotchis. This is children's pester power at work. We are anti-pester power.'

Anti-pester works. By the end of its first year, the self-financing shoe-string operation was selling two million dollars worth of toys through the most prestigious retailers in nine countries. The company looks well set to meet its goal of £12 million in sales by the turn of the century.

In 1978, Ben Cohen and Jerry Greenfield knew as much about making ice cream as you can learn from a five-dollar correspondence course. They borrowed a business plan from a pizza place, and rumour has it they weren't too sure how to balance a chequebook. They sold whatever flavours they liked and, by 1996, headed a public company with annual sales over $167 million.

All these entrepreneurs benefited to some extent from being in the right place at the right time. The late eighties were boom times and the public was hungry for novelty. Cohen, Greenfield, Graham, Ednan-Laperouse and others like them weren't business people; they were regular guys. Their off-beat methods, outrageous PR stunts and rebellious image appealed to a mild rebellious streak in consumers – especially those who'd grown up in the sixties and now had some money in their pockets. (The antics of right-wing business rebels such as Ross Perot also struck a chord, but with a completely different constituency.) To some extent, the success of these companies says as much about the consumer desires as it does about the long-term benefits of being strange.

Even in multicultural Europe, there was ample room for businesses which were radically different in their philosophy. IKEA, Benetton and Body Shop are among the most commonly known, but they are only the tip of an iceberg.

Riding the bad times

The intriguing thing about wacky companies, though, is that while they outperform their competitors in good times, they also do extraordinarily well when times are bad.

Some of our wacky companies saw their best years while navigating through tough, depressed, even chaotic, economic conditions.

Ricardo Semler, CEO of Brazil's Semco, is widely known as the most outrageous change artist in the New World. His unorthodox management techniques, like tearing up the rulebook and putting employees in charge of most decisions, helped keep his company growing and profitable during some of the worst economic conditions imaginable.

From 1986 to 1990, the São Paolo government came up with five different economic plans, while inflation fluctuated from 100 per cent to 1,600 per cent. In 1990, the Brazilian finance ministry instituted severe austerity measures and reduced the money supply by 80 per cent overnight.

In spite of this, Semco continued to grow at the fastest rate of any Brazilian company – several years during this period its sales grew by more than 80 per cent in real terms. Since 1990, it's shown a seven-fold increase in productivity and a five-fold increase in profits. In 1997, the company boasted a turnover of some £30 million.

Semler's success suggests that, somehow, internal chaos can give an organisation the flexibility it needs to deal with a chaotic outer world.

It worked in Denmark. A recession there in the early nineties would surely have spelled the end of hearing-aid manufacturer Oticon had its board not had the foresight, in 1988, to hire Lars Kolind, the self-styled king of chaos, as CEO. Founded in 1904, and a market leader for most of the century, Oticon was, by 1987, losing both market share and money. By the time the recession hit, Kolind had already worked his particular brand of magic. He'd dismantled the organisation, got rid of the office hierarchy, and even the furniture, and returned the company to profitability.

Between 1990 and 1995, during its industry's toughest ever trading period, while competitors struggled to stay in business, Oticon saw an increase of more than 100 per cent in revenue and a ten-fold increase in operating profits. In 1995, the company posted revenues of $160 million and operating profits of $20 million.

The same recession affected businesses all over Northern Europe, yet Finnish entrepreneur Liisa Joronen launched her super-empowered, no-hierarchy cleaning company SOL in 1992, during the worst recession to hit Finland since World War II. Her business not only survived, it also made a profit while competitors were struggling to stay in business at all. By 1997, SOL had doubled its customer base and increased sales revenue by 70 per cent. The figures for 1997 show revenues of $60 million and growth of more than 20 per cent annually.

None of these leaders had much choice but to fight the odds – they were working under the same tough economic conditions that affected every enterprise in their regions.

What's more interesting, from a psychological point of view, are the leaders whose thirst for challenge – or masochistic streak –

inspired them to start businesses in declining, overcrowded, low margin industries or in highly competitive ones dominated by a few big players not known for their sympathy to newcomers.

Many, like Satoshi Sakurada, did it with pocket change – and broke all the rules while they were at it. In 1972, just as both McDonald's and Burger King were aggressively expanding into Japan, Sakurada, a young Japanese salaryman who'd tried his first burger while working in his employer's Los Angeles office, quit his job and set up a fast food business. Using the capital he'd raised from friends in a single evening, he set up the kind of burger bar that would appeal to Japanese tastes – instead of bacon burgers and fries, he had customers lining up for such specially designed goodies as Nan Curry Dogs and Burdock-Root Rice Burgers.

From the start, Sakurada planned to compete on a grand scale – but in his own way. 'Most food service companies in Japan at the time were small, but we felt strongly that the business would grow and eventually comprise a large market,' he said.[6]

He was right – burgers did get to be a big deal in Japan, and MOS became a big part of the market. MOS was an immediate hit, even against the aggressively expanding McDonald's, and soon established itself as the fastest growing fast food chain in Japan (a position it held until McDonald's began an even tougher expansion campaign in 1997).

Between 1986 and 1990, sales at MOS quadrupled to $172 million, while net earnings reached $10 million.

MOS's 1997 annual report reveals a net income of $24 million on sales of US $469 million, despite McDonald's heavy marketing clout, and a major recession in Japan. MOS now has a chain of over 1,500 restaurants in Japan, and franchise outlets in Singapore, Taiwan and the People's Republic of China. In 1989, MOS invaded the burger bastion itself, opening a burger restaurant in Hawaii and a subsidiary in Delaware.

Sakurada and his team succeeded against the big multinationals not by trying to copy their strategy, but by working very hard to do just the opposite. McDonald's expanded into Japan in the manner of a 100-ton elephant – with high profile locations, heavy TV advertising and fast, cheap food. MOS, by contrast, took a more gentle approach, choosing obscure side street locations – partly to save money, but also because the best Japanese restaurants are traditionally in out of the way places – no TV advertising and no pre-cooked foods. Breaking rule number one in a fast food outlet, MOS makes its customers wait for freshly cooked food. And the customers are happy to do so – for two years running (1996 and 1997) MOS was ranked first in the Nikkei restaurant poll of best-loved Tokyo eateries.

Almost 30 years on, MOS is still running head to head with McDonald's, which reportedly has plans to grow from 2,000 Japanese outlets to 10,000 by 2007 – a threat that has prompted others, though not MOS, to get out of the burger business altogether.[7]

'If you're thinking of doing something in the fast-food industry, it's not a good idea to go with hamburgers,' said Kuniyoshi Akima, general sales manager of Dairy Queen, which has decided to replace hamburgers with pitta sandwiches on the menu at its one hundred Japanese stores because of competition from McDonald's.[8]

People at MOS aren't worried, though. Says MOS board member Masumi Saito: 'We are like the Honda of the fast food business. Toyota leads Nissan and Burger King follows McDonald's, but MOS Burger is always trying to find a different road.'[9]

Following that different road (though, of course, the road is different for each) is what gives wacky companies the confidence to stroll through aggressive competition, declining markets, thin margins and generally uncomfortable market conditions.

The American grocery industry, for example, always seems to get the trolley with the wobbly wheel. Way down at the unfashionable end of retailing, US grocery stores have long suffered from thin margins, dull marketing and chronic labour unrest.

One store, though, has – again, by breaking all the rules – thrived even in this environment. The Whole Foods chain, where employees rule and everyone's salary is posted for all to see, has 43 stores in ten states, revenues of $500 million, profit margins about 50 per cent higher than the industry average, and a return to shareholders of about 23 per cent annually.

Thin margins are also the rule in Australian music retailing. The market there has been declining since early 1997, and most chains have been forced to deeply discount their wares. One major chain has even gone bankrupt, while the others struggle to maintain a margin. One, the market leader, doesn't discount at all. Australian music fans would rather pay full price at a new chain called Sanity than get an identical CD for 20 per cent less anywhere else.

Sanity, whose founder, Brett Blundy, thought the name 'Insanity' too humdrum, charges full price for new releases, rarely advertises (so customers can feel they've discovered it for themselves), and sets up shops in towns its competitors find too small. The shops, designed like streetscapes to appeal to the latest teen zeitgeist, are bizarre enough to make anyone over 30 feel like an anthropologist, but for rock and roll fans in places like Warrnambool, Victoria, Sanity is the epitome of cool.

Founded in 1992, Sanity became the largest music retailer in Australia in just six years. By 1998, it had 133 stores and a 16 per cent market share – seven more than its closest rival, K Mart. And, while volume in the Australian music industry declined by 8 per cent in the first quarter of 1998, Sanity's sales (not even counting those from its new stores) were up by 7 per cent. The company's $1.50 shares opened at $2.10 in December 1997 and reached $2.50 by May 1998. The success of the float makes Blundy one of Australia's richest entrepreneurs, with an estimated net worth of AU$200 million.[10]

Those wacky leaders who really want a challenge, though, flock to the most notorious loss-making sector, such as airlines. Virgin CEO, Richard Branson, probably the richest working man in the UK, was once asked how to become a millionaire. His response: 'Start with a billion and buy an airline.' It worked for him. While the professionally managed Pan Am, Eastern and TWA all folded in the early nineties, Branson, who'd boned up on the airline industry in just 18 months, made money. In 1996, the Virgin Travel Group made £84 million ($142 million) in profit.

Against the odds

The American domestic airline industry is even more littered with wreckage. Since deregulation in 1978, when airlines were first allowed to compete freely, 120 American airlines have gone bankrupt. The industry as a whole lost $12.8 billion during a 1990–94 US recession.

Meanwhile, Southwest Airlines, an odd-ball little domestic carrier with low fares, good wages, ad-libbed safety announcements, and a CEO who sorts out legal disputes by arm-wrestling, has gone on to be the most profitable airline in the US, if not the world. Southwest consistently leads customer service and safety polls and has beaten every productivity measure in the industry. In 1996/97, the airline saw income jump by 53 per cent on sales that grew just 12 per cent. Southwest's stock price (traded under the NYSE symbol LUV) has jumped 300 per cent since 1990. Airlines typically trade at ten times earnings; Southwest has generally traded at 20 times earnings.[11]

An infusion of wackiness has a way of helping those least likely to succeed. In 1996, 128-year-old UK life insurance company Pearl Assurance looked doomed. Pension regulators were pursuing the company for poor compliance over its selling methods, and 16 consecutive months of falling market share had made its commercial position precarious.

During 1997, however, Pearl reported a 46 per cent increase in sales over the previous year. Staff turnover, a key indicator of the mood of an organisation, dropped from 28 per cent to just 12 per cent, and the company earned a place in Britain's *Best Employers Guide*, as one of the top 100 companies to work for in the UK.

Pearl's quick comeback stems from a radical infusion of wackiness into its culture. Richard Surface, an American, joined as CEO in 1995. His enthusiasm for changing the bureaucratic and hidebound culture was too much even for the management consultants, McKinsey & Co, he'd hired to help with the change. The consultants favoured a cautious approach to restructuring, but Surface wanted radical change. 'Pearl did not have the luxury of time on our side,' he says.

Surface overruled the consultants, cut the product line in half, replaced 12 of the 14 top executives, invested heavily in customer service training, and reorganised the sales force to a team-based system. A thousand jobs were lost in the process. The biggest change, though, was in the culture. It opened up, says Pearl training manager Helen Askey: 'People are willing to speak up if they see something wrong. Before, there was almost a fear culture here.'

Surface has also invested in some odd workplace design, with a series of themed rooms designed like ordinary sitting rooms to give back office employees a taste of the domestic environments in which sales staff meet their customers, including a living room with armchairs and a coffee table, and a garden room with astro turf and picnic tables. He's had another meeting room painted bright yellow with a stop watch on the wall to discourage slow meetings, and no one has a desk any more – people sit where they like. 'We call it "romping",' says Askey. 'It's like hot-desking, but more fun.'

How do (and don't) they measure success?

The companies in our sample have, on the whole, done very well on conventional measures of success. They are – except where they are purposely choosing not to be – fast growing and profitable.

These measures are not, however, their only, or even their most important, objectives. In fact, most of our companies take issue with at least one conventional measure of success. They have examined the numbers that most companies pursue unquestioningly, checked them against their own values, and, in many cases, discarded them.

Wacky companies are not slaves to numbers. They operate by gut instinct, common sense, and values. They have shocked many by challenging the quantitative orientation that has been the management norm for the last several decades. They've challenged not just obscure management school ratios, but also such bottom line shibboleths as market share, share price, growth and even profit.

When pressed, Southwest Airlines' vice president, people, Libby Sartain will offer a few measures that matter at the airline: 'The number of customers, our profitability, how happy our employees and customers are, and Department of Transport statistics [comparative measures of airline service standards]. But we really don't measure our success,' she says.

Southwest people, says Sartain, have little time for number crunching. 'We don't do market research studies, we don't do TQM, and we don't have a whole bunch of analysts walking around with pocket protectors and clipboards. If we're making money, if our people are happy, and our customers are happy, we're happy.'

What they don't believe in at Southwest is the mantra that bigger is better. It took Southwest twice as long to reach the $1 billion revenue mark as it did competitor America West. The latter grew quickly, but eventually went into Chapter 11, an American form of receivership.

Says CEO Herb Kelleher: 'We don't care whether we fly to Paris. We don't care whether we have a 747. What we're focused on is being profitable and job secure. If people didn't pay attention to Southwest, because it appeared to be a much smaller regional carrier, it was just immaterial to us. We set ourselves up to go into a specific niche in the airline business. If it's not profitable and not within our niche, forget it.'[12]

Market share has never been one of Southwest's objectives: 'Market share has nothing to do with profitability,' says Kelleher. 'Market share says we just want to be big; we don't care if we make money doing it. That's what misled much of the airline industry for years after deregulation.'[13]

This approach hasn't, however, prevented Southwest from scooping up market share all the same. The company, according to its own figures, consistently ranks first in market share in 88 of its top 100 city-pair markets and holds an aggregate market share of 63 per cent for the cities it serves.

'There's something called the Southwest Effect,' says Sartain. 'Every time we come into a new market, we raise the whole market, bringing in people who wouldn't otherwise fly, or fly as often, then we become first or second in that market. In most markets we're number one because we put in the most services and we keep the cost of flying low for everyone.'

Carl Schmitt, a former California state superintendent of banks, felt so strongly that bigger is anything but better, he opened his own bank just to prove it. Schmitt founded the University National Bank and Trust Company in 1980 as an experiment to test his theories – gained from years of experience in big banking – that small companies do better, not just in service, but in profitability as well.

During his tenure with Wells Fargo, one of the largest banks in the US, and his time as state bank inspector, Schmitt was struck time and again by how small banks outperformed the big ones: 'Their profitability, measured as return on assets, was consistently better than the larger banks,' Schmitt told *Inc.* magazine. 'It stood out like a sore thumb.'[14]

This, he believed, was because small banks stay focused on a specific market, and thus have lower overheads and use their funds and labour more efficiently. Unfortunately, success breeds growth, and most successful small banks eventually grow too big and lose their efficiency advantage. 'In the bureaucracy of growth, you lose your distinctiveness,' he said.

Schmitt's plan was to refuse to grow. His bank would operate with one branch and serve only Palo Alto and four nearby communities. It would not grow past a 15 per cent market share. Beyond that, Schmitt believed the bank would lose its efficiency – and his own: 'I realise what I can and can't do. One thing I can't do is manage a much bigger company.'

He was adamant about keeping his bank small, steadfastly refusing to open a second branch even when customers and staff begged him to. He finally relented, eventually opening two more 'banking floors' – he refused to the end to call them branches.

By 1991, 11 years after its launch, UNBT's return on assets was 45 per cent higher than the average return of other US banks. The bank, with assets of $287 million and a 1990 net income of $3.6 million, 'boasts that increasingly rare combination of a healthy 1.3 per cent reserve ratio and virtually no non-performing loans,' according to a 1990 *Barron's* assessment.[15] In 1996, UNBT was bought by a larger bank, Comerica, and Schmitt retired.

Shareholders and investors

Schmitt felt pressure to grow from several quarters – from employees wanting promotion opportunities and from customers wanting more products and more convenient branches. The one group not exerting pressure was the one you'd most expect to demand growth – the shareholders.

Schmitt arranged this by selecting his shareholders carefully, turning away those who wanted a quick return and stipulating that no investor could purchase more than $150,000 worth of stock at the initial public offering. 'If people have too much of their net worth tied up in this investment, it's hard to be patient,' he told *Inc.* 'I'm not trying to push investors away as much as herd the right ones in.' Those who did buy in profited. Between 1980 and 1991, UNBT's stock price rose five-fold and its return on equity stayed consistently above 14 per cent. The dividend payout was 30 per cent, as opposed to the 25 per cent normal among small banks.

Schmitt, in his initial public offering, also made sure there were enough investors to create a secondary market and give his investors an out if need be. Most didn't use it. According to *Inc.*, in 1991, 63 per cent of the outstanding shares still belonged to the people who first bought them in 1980. Sixty-five per cent of the shareholders were also bank customers.

Ice cream moguls Ben Cohen and Jerry Greenfield were also selective about their shareholders. In 1983, they needed capital for a new plant. They didn't want the loss of control involved in bringing in a venture capitalist, but bankers, brokers and other advisers told them they were too small to go public. Refusing to be bowed, Cohen dug through the files and found an obscure, never before invoked, federal law that allowed him to sell stock to Vermont residents only. The offering, if it came off, would be of a more manageable size and vastly cheaper to administer than a standard, full-scale, public offering. Besides, reports former CEO Chico Lager, Cohen liked the idea of giving first crack at ownership to the people who'd supported the company longest. He thought it nice, too, that the scheme might be legal.

They asked for minimum investments of only $100, advertised it with the shopping coupons and TV listings rather than in the business pages, and travelled around Vermont handing out prospectuses and ice cream cones at public information meetings.

A memo from Cohen to his staff described how the offering would work: 'The object of the in-state offering is to allow the average Vermonter the opportunity to invest in and hopefully profit from Ben & Jerry's – an ice cream company which the average Vermonter supported, made famous, and allowed to prosper. The premise is that the small Vermont investor should have the same opportunity to profit as the large venture capitalist.'

Says Lager: 'By selling stock "retail" to our customers we hoped to increase the percentage of the company's ownership that was in the hands of people who were aligned, we hoped philosophically, but at a minimum gastronomically, with the company.'[16]

Lager saw another advantage to having lots of small investors: 'Like us, they could straighten out the pints in the supermarket freezers and bug the frozen food clerk when the store didn't have Health Bar Crunch in stock.'[17]

The offering sold out and, by May of 1985, the price had tripled – even though the stock wasn't listed on any exchange. The company promoted a reissue with stickers on the pint packets. The underwriters took exception to the slogan, 'Get a Scoop of the Action', complaining it made the stock market seem too much like gambling. Cohen's deadpan response: 'I thought that's what it was.'[18]

A loss of control to investors is a major worry for many wacky companies. Venture capitalists and other outside investors tend to stress short-term over long-term gains, and profit at all costs. For this reason, many leaders of wacky companies prefer to avoid public offerings altogether, and either limit their growth, or finance it from their own earnings.

Both Virgin's Richard Branson and US cosmetics company founder Mary Kay Ash, 'Mary Kay Cosmetics', bought their own shares back from the stock market because they felt investors were measuring success in the wrong way. Other companies have stayed in private hands, and accepted the restricted opportunities that go with that, so they could remain free to pursue their own definition of success.

WOW Toys founder Ednan-Laperouse takes great pride in being financially independent. As their company literature states: 'We did everything on a self-financing basis, from the money we were making on designing for others,' he says. 'We don't have any venture capital money backing us and we're ploughing everything back into the company. Everyone said we were nuts – why risk your own money when you can use someone else's? Simple – we wanted full control of our destiny without moneymen telling us what to do.'

Patagonia's Yvon Chouinard has never turned to outside investors. The company has just two shareholders – Chouinard and wife Malinda – and no outside directors. Says public affairs director Lu Setnicka: 'We don't see how we can do our environmental work and answer to shareholders. They don't take it well if you tell them your decisions may lose them money.'

Some of Chouinard's decisions – to use organic instead of chemically farmed cotton, or putting 10 per cent of its pre-tax profits toward environmental causes (something it calls a voluntary Earth Tax) – may indeed lose the company money. But they rarely do. It turns out Chouinard, despite his disdain for material goods, is adamant that the goods he makes pay their way.

As an *Inc.* magazine reporter discovered: 'During a short tour of Patagonia's new surfboard start-up, Chouinard spent as much time talking about the importance and mechanics of profit as the need for social change. And as a previous CEO of Patagonia said, "The one thing I'm clear about is that Chouinard demands 10 per cent profit." Patagonia might be a social vehicle, but it runs on an economic engine. It's not a question of social good or business profit, but social good and business profit.'[19]

Thus the man who once likened handling money to 'getting doo-doo on your hands' understands that every business needs a layer of the stuff, however distasteful it may be. Chouinard, like many wacky entrepreneurs, recognises that profit is essential if he is to stay in business. What makes these leaders different is that, to them, profit is not the overriding priority.

For wacky entrepreneurs, money is rarely an end in itself. If that were the case, most would have retired comfortably years ago. For them, money is more a measure of success than an end in itself. Profit alone just isn't challenging or meaningful enough for the people involved.

For some, like Masayoshi Son, CEO of Japan's Softbank Corporation, it's just a score in a game. Says Son: 'Money is just a handy mark for judging how well you're doing. To me, to reach $10 billion in revenue was just a milestone, only a kind of target.'[20]

For VeriFone's Hatim Tyabji, 'My criteria for success was to create a new industry. Success will be a by-product of the respect we engender from customers. As a consequence of that respect revenue and profits followed. My personal definition of success is in creating a culture of caring; to engender an environment where people genuinely feel empowered. Do I care about revenue and profits? Of course. But I look at those as by-products.'

This is a common view among many of our wacky company leaders. Profit is what allows them to stay in business and thus fulfil their other goals. And that, says Ben & Jerry's co-founder Ben Cohen, is exactly as it should be: 'You can't have the biggest force in society, business, concerned only with maximising profits and still have a socially responsible society.' His partner, Greenfield, adds: 'When it's just trying to maximise profits, business lobbies for laws that would be most helpful, even if it means polluting the environment. That's not exactly in the best interest of society.'[21]

Patagonia's Chouinard agrees. His aim, he says, is to 'get ourselves to a place where we measure success not by profits but by how much good we'd done at the end of the year.'[22] Good, by any definition, is probably harder to come by than profit. It's certainly harder to account for. Ben Cohen and Jerry Greenfield tried: the company has a three-part mission statement, giving equal weight to product quality, profit, and social goals, and each year it runs an independent social audit to see how well their company is achieving its goals in such non-financial areas as charitable work and environmental impact. 'It's really important to define success,' Ben Cohen told the *Globe and Mail* in 1988. 'It means maintaining a company that maximises its contribution to the community and its employees and remains profitable.'[23]

Ten years on, the company has grown and become more mainstream, but its priorities are intact. As Mitch Curren, the company's 'info queen', told us in 1998: 'One of our goals is to spread the idea that you can run a business responsibly and make money at the same time. We hope one day businesses will be judged, not just by their financial return, but also by their social return.'

Others have less ambitious criteria for success. These vary, but usually involve meeting the needs of employees, the community, the planet – or the personal ambitions of the founders.

'For-profit business enterprises seek to enrich their owners' bank accounts,' reads MEC's (Mountain Equipment Co-op) annual report. 'MEC seeks to enrich our owners' participation in an enjoyment of outdoor activities.'

Says Joe Boxer CEO Nicholas Graham: 'Every business should have a sense of accomplishment. People have different ideas about what that accomplishment might be. And as long as you feel satisfied and feel you've made a contribution that's your reward, whether it's personal, professional or financial. A lot of people miss that point in business.' Graham's own corporate goal is, he says, 'amusing people. It's not about laughing, though; it's about making people think differently. If we can do all that and make money, great – we win.'

To Ricardo Semler, success has been achieved when he has built an organisation that 'accomplishes the most difficult of all challenges: to make people look forward to coming to work in the morning.'[24]

'We don't think we ever really attain success,' says Southwest's Libby Sartain. 'If you think you have, you become complacent.'

The costs of being different

Wacky companies pay the price of being innovators. They take bigger risks than others, set higher challenges, and face greater expectations from employees, customers and the public.

Stan Shih, CEO of the Taiwanese computer maker Acer, had, and still has, grand global ambitions even though, in 1997, he overextended his operations to the point of making the biggest corporate loss in Taiwanese history. The company recovered quickly, though, and is back on track to global leadership.

And not everything Richard Branson touches turns to gold. Neither Virgin Radio, Virgin Cola, nor Virgin Vodka had initial success in the marketplace. More recently, Branson's Virgin Rail team has struggled with the massive challenges (and consumer disgruntlement) involved in turning a former piece of British Rail into the kind of railway line that could live up to the Virgin brand name.

Branson is quick to admit his mistakes – sometimes too quick. On a live BBC Radio 5 interview, shortly after his train services had caused some high-profile delays to, among others, Labour Party delegates on their way to their party conference, he apologised to the British public for the problems with the service. Branson apologised so bluntly he then had to apologise for his language, and change his original outburst to 'We screwed up'.

One company that we had included in our original sample of

wacky companies, a British information technology company called Omni Solutions, which set up its offices according to the oriental philosophy of Feng Shui and held regular company-wide meditation sessions, went into receivership in mid-1998. The company was wacky and staff, with their at-desk head and neck massages, were undoubtedly happy, but clearly, wackiness and good feelings alone weren't enough to generate sufficient financial returns.

These are all cautionary tales. Though it may pay to be different, wackiness alone is no guarantee of success.

THE BOTTOM LINE

▶ If it's worth doing, it's worth doing differently.

▶ Profit isn't the goal, it's a by-product.

▶ The worst markets are often the most fertile ground to build a business.

NOTES

1. Craig Vetter, 'He's Not Worthy – The Curious Crisis of Yvon Chouinard,' in *Outside*, January 1997.
2. Daily Aardvark, www.aardvark.com, May 1997.
3. Edward O. Welles, 'Lost in Patagonia', in *Inc.*, August 1992.
4. Ann Gibbon, 'Mountain Equipment Blazes New Trail', in *The Globe and Mail*, 30 January 1998.
5. M. Detwiler, 'Wearing his Success on his Shorts', in *Entrepreneurial Edge*, Vol. 1, 1997.
6. 'MOS Burger: Feeding Body and Soul', in *Tradepia International*, No. 70, 1997.
7. Michael A. Lev, 'In Japan, McDonald's Means Great Marketing', in *The Chicago Tribune*, 25 February 1997.
8. Michael A. Lev 'In Japan', 1997.
9. Michael Drexler, 'A Rolling Stone Gathers No MOS', in *Mainichi Daily News*, 7 October 1997.
10. N. Shoebridge, 'Sanity's Cool-for-Kids Style Drives the Competition Crazy', in *Australia's Business Review Weekly*, 25 May 1998.
11. Kevin Freiberg and Jackie Freiberg, *Nuts! Southwest Airlines' Crazy Recipe for Business and Personal Success* (Orion Business, London, 1998).
12. Kevin Freiberg and Jackie Freiberg, *Nuts!*, 1998.

13. Kevin Freiberg and Jackie Freiberg, Nuts!, 1998.
14. Elizabeth Conlin, 'Small Business: Second Thoughts on Growth', in Inc., March 1991.
15. Elizabeth Conlin, 'Small Business', 1991.
16. Fred Lager, Ben & Jerry's: The Inside Scoop — How Two Real Guys Built a Business with a Social Conscience and a Sense of Humor (Crown Publishers, New York, 1994).
17. Fred Lager, Ben & Jerry's, 1994.
18. Fred Lager, Ben & Jerry's, 1994.
19. Collins, 'The Foundation for Doing Good', in Inc., December 1997.
20. Paul Kallender, Japan Space Net, January, 1997, http://www.spacer.com/spacenet/text/sb-a.html.
21. Daniel Kadlec, The New World of Giving, in Time, 5 May 1997.
22. Craig Vetter, 'He's Not Worthy', 1997.
23. Caitlin Kelly, 'Laid-back Firm Comes North', in The Globe and Mail, 3 August 1988.
24. Ricardo Semler, Maverick, the Success Story Behind the World's Most Unusual Workplace (Warner Books, 1993).

2 Being different is a philosophy

'When I started, I didn't realise there was a different way to be a business person. Now my business is using its credibility and power to make our world a better place to hang out in.' (Ben Cohen, co-founder of Ben & Jerry's Homemade)[1]

'You can't add value unless you have values ... We need to imagine – and then design – a system of commerce where doing good is like falling off a log.' (Paul Hawken, founder, US-based garden equipment company Smith & Hawken)[2]

'Success is a shared experience connected with lots of people. It is a bottom line with a heartbeat.' (Tom Chappell, CEO, Tom's of Maine)[3]

None of our companies are wacky simply on a whim. What may appear on the surface as bizarre corporate behaviour is, almost without exception, rooted in a deeply held philosophy. Every one of our companies has embodied in its daily decision making and activities a structured, often highly original, view about what business is and its role in the world.

Many companies, wacky and otherwise, have such beliefs laid out in mission statements, stating such worthy goals as, say, to be the foremost widget maker in Wichita, or the most respected glue stick producer in Uruguay. A philosophy is, however, much more than that: it runs deeper and affects everything a company does. It's not invented to fill a space in the annual report: it's not normally put in writing until it has been established for decades. And, unlike a mission statement, a philosophy is not an afterthought; it's likely to have been the driving force behind starting the company in the first place.

What then, is a philosophy?

- A philosophy is a set of overarching beliefs that serve as guides for everyday action. If a strategy defines what a company wants to do, its philosophy determines the how and the why.

- A philosophy drives values, culture, and an understanding of how things are done. It is central to the way the company thinks and behaves; it's reflected in everything the company does; it is reinforced throughout the organisation in words, deeds and symbols.

- Unlike a strategy – which is often treated like a state secret – a philosophy is understood (consciously or intuitively) by all employees, and by most other stakeholders as well. Most wacky companies go to great lengths to ensure their philosophy is understood by everyone they deal with.

- And, unlike a strategy, a philosophy doesn't change with business conditions. It's not a short-term way to deal with particular issues. Rather, it's a foundation for dealing with any issues that arise. A philosophy, though it may adapt or grow, cannot fundamentally change without radically altering both the way the company operates and its fundamental sense of identity.

- A philosophy is what gives a company soul or, as Paul Hawken, the founder of American garden equipment company Smith & Hawken, would have it, a philosophy gives a company *meaning*.

To Hawken, whose company is well known for its position on environmental and social responsibility issues, business as a whole needs a philosophy – if only to give commercial activities some meaning beyond the purely financial. As he wrote in a 1989 article: 'One of the challenges facing American business is to add meaning to commercial life. That's difficult for a company to do unless it is able to impart to its employees the meaning of the company. A lot of companies have lore; they have history; they have tradition; they have huge markets; but they have no meaning.'[4]

Most wacky company philosophies haven't been committed to paper – or at least not anything that could be framed or reprinted in the annual report. No committee ever agonised over the phrasing of such telling off-the-cuff statements as 'Kick butt and have fun' from Sun Microsystem's CEO Scott McNealy, or Quad/Graphics' 'Have fun, make money. Don't do business with anyone you don't like.'[5]

If most of our wacky companies haven't written down their philosophy, their vision or their values, it's because they don't need to. Stakeholders understand the philosophy because people in the company manifestly live it and other people can see them do so. Only when the company gets to the size where the leader cannot be a personal role model to every employee do companies typically begin to write down their beliefs, values and view of the world. Even then, a written philosophy is not strictly necessary because, by the time a company gets that large, there are usually more than enough disciples available to personally demonstrate the values to the next generation of employees.

IKEA founder CEO Ingvar Kamprad committed his philosophy to paper in 1976. His *Testament of a Furniture Dealer* still forms the basis for company operations, even though IKEA now operates in 28 countries and has a turnover in excess of £865 million. In *Testament*, Kamprad urges his co-workers (he doesn't call them employees) to be 'a group of constructive fanatics who, with unwavering obstinacy, refuse to accept the impossible'.

Kamprad's is a homespun philosophy that combines the virtues of simplicity and making do (the company led the way in using recycled materials in furniture, for example) with determination and a deep-seated commitment to equality and innovation. It's rooted in Kamprad's background. He grew up in one of the poorest parts of rural Sweden during the depression, and to this day admires the values of thrift and hard work he saw there. His childhood experiences also fuel his main objective – to contribute to a more democratic society by making decent furniture that most people can afford.

The people at Southwest Airlines haven't written down their whole philosophy, though they did take some time out from planning parties to write up a mission statement – then delivered a copy to each employee as a prize in a box of Cracker Jack.

Southwest's people, though, behind all their games, joking and jumping out of overhead bins, operate according to a set of values not that far removed from Kamprad's. Theirs too is homespun, conservative and consistent, with special attention for the little guy. At the core of Southwest's unwritten philosophy are: care and consideration for colleagues – including recognising individual contribution, allowing people to be themselves at work, and permitting staff to take risks; hard but meaningful work; a conservative, pay-as-you-grow, stance on finances; and making air travel available to people who couldn't otherwise afford it.

Kevin and Jackie Freiberg, authors of a book on the company, argue that Southwest's secret ingredient is not the humour and flakiness the company is so well known for, but its sense of discipline. 'Throughout its history, Southwest has consistently adhered to a clearly defined purpose and a well thought out strategy for accomplishing it. As simple as it sounds, Southwest exists to make a profit, achieve job security for every employee, and make flying affordable for more people. Even at the height of its success, Southwest exercised the discipline not to stray from its strategy.'[6]

What drives wacky companies?

One useful way to explore the difference between wacky companies and others is by examining what they focus on. All companies can choose to focus on either employees or customers, and on whether they run their business through systems or through values.

Both IKEA and Southwest are what we would call values driven/ employee focused companies, sitting, with most of our wacky companies, in quadrant four of the values/systems matrix in figure 2.1.

Quadrant 1: Customer focused/systems driven

Most companies in the past two decades have been struggling to make themselves more systems driven and customer focused. Most of the widely used management techniques, from management by objectives (MBO) through total quality management (TQM) to business process re-engineering (BPR), are about creating more

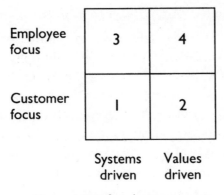

Figure 2.1 Values/systems matrix

efficient systems – systems aimed, primarily, at improving performance for the customer. Ricardo Semler, CEO of the highly original
Brazilian company Semco, tried this route when he tried to turn
around his moribund family firm in the mid-eighties. He was
frustrated, though, that the more management techniques, checks
and balances he applied, the less productive and creative his
workforce became. He eventually dropped the idea, and moved a
full 180 degrees to quadrant four.

Quadrant 2: Customer focused/values driven

These companies provide superior performance for their customers.
However, instead of creating and imposing detailed systems, they
apply a set of strong and widely understood values. These values
drive the business. When employees understand the values and are
given what they need to make them work, they create the necessary
systems themselves. This was a characteristic of virtually all of the
companies examined in a recent global study of long-term high
performing companies. (See 'The value of values' below for detail.)[7]

It is also a characteristic of MOS Burger, and it's the fundamental
difference between MOS and virtually every other fast food chain.
Burger chains like McDonald's epitomise a systems driven culture,
with their precise timing and portion controls. Fast food chains
typically control, measure and systemise every action and process to
within an inch of its life. It's not good food or even clever marketing

that made the Golden Arches such a worldwide presence: it was punch clocks and portion control. Yes, McDonald's has values, but these are not the primary drivers of the business.

MOS Burger has been able to compete head to head with McDonald's in Japan by doing precisely the opposite. MOS is led not by systems, but by values – by a deeply held oriental value system than runs counter to most western notions of the way a big business behaves. Founder Satoshi Sakurada explains: 'My philosophy is very Oriental. It's based on what are called the "Seven Principles of Good Relationships". These include, for instance, sincerity, honesty, gratitude, and courtesy – virtues that we work hard to instil in our staff. These principles are especially important today because we are all so busy in our daily lives that we forget such virtues. But it's these simple virtues that comprise the foundation of good service. Another personal influence can be expressed by the Chinese proverb translated into English as "The same source nurtures the body as well as the spirit".'

This philosophy translates into various practical aspects of MOS operations, including using organic produce, cooking food to order, refusing to fight price wars at the expense of quality, and developing relationships with diners in each neighbourhood, rather than saturating the TV screens with big promises. It's also the reason MOS gives Japanese consumers what they like, rather than trying to win them over with western products. It all comes down to Sakurada's belief in the right way to do thing. MOS also stays intimately involved with all franchisees, providing intense training to ensure they understand and apply the philosophy; and has developed its own network of farmers to ensure quality of supply.

Another aspect of customer focused/values driven companies is consideration for what their customers can afford. Many of these companies, notably Mountain Equipment Co-op and IKEA, exist to make products available to people who couldn't otherwise afford them. Southwest Airlines also play that role. As CEO Herb Kelleher once said, 'We're not competing with other airlines, we're competing with ground transportation.' However, as Kelleher insists on putting employees first in order to better serve customers, his is, strictly speaking, an employee driven organisation.

The value of values

A 1997 study of 31 top performing international organisations discovered that virtually all of them were values, rather than systems, driven.

For these companies, values provided a short-cut to effective decision making. They also helped establish relationships with customers, suppliers, advisers and even acquisition candidates. The study showed that values, if adhered to, are good for a company's reputation and can also be a good means of assessing whether people fit the organisation. They can also help a company stay on track. As Archie Norman, then CEO of leading UK grocery retailer ASDA, pointed out: 'One of the purposes of a strong sense of values with a strong sense of involvement is not that it'll stop you making mistakes, but that you'll as sure as hell find out when you do, because you feel it.'

The companies studied used their values to harness and channel emotions among stakeholders. They used values as a means of motivating people to act on their own initiative, and they projected those values at stakeholders as a means of building positive goodwill and lasting relationships.

The values varied a great deal among companies; critically, though, they were consistent within each company.

The CEOs spoken to were almost universally dismissive of the standard mission statement. Several do have pithy statements of purpose, however. Southwest Airlines', for example (it featured in that study, too), is 'to deliver positively outrageous service at unbelievably low prices'.

The values of these top performing companies, stated or understood, generally:

- reflected the gut feelings of everyone in the business, not just the top management team
- reflected reality, rather than hopes and wishes
- were used in everyday decision making
- were few in number (seven at most) and powerful.

The authors also found that companies become value driven when leaders:

- set an example
- ensure all messages about values are consistent
- continuously look for opportunities to reinforce the values
- manage by general principles, rather than by rules.

Quadrant 3: Employee focused/systems driven

A third category of companies is typified by professional practices, such as lawyers, accountants, advertising agencies and consultants. Systems are important in these businesses: lawyers and accountants, in particular, are expected to adhere to the strict rules of their profession. And even advertising agencies spend a great deal of effort trying to systematise their creativity. These organisations are often narcissistic, existing primarily not for the customer, but for the intellectual and financial indulgence of the professionals who inhabit them. Especially in the case of highly creative advertising agencies, the customers of these companies can, at times, feel like little more than a vehicle for the gratification of egos. The system works because the organisation has expertise the customer needs.

American advertising agency Chiat/Day was, in its day, accused of taking this attitude. During the eighties, the agency was widely regarded as the defining force in creative advertising, though it also had something of a reputation for having a take-it-or-leave-it approach to creative work.

Adweek reporter Greg Farrell argues that, while this reputation was exaggerated, 'Chiat/Day nevertheless tends to show a lot more spine in defence of its product than most agencies its size. It is precisely this commitment to quality that gives the agency its competitive edge while at the same time undermining it as a reliably predictable business venture.'[8]

Founder Jay Chiat also felt the reputation was overstated. As he told *Adweek*: 'Sometimes I think we have an image of being hard-nosed contrarians who say, "Do it our way or not". I mean, we listen. It's the client and it's advertising and nobody here is independently wealthy, so it's not as though we're trying to be stupid. It's that if you're really going to talk out of only one side of your mouth, then you have to continue to do it, or your people won't believe it. And then they won't want to perform any more.'[9]

Interestingly, one of our strongest examples of an employee focused/systems driven company is not a professional service at all, but a manufacturing plant in the Southern US. Springfield Remanufacturing Corporation isn't just employee focused, it's employee owned, and so obsessed with systems its entire staff (including the floor sweepers and the CEO) sit down together for a half hour each week to check out the latest financial figures.

Employee focused/systems driven organisations usually have pragmatic philosophies, with few ambitions outside their walls. As CEO Jack Stack says, 'We are trying to get a bunch of people through life. We are not trying to change the world. We work together, we play together, we win together.'[10]

Quadrant 4: Employee focused/values driven

Most of our wacky companies fall into this category. At its extreme are employee-owned companies, which are not too far removed from the employee owned co-operatives popular earlier this century in that their primary motivation is to create and protect employment.

Employee-focused companies exist primarily by and for employees, and are driven by the belief that people come first. Besides a high level of profit sharing and employee ownership, these companies tend to offer generous benefits and go to great lengths to avoid lay offs.

For these companies, when it comes down to a choice between employees and customers, the customer comes second.

At Southwest Airlines, explains corporate secretary and executive vice president Colleen Barrett, 'that means that the company will support an employee who goes out of his way for a customer. No employee will ever be punished for using good judgement and common sense when trying to accommodate a customer – no matter what our rules are.'[11]

Such a policy is especially important in the airline industry. As former flight attendant, now administrator, Kathy Pettit says: 'How can I be expected to do the right thing when I'm locked in a tube with hundreds of strangers, all the while knowing that if something happens to go wrong, my company will not back me?'[12]

The principle is simple: if employees are well treated and supported, they are better equipped to provide legendary service to customers. Southwest, by putting customers second, stays consistently at the top of customer service polls.

The concept was (arguably) first coined in 1992, when Hal Rosenbluth, CEO of Rosenbluth Travel, wrote a book called *The Customer Comes Second and other Secrets of Exceptional Service*. In it, he argued that putting customers second – focusing on the needs of employees and creating a genuinely humane workplace – could lead to better customer service.

So, just as rude Southwest passengers will be asked to fly with another airline, clients who are repeatedly rude to Rosenbluth associates may be asked to find another travel agency.

Putting employees first also works well for shareholders, even though most of these companies place them third in their affections, after customers.

Howard Schultz, CEO of US coffee house chain Starbuck's, explained to his initial investors: 'I told them our first priority was to take care of our people, because they were the ones responsible for communicating our passion to our customers. If we did that well, we'd accomplish our second priority, taking care of our customers. And only if we achieved both of those goals, would we be able to provide long-term value for our shareholders.'

Smart investors were quite happy with third place. In 1992, Starbuck's shares went from $17 to $33 in their first three months of trading. For the next six years, the coffee chain's earnings grew by 50 per cent a year, every year. By 1998, Starbuck's was opening a new store every day somewhere in North America.

Starbuck's is not an anomaly in this. Every year, *Fortune* magazine presents its choice of the 100 best companies to work for in America; companies which have, in its editors' view, the happiest, best cared for employees in the country. In 1998, 61 of these companies had been publicly traded for at least five years. Of these, 45 yielded significantly higher returns to shareholders than the Russell 3000 – a widely used index of top performing large and small US companies. The 61 employee-focused companies averaged annual returns of 27.5 per cent versus 17.3 per cent for the Russell 3000. Over the previous ten years, the 61 companies averaged returns of 23.4 per cent – almost 10 percentage points more than the Russell 3000.

In employee focused/values driven companies, highly empowered employees internalise the values, and create systems based on those values. However, this is not to say they can't be highly systematic. Southwest Airlines, whose teams can land, unload, reload, and send off an aircraft in just 20 minutes, relies heavily on efficient systems. The point, though, is that the systems don't come first, the values do. The values determine which rules and systems are necessary, and only those are adopted.

These companies also have within their ranks the traditional philanthropic companies – those based on Victorian values of thrift and philanthropy and the idea of looking after one's own. These include companies like Wal-Mart, where staff work for low wages, but retire wealthy thanks to stock options; or Wisconsin printer Quad/Graphics where, it appears, almost every imaginable employee need is taken care of: Quad/Cuisine runs the cafeteria and sells take home dinners; there's Quad/Education for company training; and Quad/Med, a clinic for staff and their families; Quad/Travel books holidays and business trips; Quad/Care watches the kids; Quad/Galleries is an in-house art gallery; and Quad/Pop keeps up a steady supply of free popcorn; Quad/Gardens does the landscaping and maintains Quad/Camp, a nature preserve with a baseball diamond and volleyball courts.

This cradle-to-grave approach to employees recalls the well-meaning, but paternalistic philosophies of such Victorian business philanthropists as Milton Hershey. Hershey, the turn of the century founder of what is now America's biggest chocolate and candy maker, was more than your typical factory owner. Combining good works, old-fashioned virtues, good business sense and the concept of good healthy fun, he created, in that era of company towns, a kind of industrial Utopia.

Hershey was somewhat ahead of his time, insisting that, even for factory workers, 'there is more to life than just work. That beauty, nature and wholesome leisure-time activities are essential ingredients to a full life.'[13]

So, in his purpose-built town of Hershey, Pennsylvania, the roads have names like Chocolate Street and Cocoa Avenue, and the street lamps are shaped like Hershey kisses. There's an elaborate community centre where Hershey's present-day employees can use a big fitness centre and swimming pool free of charge, two cinemas, a museum of American life, a sports arena (where the Hershey Bears professional ice hockey team plays), five golf courses, and Hershey Park. According to an article in Business World in 1903, his town had 'no provisions for a police department, nor for a jail. Here there will be no unhappiness, then why any crime?'

In Europe at the time, Quaker families (and, coincidentally, also chocolate makers) such as Cadbury and Rowntree took a similar view of employee welfare. Today the approach lives on in companies like Rhino Foods, best known as the supplier of cookie dough to Ben & Jerry's. While its most famous customer struggles with external social responsibility, Rhino Foods applies its values closer to home, choosing to assist its employees before becoming involved in community organisations. Says owner Ted Castle: 'We believe we're creating 83 healthy people out in the community. If every organisation did that, there probably wouldn't need to be so many [community service] groups out there. We want to care and nurture our own employees first, and if we're successful at that, then we nurture other people.'[14]

Traditionally, then, employee focused/values driven companies keep their values close to home, concentrating on their immediate sphere, and looking out for their employees first.

Since the early 1980s, however, a new kind of values driven company has emerged – one that is profoundly values driven, but focused not so much on customers or employees, but on broader issues of society and environment.

It could be argued that these two groups of companies – the internally focused and the externally focused – while both values driven, are at different stages of evolution. Companies at earlier stages of development, if they can afford to be values driven at all, tend to look to the needs of their own people; as they become more advanced, more values driven – and usually wealthier – they find they can look further afield at external needs.

The hierarchy of business needs (next section and figure 2.2) is a useful model for explaining the stages a company goes through, and the priorities it sets, once it has chosen to be led by its values.

---

6 Organisational self-fulfilment
An integrated approach to all stakeholders.

5 External community conscience
Wanting to contribute to society more broadly, with
a strong emphasis on maintaining corporate reputation.

4 Compensatory community conscience
Behaving responsibly toward society and the environment
by attempting to atone for the company's own impact.

3 Internal community conscience
The company as vehicle for developing and rewarding
the people within it.

2 Security
Building for the future; these companies would put
their immediate creditors first.

I Survival
Cost-management, paying the bills, staving off the competition.

Figure 2.2 Hierarchy of business needs

Companies don't normally work their way up the chain; instead they struggle with conflicting needs on various levels, until they reach the self-fulfilment stage (which can be defined as that point where the company has got a handle on conflicting demands).

The hierarchy of business needs

The lower levels (stages 1 and 2) are the business equivalent of hunter-gatherer societies. Still trying to keep the wolf from the door, they have little opportunity to look to their wider role.

Wacky companies have all advanced beyond the basics of stage 1 and stage 2. Companies like SOL, IKEA, Richer Sounds, Rhino Foods, Quad/Graphics and Hershey Foods have reached stage 3, where their efforts focus on internal activities and on taking care of their own.

The fourth level, which we call compensatory community

consciousness, is occupied by companies that have expanded their concerns to the outside world, but focus their efforts on compensating for or reducing the damage they've done. This goes far beyond the picking up after oneself that is legislated and expected. These companies are highly aware of their impact, often guilt-ridden, and will place putting things right above generating profits. The Body Shop, for example, is as well known for its efforts to improve the lot of animals, the environment and endangered cultural groups, as it is for its products.

Another such company is AES, an American power plant operator founded by an unlikely partnership between Dennis Bakke, a devout Christian, and Roger Sant, an environmentalist who has been active in organisations like the Worldwide Fund for Nature and the Environmental Defense Fund. Together they have created an international, multi-million dollar organisation based on the principles of teamwork, employee empowerment, and – though it's something of a stretch for a heavy utility – environmental responsibility.

According to *Fast Company*, AES tries to compensate for its emissions, not just on a local, but also on a global scale. It recently planted 52 million trees in Guatemala, the number it calculated were needed to offset 40 years of emissions from a new plant in Connecticut. As it expands globally, AES has extended its concerns to social, as well as environmental, initiatives, such as building and running schools, medical centres and food banks in the areas where it operates.

AES puts its values first, even at the risk of annoying investors. In 1991, when Bakke and Sant went public with both their share issue and their business philosophy, the US Securities and Exchange Commission required them to list their values as a 'risk factor'. The prospectus warned potential investors that: 'If the Company perceives a conflict between values and profits, the Company will try to adhere to its values – even though doing so might result in diminished profits or foregone opportunities.'[15]

The people at outdoor equipment manufacturer Patagonia take a similar approach; not so much because they think it's a good idea, but because they believe the world will end otherwise. Patagonia's activities are fuelled by a powerful philosophy that overrides every decision made in the company. It's one of minimal environmental impact, long-term sustainability, and of environmental responsibility at every level.

Patagoniacs, as they like to call themselves, are environmentalists, which is to be expected in the outdoor equipment business, but they don't practice the pale green shade of environmentalism currently fashionable in North America. Rather, they take the more extreme view that the world isn't just nearing, but is already in the midst of, an environmental crisis. Says public affairs director Lu Setnicka: 'As a company, we think that what's happening in the natural world is at a crisis level. We are trying to find solutions to that.' And, more optimistically: 'We think of business in the long term. When you know you are going to be around, not just for the next year, but for the next 100 years, you make very different decisions.'

So firm are they in their environmental beliefs that, confirms Setnicka, the company offers courses to its employees in non-violent activism and may even post bail if they get arrested as the result of their involvement with an environmental cause – provided they have taken the course. 'It's a course in non-violent civil disobedience. It helps our people understand what people on the front line are doing,' she says.

How does that mesh with running a multi-million consumer goods company? 'Everything we make pollutes,' wrote founder Yvon Chouinard in the company's 1991 product catalogue. 'Other than shutting down the doors and giving up, what Patagonia can do is to constantly assess what we are doing and work toward reducing the damage we do.'

Reducing the product line and concentrating on multi-purpose, durable items that consumers would need fewer of was part of the solution. However, such is the fashion for outdoor gear that, despite a product and marketing policy that encouraged reduced unit sales, Patagonia sales continue to grow.

'Patagonia is an experiment, really, an attempt to prove being ecologically responsible works,' says Chouinard. 'And every time we've done the right thing, it's ended up making us more money.'[16] 'We can all look back and be proud of this grand experiment we've been involved in,' adds Setnicka.

The companies at level 5 are also part of a grand experiment.

These companies – Ben & Jerry's, the Body Shop and Smith & Hawken, among others – have taken a larger step out into the world, concerning themselves, not just with the results of their own actions, but with the needs of society as a whole.

These companies are founded on the belief that there is a different, more ethical, way to do business. All are convinced that it is possible to both do well and do good – or, as Ben Cohen puts it, 'to lead with your values and make money too'.

Ben & Jerry's Homemade, founded in 1978, has always operated according to the principle that a business owes as much to the outside world as it does to its shareholders. That, coupled with co-founder Ben Cohen's desire 'to make the world a better place to hang out in,' inspired the founders to aim 7.5 per cent of their pre-tax profits, and a great deal of ice cream, at a whole raft of social and environmental causes – from nuclear disarmament to child welfare, voter registration and farm aid. The company has also always made a special effort to buy from minority or disadvantaged suppliers.

However, by the time they'd been in business for a decade or so, Cohen's vision had reached beyond this. According to former CEO Fred Lager, the founder took the position that: 'It's not a question of making great ice cream, making some money, and then doing socially responsible things. Caring about the community has to be imbued throughout the organisation so that it impacts every decision we make.'[17]

Cohen's idea was to redefine the bottom line, to include both an economic and a social component, so as to measure the company's performance not just by profitability, but also by what it had contributed to the community, arguing that: 'We can't just optimise profits. We need to optimise the community as well.' This concept, which Cohen dubbed 'Linked Prosperity', gave rise in 1988 to Ben & Jerry's Mission Statement, which gives equal weight to product quality, social activism and profitable growth.

As Cohen explained to his employees at the time: 'Most people suspend their values about contributing to society when they go to work, believing that it's something they're only supposed to be concerned with in their free time at home. It's when we're at work that we're most powerful, because we're organised and we have the financial resources of the company behind us. The results we can achieve within the company, working together, are far greater than those we could accomplish working as three hundred individuals on our own.'[18]

Their contributions were many and varied. Ben & Jerry's Foundation, established to distribute the funds the company earmarks for charity, has, says former CEO Fred Lager, 'an intended bias toward weird and offbeat projects that are unlikely to get funding from traditional sources.'

In 1988, Ben & Jerry's launched a product called Peace Pops: vanilla, covered in chocolate, wrapped in an anti-nuclear campaign (copy on the package informed readers about a defence budget reduction campaign), and notorised ice cream scoopers so customers could register to vote at some of their shops; 1989's flavour was Rainforest Crunch: the nuts were said to come from rainforest trees (those that weren't already in Anita Roddick's shampoo) and sales were geared to benefit preservation efforts.

In 1990, Ben & Jerry's sponsored an exchange of young community workers with a group in the Soviet Union; two years later they opened a scoop shop and manufacturing facility in Russia. Other campaigns, run in shops and on packaging, involved supporting small farmers, fighting child poverty, and campaigning against a nuclear power plant. A billboard for the latter campaign read: 'Stop Seabrook. Keep our customers alive and licking.'

Such companies, however much they'd like to be ideal employers, can leave employees feeling neglected at the expense of worthy causes in the outside world. Ben Cohen is aware enough of his own company's shortcomings in this regard to publish some of his staff's criticisms. In his own book about the company, he quotes the concerns of plant worker Daisy Sweet, who says: 'Before I came here I'd heard the company did a lot for the community. But I didn't know how much they went outside the community. They do give money to good causes. But I think they should concentrate on their own people first. For one thing, the pay stinks. Here we are fighting to get decent wages and the higher ups are giving all this money away. I think they could do more for their employees before they look outside.'[19]

Former Smith & Hawken employee Meredith Maran recalls a similar atmosphere at that socially responsible company: 'While Paul

[Hawken] accepts awards for environmental and social responsibility, his employees are working long hours for unglamorous wages, feeling insecure, unheard, unappreciated. I muster my courage and tell Paul that people are afraid of him – too afraid to tell him so.'[20]

Does philosophy pay?

Yes, says Ben and Jerry's former CEO Fred Lager, though he lets the numbers do the talking: 'When the board had first talked about the social mission back in 1988, we had debated what impact it would have on the profitability of the company. By the end of 1991, we had our answer. Sales for the year were up another 26 per cent, to $97 million. Profits were up 43 percent from the previous year, to $3.7 million. In 1992, sales jumped another 36 percent, to $132 million, while profits increased a whopping 79 percent, to $6.7 million.'[21]

In a 1992 letter to shareholders, Ben Cohen wrote: 'The most amazing thing is that our social values . . . have actually helped us to become a stable, profitable, high-end growth company. This is especially interesting because it flies in the face of those business theorists who state that publicly held corporations cannot make a profit and help the community at the same time, and moreover that such companies have no business trying to do so. The issues here are heart, soul, love and spirituality. Corporations that exist solely to maximise profit become disconnected from their soul – the spiritual interconnectedness of humanity. Like individuals, businesses can conduct themselves with the knowledge that the hearts, souls and spirits of all people are interconnected, so that as we help others, we cannot help helping ourselves.'

Purchasing manager Todd Kane agrees: 'During the first several years of Ben and Jerry's existence, the common view of the social mission was that it took away from the company's profitability and caused extra work. Now there's a general understanding that what drives our financial success is being a different kind of company. People understand that the more kinds of values-led things we do, the more we contribute to our success.'[22]

Tom Chappell had a similar experience. The founder of personal care products company Tom's of Maine is a deeply religious man and probably the only manager ever to earn a master's degree from the Harvard Divinity School while CEO of a major company.

Chappell invited one of his Divinity professors to attend a board meeting and help formulate policies for his company. 'At board meetings, most companies ask questions like "Where are we going and how are we going to get there?" I wanted us to ask questions like "Who are we and what are we all about?"' This led to a reassessment of a number of company policies. 'In the past, when we talked about goals, we argued about profit and social and environmental responsibility as an either/or issue, but we agreed all were important. Now, we're about doing things in such a way that we do all three.'

This re-evaluation led to a number of new policies that would, on the face of it, seem designed to cut profits. These include donating 10 per cent of profits to charity, ending the workday at 1 p.m. on summer Fridays, encouraging employees to spend up to 5 per cent of their paid time working with non-profit groups, and refusing to use animal testing, even though the refusal cost them an important dental association endorsement. (Tom's, whose leading product is toothpaste, was unable to get the American Dental Association's (ADA) seal of approval because for the ADA, the only acceptable test involved animals. Tom's eventually gained the seal by running tests on volunteer college students.)

All this do-gooding should cost money. It didn't. Tom's Web site reports close to 20 per cent growth yearly since the new policies have taken effect. Market share is increasing, as are profits.

The value of a deep driven philosophy

What's so important about a philosophy? The experiences of wacky companies suggest a deeply held, special perspective on the world and what matters in it gives businesses a number of advantages. Among them are the following.

A philosophy reduces the need for regulations

Internally, a strong underlying philosophy generates a strong company culture, which in turn generates a set of values that employees, managers and other stakeholders understand, approve of, and instinctively use as a framework for their decisions. These values reduce the need for policies and regulations.

Practically speaking, a philosophy means people know what to do without being told. This is essential for companies that have, like so many of our wacky companies, flattened their organisations and got rid of most of their middle managers.

Rules just aren't necessary: with a solid set of values as a framework, people can be trusted to design suitable systems – provided they have an emotional as well as intellectual grasp of what the system is intended to do.

A philosophy can help a company cope with change

A philosophy can help a company cope with change by keeping it on track. It defines priorities and provides a basis for decision making in the face of unexpected new opportunities or crises. 'A strong culture is sort of an anchor for letting people loose to create a lot of change, not to impede it,' says Rosabeth Moss Kanter of the Harvard Business School.[23]

A philosophy lets you know when you're doing the right thing

A philosophy also provides guidance when businesses are faced with a choice between profits and ethics. Most ethical choices boil down to a choice between the interests of various stakeholders or between potential profit or growth and the needs of others. A philosophy defines the priorities.

Virgin's Richard Branson, for example, when trying to decide whether to buy record label EMI, decided not to because the lay-offs involved would run counter to his values.

Tobias Communications, a publisher in New Orleans, as another example, purposely steers away from the more profitable Christian market to get its secular looking Christian oriented goods into a wider market. Though profitable by conventional measures, the real purpose, says president Pastor Mark Joeckel, is to get positive messages to people he believes most need it. 'We could do better financially if we sold to Christian bookstores. Actually, you can make a large profit within the Christian market. Christian CDs sell for about four dollars more than others do. But we didn't want to do that. We've been preaching to the choir for 500 years. We want to get the message to people who really need it.'

Outdoor equipment manufacturer Yvon Chouinard puts environmental responsibility before profit. So, the day he saw a once pristine climbing route scarred by overuse – in part by climbing products his company produced – he stopped making them, even though, at the time, they comprised 70 per cent of his sales.

In 1995, when the company's first environmental audit showed that cotton was the most polluting material Patagonia used, Chouinard demanded that the whole operation switch to organic cotton. 'The environmental audit showed that, of all the fibres used, it was conventionally grown, 100 per cent "pure" cotton that caused the most environmental damage. Now that we know, it would be unconscionable for us to do anything less,' says Chouinard.[24] 'It cost us money, we took a hit on it. But we could no longer continue the way we were if we knew there was an alternative. The core values guided us,' says spokesperson Lu Setnicka.

At Ben & Jerry's, Ben Cohen insisted that top pay be restricted to five times the salary of the lowest paid worker. When Fred Lager argued that it was difficult to hire the management expertise needed at what was sometimes less than half the going rate, Cohen responded: 'There's no limit at all on what the upper managers can get paid. All they have to do is make sure they raise the bottom first.'[25]

The ratio was eventually upped to seven to one, then dropped altogether in early 1997, though, according to info queen Mitch Curren, it's still only about fifteen to one – versus the hundred to one she says is common in American companies of a similar size.

IKEA was among the first companies to risk the ire of the religious right and market directly to gay couples. In 1994, the company placed an ad on American TV which featured two men shopping for a table together. It was one of a series designed to show that all kinds of people, such as gay and mixed race couples, shop for furniture at IKEA.

A philosophy will also let you know when you've got it wrong. As Tom Chappell, founder of Tom's of Maine, a toiletries company with a strong social and environmental ethic, observes: 'We've learned that if any decision is made that goes against our beliefs then we don't look like ourselves and we won't maintain our level of success.'[26]

Chappell puts his money where his mouth is: he shuts down his factory four times a year at a cost of $100,000 each time, to ensure that all employees attend meetings about environmental and other social issues.[27]

A philosophy attracts like-minded customers, creates genuine differences in the marketplace – and saves a packet on marketing

A clear and different philosophy attracts like-minded customers who choose brands, increasingly, as a reflection of their own values.

Fred Lager, one of a series of Ben & Jerry's CEOs, noticed that all this 'hippie do-gooder stuff', like signing up minorities to vote and buying from disadvantaged suppliers, was good for sales. The company's socially responsible mission, was, he observed 'proving to be an effective marketing strategy. There was no doubt that our customers were more inclined to buy our ice cream and support our business because of how we, in turn, supported the community.'[28]

For others, it's an irreverent or rebellious philosophy that reinforces customers' personal values. Virgin's early rebel image had many people buying tickets as a political statement.

Joe Boxer's underwear gives its wearers humour by proxy – so much so that American teens have taken to wearing their jeans extra baggy, just to show the label. The company's willingness to go completely over the top, again and again, is something that consumers like to be associated with, if only vicariously. 'We're the number one boxer short company in America, not because we spent a lot of money on advertising, but because we entertain people,' says Graham.

Whatever the philosophy, if it's done right, it can provide the kind of added value most marketers could only dream about. Peter Laundy, a marketing consultant with Laundy Rogers Design in New York, explains why most marketers will just have to keep on dreaming.[29]

Laundy, who designs marketing communications programmes,

contends that most companies have traditionally pursued their markets through creating and stressing the most trivial differences between their products and those of their competitors. He calls this practice image positioning, as it is based more on the image of the product than any real attributes it may have. Image positioning works to an extent, he says, but – no surprise here – most consumers have become, quite justifiably, cynical about marketing claims. Image positioners, he adds, also tend to be so concerned with winning that they pay more attention to their competitors than to their customers.

Other companies, including many of the wacky companies we've been studying, such as Ben & Jerry's, the Body Shop and Smith & Hawken, don't rely on image positioning. Rather, because they have built real differences into their products and their organisations, and consumers have real, rather than imaginary, reasons to buy from them, they don't have to dress up and praise their offerings.

Laundy calls these companies character expressers – they express their character in everything they do, and they rely on their character to give them marketing edge.

All our wacky companies are character expressers. Their philosophy creates genuine differences between their offerings and others on the market, so they don't need marketing fluff or analysis to dress them up. They don't target, segment, run focus groups, demographic analysis or psychometric profiles; they rarely buy advertising and they don't do market research. Just as it's clear from their actions who they are and what they stand for, wacky companies know who their customers are and what they want.

Anita Roddick, for example, never promised anyone a rose garden. Her company, the Body Shop, revolutionised the cosmetics industry by refusing to sell fantasy. It was the first mainstream beauty products supplier not to patronise its customers with images of unattainable glamour. Cynical shoppers, resonating to unexpected honesty, lapped it up.

Ben & Jerry's also marketed honesty. While the rest of the superpremium ice cream market was offering fake European glamour and hyper-elegant, often suggestive, presentation ('Häagen Dazs is a New York creation – it means precisely nothing in Danish), Ben & Jerry's broke the rules with an uncontrived, funky, small town image. They made flavours they liked – the sort of flavours kids might come up with if left alone in the kitchen – and left off the sex and glamour.

The entire script of one of their first TV ads ran:

> 'Hi, I'm Ben.'
> 'And I'm Jerry.'
> 'We may not have enough money for a 30 second TV spot, but we sure make some of the best ice cream you ever tasted.'

A 1983 press release read: 'Two Crazy Vermont Hippies Invade Boston with their ice cream. While the invasion . . . might not be termed a full-scale attack, Ben and Jerry figure that it will at least pay for the gas.'

The image struck a chord with America's ice cream eating public in a way that their quasi-European competitors didn't. It was honest, and they were only offering what they genuinely could deliver – good ice cream and a decent way of doing business.

Another useful feature of offering reality is that it provides free publicity. That's why wacky companies typically spend so little on advertising – what they are doing is genuinely interesting and different enough that the media pays attention.

Advertising agencies would, it seems, be left out in the cold by this new approach, but one UK ad agency is ahead of its clients in the move away from spurious imagery to character-based marketing. Instead of simply advertising a product, St. Luke's seeks to help determine what the client's ethos is, then convey that ethos to a wider audience. It's a service that can challenge the way the client does business.

'The old fantasy, dream, aspiration advertising is worn out,' says co-founder David Abraham. What an advertising agency needs to do now is shift towards helping clients understand and design their relationship with stakeholders. St. Luke's even has an acronym for it: TRS – their Total Role in Society.

'In a lot of advertising consumers are asked to live in almost a fantasy world,' says Abraham. 'What we're saying is, let's try to make it closer to reality. All brands and companies exist in a social context. It's time we recognised that fact.'

It's a brave step. And some people will question its sincerity. But co-founder Andy Law insists it is not about being politically correct for its own sake: 'St. Luke's is not a nicey, nicey advertising agency,' he says. 'Good advertising is provocative sometimes. But we do believe all organisations should conduct themselves ethically.'

Still, David Abraham hasn't forgotten the criteria by which the majority of clients still judge advertising agencies. 'At the end of the day, are we still trying to sell more stuff?' he asks. 'The answer is yes.'

Tom Chappell, the co-founder and president of eco-minded toiletry maker Tom's of Maine, summarises a character expresser's point of view when he says: 'Success means never letting the competition define you. Instead, you have to define yourself based on a point of view you care deeply about.'[30] So does VeriFone's Hatim Tyabji, 'You won't see a strategy du jour,' he says. 'You won't find us reacting to the last announcement of a competitor. Consistency – and doing what is right – is a mantra around here.'[31] 'What we're trying to cultivate in this company is moral authority. When I have moral authority, I can do anything. That concept is not understood very well in corporate life. People look for bullshit authority, not moral authority.'[32]

Benetton, the Italian clothing company, appears to have taken a step beyond character expression into a bizarre category of its own, with marketing that is entirely about social context, without even a mention of the product.

Since 1988, the company has run controversial, at times shocking, print ads featuring jolting images of newborn babies, war zones and AIDS patients, that have nothing to do with the company's products, but a lot to do with generating press coverage, media awards and public furore. The ads may even have sold a few sweaters – Benetton is a quickly growing global company with 7,000 stores in 120 countries.

Though Benetton is not precisely a character expresser – there's too much distance between its products and its marketing for that – its leaders have a similiar head first, trust your instincts, high risk attitude to marketing. 'Research? We try to do the very opposite,' says Oliviero Toscani, the photographer behind most of Benetton's more outrageous ads, on the company's Web site. 'We try to make our ads personal. If you do research, you get yesterday's results. If they did research five hundred years ago, they never would have discovered America. They would have found out the world is flat. You have to have the courage to make mistakes. Everything we do is about impulse, about guts. That's what built Benetton; Luciano [Benetton] didn't test the market for a taste in coloured sweaters.'

A philosophy is hard to copy

Because wacky companies offer the world their real selves, rather than a market oriented image, they are very hard to replicate.

Many have asked: 'If those idiots Ben and Jerry can do it, why can't we?' And many have tried, notably an early competitor who came out with a product called Steve's Ice Cream, mimicking Ben & Jerry's right down to the homey packaging. The trouble was, despite the picture on the box, there was no Steve. At Ben & Jerry's there were, and are, a real Ben and a real Jerry, and with them, the values, complexities and idiosyncrasies that make the whole thing work.

Similarly, IKEA's success formula is not a formula, but a whole array of details that give life to the founder's business philosophy. IKEA is not just about inexpensive furniture or clever design, either of which competitors can, and have, copied. Rather, it's a whole myriad of innovations and clever ideas: some big – like using warehouse-sized stores and installing restaurants – some small, but as important, as naming every little grapple-grommet they sell.

One of the clearest examples of how difficult it can be to copy a wacky company was British Airways' attempt to introduce Southwest Airlines' style humour. One manager, who has since left the company, adopted the title of 'Corporate Jester' and even had it printed on his business cards beneath the regal British Airways logo. The appointment, he told journalists at the time, was based on the Shakespearean tradition and grew out of the job description for King Lear's Fool. The role, he said, would enable him to ask awkward questions of senior management and to act as a foil against complacency. The idea may have worked, on stage or in almost any of our wacky companies, but in the formal setting of British Airways, it appeared only ridiculous.

A clear and different philosophy attracts like-minded employees

Employees, too, care increasingly about the character and values of the company they work for. Companies with strong values-based philosophies, like Ben & Jerry's, the Body Shop and Smith & Hawken, can generate high levels of employee loyalty and motivation. They also find it easier to recruit than their competitors and face low rates of staff turnover and absenteeism.

A clear and different philosophy attracts like-minded stockholders

Private investors are increasingly choosing investments that reflect, or at least don't run counter to, their own values. The biggest impact of this has been seen in the growth of ethical investment funds (also known as screened portfolios or socially responsible investments) which allow ordinary people to tie their savings and pensions to their political, environmental or moral beliefs. According to the Social Investment Organisation (SIO), a Toronto-based non-profit organisation set up to promote socially responsible investment, a growing number of investors are beginning to realise that it makes little sense to donate time and money to charities or environmental groups while investing in the very organisations they're campaigning against.

Ethical investors, according to SIO executive director Robert Walker, have three basic motivations. Some simply don't want to invest in companies whose activities run counter to their moral values, and choose funds that screen out companies engaged in, say, tobacco or weapons manufacture. Others use their investments as a way to encourage companies to change their behaviour and compete on their social and environmental records as well as their financial performance. An increasing number of social investors now also view socially responsible investment as a tool for social transformation, as a way to take control of capital and help create a more socially and environmentally sustainable society.

Of course, no matter how lofty their ambitions, investors still want a decent return, and they do get it. Ethical investments, according to Walker, perform about as well as any other mutual funds: 'Recent US studies show that screened portfolios perform just as well as unscreened.'

The move to ethical investments is affecting corporate behaviour, adds Walker. 'Corporations are listening and they are concerned. Screened portfolios, ideally combined with shareholdership, can prompt corporations to review and change policies, programs and practices. For some, socially responsible investment and corporate social responsibility are only a matter of public relations and positioning to take advantage of changing business-operating environments. But others have recognised they will not prosper over the long term if employees are not satisfied, if communities are under stress, and if the environment is allowed to decay. These corporations need to be rewarded for taking action and implementing progressive programs.'

Selling the philosophy

It can be difficult to get others on board with a wacky new philosophy of business. It's especially difficult when trying to change the culture of an existing company. Though shop floor employees are generally warm to the idea of a more caring, fun, or empowered workplace, senior managers can be hard to persuade. Sometimes the only solution is a parting of the ways.

SOL's Joronen, for example, found it was all but impossible to sell her new methods to the old guard. Her only option was to buy the company she wanted to manage and run it separately from the rest of the family business. Semco's Semler found quick agreement by firing most of his senior managers in a single day. At advertising agency St. Luke's, the London office manager hived off his branch from the rest of the company by drawing an imaginary line in his office and asking anyone who wanted to join him to cross it.

Most of our wacky companies have little difficulty persuading new recruits of the value of their philosophy because most employees, including senior managers, are self selecting – they chose the company because it fits with their values. They do, however, have to convince at least some outsiders to come on board with their new way of thinking.

Outside investors can take a lot of persuasion. Not necessarily because they think wacky entrepreneurs are crazy (though they may well think that), but because, in spite of the growth in ethical investment funds, decision makers at the traditional sources of funding generally don't believe that talk of vision, values and philosophy has any relevance to their investment decision.

This is what Starbuck's CEO Howard Schultz was up against when he first planned to take his company public in 1991. The investment bankers came courting and, writes Schultz, 'it was flattering to be the object of so much attention'. The bankers were all very impressed with the coffee chain's financial information but, says Schultz, 'Almost all of them seemed to tune out when I started discussing our company's mission statement – how we treat our employees like partners and our customers like stars. If they were taking notes, their pens stopped moving when I brought up values, as if I were indulging in rhetoric unrelated to Starbuck's financial performance. . . . Experience has taught me that it's easy to talk about values, hard to implement them, and even harder for an outsider to determine which values are heartfelt and which are window dressing. Wall Street cannot place a value on values.'[33]

Luciano Benetton doesn't soft peddle around his stakeholders. Besides the disturbing ads his company is so famous for, it also funds *Colors*, a magazine filled with apocalyptic images of the world and what's wrong with it but, as with most of Benetton's marketing, not a mention of the company's products.

The stakeholders' reaction? 'They went insane,' says *Colors* founding editor Tibor Kalman. '[Photographer] Toscani does an ad with a white baby being breast fed by a black woman, and of course the franchise holders and the managers go insane. There were huge battles going on all the time. Those poor people were trying to sell sweaters. But Luciano Benetton would say to them, "Shut the hell up; what we are doing is something important here."'[34]

THE BOTTOM LINE

▶ A philosophy is what creates differentiating values.

▶ A philosophy is hard to copy.

▶ Employees and values are more important than customers and systems.

NOTES

1. Kelly Caitlin, 'Laid-back Firm Comes North', in *The Globe and Mail*, 3 August 1988.
2. The editors, 'Coming of Age', in *Inc.*, April 1989.
3. Anna Muoio, 'The Secrets of their Success – and Yours', in *Fast Company*, June/July 1997.
4. The editors, 'Coming of Age', in *Inc.*, April 1989.
5. Robert Levering and Milton Moskowitz, *The 100 Best Companies to Work for in America* (Doubleday, New York, 1993), p. 385.
6. Kevin Freiberg and Jackie Freiberg, *Nuts! Southwest Airlines' Crazy Recipe for Business and Personal Success* (Orion Business, London, 1998).
7. Walter Goldsmith and David Clutterbuck, *The Winning Streak, Mark II* (Orion Business Books, 1997).
8. Greg Farrell, 'Chiat's End Game', in *Adweek*, 12 July 1993.
9. Greg Farrell, 'Chiat's End Game', 1993.
10. Robert Levering and Milton Moskowitz, 1993, p. 422.
11. Kevin Freiberg and Jackie Freiberg, *Nuts!*, 1998.
12. Kevin Freiberg and Jackie Freiberg, *Nuts!*, 1998.
13. Robert Levering and Milton Moskowitz, 1993, p. 173.
14. Gillian Flynn, 'Why Rhino Won't Wait until Tomorrow', in *Personnel Journal*, July 1996.
15. Alex Markels, 'Power to the People', in *Fast Company*, February/March 1998.
16. Craig Vetter, 'He's Not Worthy – The Curious Crisis of Yvon Chouinard', in *Outside*, January 1997.
17. Fred Lager, *Ben & Jerry's: The Inside Scoop – How Two Real Guys Built a Business with a Social Conscience and a Sense of Humor* (Crown Publishers, New York, 1994).
18. Ben Cohen and Jerry Greenfield, *Ben & Jerry's Double Dip: Lead with Your Values and Make Money Too* (Simon & Schuster, New York, 1997).
19. Ben Cohen and Jerry Greenfield, *Ben & Jerry's Double Dip*, 1997.
20. Meredith Maran, *What It's Like to Live Now* (Bantam Books, 1995).
21. Fred Lager, *Ben & Jerry's*, 1994.
22. Ben Cohen and Jerry Greenfield, *Ben & Jerry's Double Dip*, 1997.

23. John Case, 'Corporate Culture', in *Inc.*, November 1996.
24. Yvon Chouinard, Patagonia Web site, 1997, http://www.patagonia.com.
25. Fred Lager, *Ben & Jerry's*, 1994.
26. Anna Muoio, 'The Secrets of their Success', 1997.
27. Daniel Kadlec, 'The New World of Giving', in *Time*, 5 May 1997.
28. Fred Lager, *Ben & Jerry's*, 1994.
29. Peter Laundy, 'Image Trouble', in *Inc.*, September 1993.
30. Anna Muoio, 'The Secrets of their Success', 1997.
31. J. Kutler, 'VeriFone's Unconventional Chief', in *American Banker*, 20 April 1995.
32. W. Taylor, 'At VeriFone It's a Dog's Life (And They Love It!)', in *Fast Company*, November 1995.
33. Howard Schultz and Dori Jones Yang, *Pour Your Heart Into It* (Hyperion, 1997).
34. Allan Casey, 'Tibor Kalman', in *Adbusters*, Autumn, 1998.

3 Dismantling the organisation

'If you want my advice, take a deep breath, pluck up your courage and feed the policy book to the shredder one page at a time.' (Ricardo Semler, CEO, Semco Brazil)[1]

'To keep a company alive, one of the jobs of top management is to keep it dis-organised.' (Lars Kolind, CEO, Oticon)[2]

'Why go to someone with a title when you can go to someone with an answer?' (W. L. Gore associate, Tom Fairchild)[3]

'I get the most excited when I see a complete industry confused.' (Hal Rosenbluth, CEO, Rosenbluth International)[4]

It's an old business school adage that 'structure follows strategy'. Like most business school wisdom, it's wrong. Structure actually results from philosophy. The traditional pyramid organisation grew out of societies that were composed of multiple layers and were simply the reflection of the 'natural order'. As that natural order breaks down, it's not surprising that rigid, multi-layered hierarchies become harder and harder to manage. It's true that companies do try to rearrange divisional and departmental structures – often frequently – in line with changing business goals. But that's the equivalent of rearranging the position of open-plan cubicles (or moving the deck chairs on the Titanic – choose your own metaphor). The underlying shape or pattern of the organisation is largely unaffected.

It is the business philosophy that defines how people form groups and the relationships between groups. Like any complex organism, a company is made up of thousands of small groups, linked together to form a whole. What makes the organisation function is not the gross structures (the hierarchy charts) but the way these small components behave together. (A person and a mannequin may look the same, but it's what goes on at the miniature level that counts.)

Changing the external shape of a hierarchical organisation will do little towards changing the behaviours of groups and individuals within it. Left to their own devices, people used to hierarchies will invariably create subtle layers of differentiation and rely on command and control to make things happen. Wacky companies have different structures and shapes because their philosophy is different.

Twenty years ago, in places as far apart as Japan and Brazil, there were wacky companies whose structures were based on a fundamental belief that other companies were far too soft in imposing discipline and hierarchy. They put new recruits through at least a year of humiliation and self-discipline to instil the kind of group values that would allow for a culture of radically greater than normal control. Sadly (they would have made a great contrast) we could find no trace of these companies in 1998. In their case, being different was not enough to ensure survival, it seems.

Most wacky companies today are relaxed-looking places, where staff dress like they're at summer camp, everyone uses first names, and it's difficult for a casual visitor to tell who's in charge. In our research, we found, variously, puppies under tables, bare feet on desks, putting greens in offices, popcorn machines in factories and, in one case, surfboards in the mailroom.

What we didn't find were: job titles, corner offices, organisational charts, executive furniture, assigned workspaces, punch clocks, neckties, or anyone willing to answer to 'Mister'.

At Oticon, SOL, VeriFone and Chiat/Day we couldn't even find any desks – employees there work from rolling carts, shared workspaces, cafeterias, or crouched on the floor.

Wacky companies may look like badly run student houses, but competitors underestimate them at their peril. For all their chaotic appearance, these are highly efficient, fast moving, hard working, effective organisations – or, as Oticon's Lars Kolind would have it, 'dis-organisations'.

Wacky companies go to a lot of trouble to disorganise themselves, in many cases becoming increasingly chaotic looking as they mature and evolve. And wackiness is not kid stuff – it takes thought, experimentation and a great deal of nerve to create the kind of chaos that works.

Most companies start small, tackling the symbols of bureaucracy – the job titles, perks and dress codes. They then go on to tackle the bureaucracy itself, shredding the paper and tossing out the rule books.

The next step is to dismantle the company's hierarchy, removing layers of management, flattening the organisation and decentralising control. They mix it up too – encouraging people to try doing each other's jobs.

The wackiest among them go on to get rid of their structure altogether, doing away with job titles, roles, job descriptions and, if not the bosses themselves, at least the concept of bosses.

At this point, many look about them and find they don't even need the office any more, and call in the movers to cart away the desks, partitions, walls and chairs.

Employees in wacky companies need a certain amount of imagination to figure out what they do, whom they do it for, and where they do it. But they do do it – in most cases, faster, cheaper, and better than they ever did before.

Lightening up – cutting the crap

The first things to go in wacky companies are the trappings of status – executive washrooms, reserved parking places or special executive furniture. At Finnish cleaning company SOL, the symbols of hierarchy that would normally distinguish a manager from a worker are conspicuously absent. Slogans such as 'Freedom from the office', 'Freedom from status symbols' and 'Kill routine before it kills you' drive the point home.

No one at SOL gets special treatment. SOL's open plan office in Helsinki has virtually no hierarchy. Desks are communal – employees roam around the building settling wherever the space is most amenable to the task they are undertaking – and no one has a secretary. In fact, no one has a job title. Each employee has an area of the business that he or she is accountable for, such as bookkeeping or employment records, but no one has an official title.

Joronen herself does without an assistant, as she expects her staff to. 'We do not have secretaries or other service people in SOL. Everyone writes their own letters, sends faxes, makes copies, makes the coffee for customers, and answers the phone. I must be the role model for everyone, and always do everything myself.'

Nor are there any secretaries, receptionists or personal assistants at the Brazilian manufacturing firm Semco. Everyone, including top management, fetches and carries, welcomes guests and makes their own tea. 'We don't believe in cluttering the payroll with ungratifying dead end jobs,' says CEO Ricardo Semler.[5]

When Semler took over his family manufacturing firm and set about deconstructing the organisation, he, too, started with the symbols. With the agreement of office staff and managers, he knocked down the office walls, re-designed the workspace and got rid of individual offices.

'My own work area got much smaller,' he says, 'and I still can't find that sofa I used to have.' Next to go were the reserved parking spaces, followed by embossed business cards, private dining rooms and rank-related office furniture. 'No longer would it be possible to discern a person's status by the grade and grain of his office furniture or the plushness of the carpet,' wrote Semler in his company history.[6]

At Bloomberg, a New York-based news services company, there are no titles, even on business cards. Management dropped job titles altogether in 1992, partly because they were seen as divisive among the workforce, but also because they created an expectation of promotion every couple of years, which could only be fulfilled by creating more and more titles and smaller and smaller fiefdoms.

At Ben & Jerry's Homemade, there are job titles – people can pick what they like. Tsar, guru, queen and emperor are popular – co-founder Ben Cohen likes 'Primal ice cream therapist'. 'A hierarchy does exist, but it's something we can break through, dull and blur the edges of,' says info queen Mitch Curren.

A title like primal ice cream therapist may not carry a lot of weight, but symbols do, and wacky companies know better than to underestimate them. If, as so often happens in conventional companies, the values and mission statement shout egalitarianism, while formal titles, reserved parking places, suits and ties indicate that nothing has changed, employees will take the symbols, not the statements, as the more accurate reflection of reality.

These symbols include names – in wacky companies everyone is on a first name basis – dress codes, titles, modes of address, and social habits denoting status. Even where the national culture favours formality in most things, our wacky companies are invariably that much less formal than the pervading social norm. In Europe, for example, where many languages use both a familiar and a formal form of the word 'you', IKEA staff invariably use the familiar. And in Taiwan, employees at computer maker Acer took some time getting used to calling their CEO Stan, rather than Mr Shih, but they do. It's this easing up on the normally rigid Chinese organisational formality – where employees are often made to wear company uniforms and even senior managers are required to punch into time clocks – that many believe is part of Acer's success.

Dress is the most powerful symbol of corporate rigidity left in most English-speaking countries. That's probably why most of our wacky leaders are so rarely seen in suits. Ben Cohen, probably America's wealthiest ice cream seller, is rumoured not to own a suit. Nicholas Graham, CEO of off-beat underwear company Joe Boxer, favours bright colours and polka dots and says he likes having his own business because 'it gives me the freedom to dress as a goofball'.[7]

SOL's Joronen takes her symbolic role seriously and acts as sort of a colour-coded role model. Because the colour yellow symbolises the positive sunny service culture she encourages at SOL, Joronen always wears yellow. She wears the same yellow company jackets her employees wear and even her swimsuit, bicycle and evening dress are yellow.

Southwest's Herb Kelleher is known for his preference for casual wear even at the expense of executive image. He often goes to board meetings in jeans and a sweatshirt and has appeared in front of Southwest's troops and the media as, among other things, Elvis, Corporal Klinger, General Patton, and a Harley rider.

It's hard to be exceptionally casual in ultra-laid back southern California, but Patagoniacs manage it, with corporate wear that includes baggy surfing shorts and bare feet. According to the editors of The 100 Best Companies to Work for in America, one applicant knew it was her kind of company when she saw a staff member nursing an infant at the board room table.

Richard Branson's informal dress sense is just one of the many ways he stands out from the pinstriped crowd – and he turns this, too, to his advantage. In the early days of Virgin, the company ran into a cash flow crisis that threatened to put it out of business. Branson arranged a meeting with his account manager at Coutts, one of the oldest and most conservative British banks. When the day arrived, the young entrepreneur turned up for work dressed as usual in jeans and a T-shirt. 'Richard,' said one of his colleagues, 'don't you think it's time to put a suit on?' 'If I suddenly turn up at the bank wearing a suit and tie,' said Branson, 'they will know we're trouble.' In the event, Branson strolled into the meeting in his jeans, and informed his bankers that the business was expanding so quickly that he needed a bigger overdraft to keep up with orders. The bank took one look at the scruffy, self-assured youth and agreed.

Whether it's a relaxed dress code or a relaxed social code, an informal atmosphere can have a powerful symbolic effect. It tells people that 'we want you to be yourselves, not uniformed robots, and we want you to be happy and comfortable at work'.

Many mainstream companies have been surprised to learn how important this approach is to their staff – and how motivating. Matt Weinstein is CEO of Playfair, a San Francisco area consultancy that specialises in team building and encouraging fun at work. He found with one client that, when given a choice of treats including parties or cash bonuses, employees almost unanimously chose casual Fridays – a perk that, incidentally, costs the company nothing. However, this enthusiasm calls into question why the companies need to impose formal dress code in the first place.

Dress-down Friday – a ritual response

The trend in recent years for companies in the US and Europe to allow employees the 'perk' of dressing down once a week is yet another example of how traditional businesses adopt the form, but not the philosophy, of wacky companies. Far from being a great motivator, Dress-down Friday can reinforce employees' sense of being obliged to conform the rest of the week. In organisations where dress-down day is a privilege earned by meeting departmental targets, having to come to work in a suit, while others dress casually, becomes a degrading punishment.

In a company co-founded by one of the authors of this book, dress code is left entirely to the discretion of the individuals and teams, on the grounds that they know what's appropriate and when. A proposal from the chairman that once in a while it would be fun if everyone had a Dress-up Friday, with tuxedos and ball gowns, still hasn't been adopted . . .

Ricardo Semler rejects dress codes, because, he says, they 'are all about conformity'. Semler argues that a corporate uniform inevitably leads to other forms of officially imposed conformity, such as a uniform language, behaviour and possibly even thinking – any of which can stifle the creativity and flexibility essential to a vibrant organisation.

That's what Acer's Stan Shih discovered. He agrees with the North American perception that Asian workers can be hesitant about speaking their minds before their organisational superiors. He insists, however, that this behaviour is not culturally ingrained, but merely a function of the typically rigid Asian organisation structure. Simply loosening up the hierarchy, leaving doors open and using first names has, he's found, freed up the communication flow. Now ideas fly freely in person and via e-mail, and employees do speak their minds. William Lu, the CEO of Acer Computer International in Singapore, says: 'Sometimes we have to go to people one by one to get their opinion, but it's rare.'[8]

Working the hours

People in wacky companies are also free to set their own hours – you won't see a punch clock in any wacky workplace. For Ricardo Semler, it took passing out on a supplier's factory floor to notice that there's not that much to be gained from allegiance to a clock. Taken ill while visiting a pump factory in New York, Semler underwent a battery of tests to determine the cause of his illness. The diagnosis: the most advanced case of stress the doctor had ever seen in a 25-year-old.

Semler went home determined to change the way he ran his own life, and the way he ran his business. He tossed out the ingrained notions that effort and results are related, and that the quantity of work is as important as its quality. He tore up his rule book, dismantled the company time clocks and abandoned the highly controlled, number-crunching management style he'd been using to try to get his family business back on track. 'It was no longer a case of count the numbers and the profits will look after themselves,' he said. 'The new doctrine was "forget about the numbers, we've got better things to do".' He called the malady 'time sickness' and posited that it was caused by four things:

1. The mistaken belief that effort and result are directly proportional.
2. The idea that the quantity of work is more important than the quality.
3. Using change and events to justify poor time-management.
4. Fear of delegation and fear of being replaced.

Semler abolished set office hours for management on the grounds that it was the quality of the work done rather than the time spent doing it that mattered. Later, he applied the same principle to shop floor work hours, though he left it up to the work groups at each plant as to whether or not to adopt flexi-time.

Semler also encourages salaried staff to take time off when they need to – down time to learn new skills or recharge their batteries that he calls 'Hepatitis Leave'. The name came about when some executives said they didn't have the time to think anymore. Semler asked what would happen if they had hepatitis and were forced to spend two months recuperating.

Almost all the companies in our sample work on some form of flexi-time. It's a function of trusting the employees and giving them the freedom to do what they think is best. At Patagonia's Ventura, California head office, for example, the surfboards leaning against the mail room wall are not product samples – they're there so staffers can surf when the surf's up, even if that happens to be 3 p.m. on a Tuesday. Says Patagonia's director of public affairs Lu Setnicka: 'Yes, people still take time off to go surfing. [We tell employees] you're the one who knows best how to do your work, you can manage it best. You get feedback, and have deadlines, but you don't have people leaning over your shoulder tapping their feet.'

Setting their own hours also enables employees to have a life outside the office. For employers, that means being able to attract a pool of talent that would otherwise not feel able to work, and getting better results from working parents who aren't wracked with guilt.

Here's how it works for SOL team co-ordinator Jukka Suuniitty: 'Yesterday I came in at about 11 o'clock. Today I came in about 7 o'clock. It depends on the situation at home. I have two little children and they are ranked very high in my priorities. My idea is that I try to balance things. Normally I come in every day. Sometimes I take work home if there is an urgent project that has a deadline. Also, I have days during the week that I might stay at home with the kids. It has taken many years to forget the old way of doing things and start to believe that you intuitively know how much you should work without checking the hours every day. I don't count the hours anymore,' says Suuniitty.

Leapfrog Research and Planning Ltd, a Windsor, UK, based market research company runs not so much on flexi-time as 'kid time'. The company, which conducts consumer interviews and focus groups for such clients as Tesco, Coca-Cola and Camelot, is based on the concept of flexibility: people take personal time when they need it, no questions asked.

The management at Leapfrog, like so many of the wacky employers in our example, recognise that flexible workdays aren't just nice, they're necessary. It may sound crazy to give employees time off to take their children shoe shopping or to run in an egg and spoon race at a school sports day, but consider the options: working with an office full of stressed and guilt-wracked parents, or not hiring parents at all. Neither option appealed to Judy Taylor, Leapfrog MD and mother of four, and her business partner Andrea Berlowitz. They set up their company to make juggling work and home, if not easy, at least manageable – not for altruistic reasons, but because they needed the talented people who would otherwise stay home to raise families.

Here's how it works:

- at peak times – Christmas, summer holidays and the end of the school year – an assistant co-ordinates diaries so everyone has the personal time off they need
- executives work in pairs so there is always someone in the office who's up to speed on a project when a client calls
- regular status meetings keep everyone up to date on all accounts
- the details of every job are computerised
- everyone is entitled to personal time off regardless of office position or family situation.

The flexibility also appeals to people who may not have children, but do have lives, and to people who, for whatever reason, just need a break. Says Taylor: 'If someone wants a day off because they're hacked off, that's OK. We get more out of people that way.'[9]

Most wacky companies are replete with family friendly policies. Not just flexi-time, but on-site day care and other family friendly perks.

A number of California high-tech companies, whose employees are often too busy to have children anyway, have introduced a new twist on family centred policies by allowing staff to bring their pets to work, adding a whole new angle to 'the dog ate my homework' story. The Sacramento Bee advises the use of baby gates and obedience courses for office pets. This may not be entirely effective for Burton A. Burton, the CEO of Casablanca Fan Company, who likes to bring his pet – a boa constrictor – to work. At Bay area software developer Digital Renaissance, the only criterion is that employees' dogs get along with the boss's dog.

Clearly, dismantling the punch clock can free people to do their best at work and still enjoy a private life. For others, though, blurring the edges of the working day can mean working at least as much, if not more, than they did before. Ben & Jerry's Homemade is, for example, widely regarded as one of the most fun-loving employers in America, with benefit packages that include on-site childcare and free ice cream. Info queen Mitch Curren has been with them since the late eighties. When asked what it's like to work there, she said, without hesitation: 'Exhausting.' 'Being committed, means working more than you should,' she explains.

The commitment is usually as much to one's peers as to one's boss. Susan Boltinghouse, a controls engineer at off-beat California robotics company Odetics, admits to putting in long hours: 'In my division there's a fair amount of peer pressure to do that. It has never come from management but when your peers are working particularly hard, you kind of feel like you had better do that as well.' Odetics software engineer Marti Cassell-Fix adds: 'People put in a lot, and some of us don't get paid for our overtime. There is that peer pressure to work, but you always want to; you enjoy what you're doing.'[10]

Sometimes flexible work hours can pit companies against the authorities. France's legislated 39-hour work week has had labour ministry inspectors out photographing number plates in company parking lots after hours – behaviour that has prompted business leaders to ask whether these limits really should apply to professionals and managers.[11]

At AES, a highly empowered power plant company, co-founder and CEO Dennis Bakke doesn't feel this kind of clock-watching should apply to anyone, and objects to American labour laws that require that non-management workers be paid strictly on an hourly basis. He argues that an all salary format, which he uses in jurisdictions that permit it, allows for the empowerment and freedom his company encourages. Hourly pay laws, he argued in a letter to a US Secretary of Labor, 'are one of the major hindrances to creating a fun, meaningful and empowering workplace.'[12]

SOL's Liisa Joronen feels so strongly about not keeping tabs on staff hours she's prepared to break the law. Finnish law requires all employers to keep detailed records of employees' hours. Joronen keeps no records at all, and does not intend to. 'We don't have overwork in this company,' she says. 'I will never keep records of my peoples' hours. I will go to jail before I do that.'

Julian Richer, CEO of UK retailer Richer Sounds, does monitor his staff hours, but only to ensure they don't work too much. Those with six-day weeks or ten-hour days on their time sheets will have to explain themselves to the boss. 'I believe work should be fun. I also think we should do less of it,' he says.[13]

No rules

Wacky companies don't need strictly defined work hours, just as they don't need most rules. As detailed in Chapter 2, an overriding philosophy and a strong set of values provide all the direction most people need. At IKEA, for example, 'there are very few rules and guidelines but a very strict framework,' says IKEA Sweden purchasing manager Sven Kulldorf. 'I would say rules are not something that make an organisation hot. We don't like rules.'

Neither does British vacuum cleaner designer James Dyson. His employees have only two rules: no smoking and no ties. Dyson once told the board of an American company that ties make you go deaf in your old age. There's no evidence that they heard him.

Three basic rules seem to be common to most wacky companies:

- understand the values
- use your common sense
- cut the bureaucracy.

Those who try it, like it. Oscar Prieto, a manager with power plant operator AES, experimented when his company took over a newly privatised hydroelectric plant in Cabra Corral, Argentina. 'We broke all the rules,' says Prieto. 'No overtime. No bosses. No time records. No shift schedules. No assigned responsibilities. No administration. And guess what? It worked!'[14]

Rules, paperwork, forms, regulations – unless they have a clear benefit to workers, customers or society at large, wacky companies get rid of them. You might call these things bureaucracy; Julian Richer calls them crap. His 'Cut the Crap Committee' meets monthly to seek and destroy excess regulations and procedures. 'If a rule isn't really necessary, strip it away,' he says.[15]

At Danish hearing-aid manufacturer Oticon, the war on bureaucracy started with a war on paper. The company has reduced paperwork by 80 per cent since banning filing and memos and scanning and shredding all incoming mail. The shredded remains now tumble symbolically down a transparent chute through the company cafeteria.

James Dyson has also banned memos. They are, he says, 'just a way of passing the buck'. He's equally unimpressed with e-mail. 'The graphics are so appalling I just can't get interested enough to read them,' he says.

Bureaucracy isn't just unnecessary; it can be downright dangerous, argues University National Bank and Trust founder Carl Schmitt. 'What will kill this company first is a bunch of people running around with their noses stuck in rule books and manuals.' More than just contributing to a starchy atmosphere, he claims, rules allow people to avoid taking responsibility for their actions, sapping the challenge out of any job.[16]

Ricardo Semler found that rules also sapped innovation – something he needed in his moribund manufacturing plant. 'The desire for rules and the need for innovation are incompatible,' he says. 'It's order or progress. Rules freeze companies inside a glacier; innovation lets them ride sleighs over it.'

Semler is something of a born again bureaucracy fighter. In the early days of his tenure at Semco, he added a great many rules as he implemented new systems based on the management theories of the time. As he describes in his book *Maverick*: 'Our residential managerial wizard installed dozens of new procedures and invented new forms almost daily. Files were rigorously organised ... Employees' bags were searched. Everyone was issued with a plastic ID card ... Production schedules were displayed on boards in our new planning and control department. Members of our new time and methods department were dispatched around the plant, searching for ways to speed our workers up.'

It didn't work, nor did it sit well with Semler. 'I couldn't help thinking that Semco could be run differently, without all those numbers and all those rules. What if we could strip away all the artificial nonsense, all the managerial mumbo jumbo? What if we could run the business in a simpler way, a more natural way?'[17] He did, and it worked. Semler has abolished most of the controls, like security checks, dress codes and time clocks, which are still the norm among his competitors. He also got rid of the company rule book. He knew it was a waste of time when he handed managers some new pages for it. When he later asked their opinions about the new rules, he was surprised to hear that they thought they were fine – especially as he had stapled the pages together so no one could read them.

Today new hires at Semco don't get a long list of dos and don'ts. Instead, they are given a 20-page booklet called the *Survival Manual*, containing many cartoons but few words. It is a testament to the fact that, at Semco, the main rule is: use your common sense.

Fighting bureaucracy

Wacky leaders are able to cut the crap so ruthlessly because they don't care about most of the things professional managers worry about. They spend their time working on what's important to them, and trust their staff to muddle through on anything else that comes up. By contrast, professional managers spend a great deal of time preventing undesirable things from happening – usually by stopping other people from doing things.

Harry Quadracci, the founder and CEO of Quad/Graphics, a \$375 million a year Wisconsin-based printing and technology company, has seen this innovation stifling process happen all too often. 'Everybody manages quite well. Whenever anything goes wrong, they take immediate action to make sure nothing will go wrong again. The problem is, nothing new will ever happen, either.'[18]

Fighting bureaucracy is like rowing upstream. The moment you ease off, you drift back downstream rapidly. It is always easier to allow routines to develop and to create systems to deal with individual problems than it is to step back and consider what could be done to make systems unnecessary. See figure 3.1.

To IKEA Sweden purchasing manager Sven Kulldorf, 'Bureaucracy is like a cancer, it grows from itself. It's easy to think that if we control this then we can eliminate the problem, but there are always hundreds of areas that we have to control. Like a cancer you have to take a knife and cut it away. We have to work at it continuously.'

The principal weapon in the wacky leader's armoury is his or her own example.

Simplexity

Wacky leaders have a talent for simplexity. The term, used by one of the authors in an earlier book,[19] means simplifying complex issues to the point that they're manageable. It's done, not by glossing over issues in the manner of a political soundbite, but by breaking them

---

What creates bureaucracy?

- Systems that go unchallenged
- Systems that aren't owned and controlled by the people who use them
- People who are not in control of their jobs (so they have to find ways of controlling other people's)
- Structures that don't allow for initiative
- Lack of personal direction and purpose

How do you kill bureaucracy?

- Challenge every system
- Let people design and control the systems they think are necessary
- Make people responsible for their own jobs
- Leave room for initiative
- Design jobs with inherent direction and purpose

Figure 3.1 Bureaucracy and how to eliminate it

down to the point that they can be dealt with by a combination of simple solutions. It means simplifying without being simplistic.

It worked for Patagonia's Yvon Chouinard, whose guiding principle of design was originally expressed by the writer Antoine de Saint Exupéry: 'Have you ever thought, not only about the airplane but about whatever man builds, that all of man's industrial efforts, all his computations and calculations, all the nights spent working over draughts and blueprints, invariably culminate in the production of a thing whose sole and guiding principle is the ultimate principle of simplicity?'

Patagonia's clothing and equipment designs still follow this principle of ultimate simplicity, as do those of IKEA, Dyson and many of our wacky companies.

IKEA's faith in simplexity extends to its systems. As Ingvar Kamprad explains in his testament: 'The key concepts behind simplicity are words like efficiency, common sense and doing what comes naturally. If we do what feels natural, we will avoid complicated solutions. The fewer the rules and the shorter the instructions, the easier and more natural it is to stick to them. The simpler the explanation, the easier it is to understand it and carry it out.'[20]

The reigning masters of simplexity are Southwest Airlines. Herb Kelleher and his thousands of employees run an immensely complex organisation dealing with millions of passengers, government regulations, union agreements, complex technology, and intense competition – and have succeeded by making their operations so simple no one else has been able to copy them.

On the face of it, there's little to stop competitors from simply copying the strategy: keep planes full and flying, keep costs and fares low, and keep customers and employees happy. Southwest's methods are no secret; the system doesn't depend on patents or proprietary technology and the airline serves a growing, fairly unregulated, market. Yet, though many have tried, no competitor has ever successfully mimicked Southwest's formula. Possibly, because, like IKEA, Southwest's secret isn't really a formula at all.

Everything Southwest does, in its technology, personnel policies and customer service, from cutting out bureaucracy, to communicating in person rather than through memos, to letting employees make decisions on the spot, is ruled by a guiding principle: keep it simple.

Southwest uses only one type of aircraft – the Boeing 737. Besides generating bulk deals from Boeing, this streamlines training, crew scheduling, parts inventories, mechanical expertise and turnaround procedures. Southwest only has one class of seats. In fact, customers aren't even assigned seats. There are no meals and, since 1995, not even any tickets. Simplicity increases speed and cuts costs, so the company is always looking for ways to simplify things.

Said chairman Herb Kelleher in a 1994 interview: 'Business has gotten so complex that we've forgotten the basics: do what your customer wants, be happy in your work . . . all these little things. The way I dignify it is to say "Remember Einstein's criterion: if you've got a choice between two theories, neither of which is overtly provable, pick the simplest one. It's always right!"'[21]

Southwest's marketing strategy is also insanely simple: no image positioning or glamour here – what they offer are cheap deals and a good time getting there.

Underwear mogul Nicholas Graham has shocked the New York fashion industry – a fraught and fractured, highly complex industry – and succeeded with an insanely simple strategy. Graham, in an age of increasingly pointed target marketing, doesn't target. He appeals to the masses – starting with a product that everyone needs (underwear), adding something that everybody likes (humour), then making sure everybody knows about it through outrageous publicity stunts.

'To be a true brand is to not have a demographic. I'm in demographic denial,' says Graham. 'A true brand should be able to encompass any social structure and income level.'[22] It's simple, and it works.

Wacky leaders operate at two levels of complexity. At one level, they are typically able to step back from a problem and see it from several perspectives before choosing the one that makes best sense for them. At another level, they promote simple concepts, such as the homilies in Kamprad's little book. Both approaches are useful in keeping bureaucracy at bay – they create a kind of pincer movement on bureaucracy.

At one level Southwest's Herb Keller spends most of his time lobbying against airline regulations in Washington – a highly complex procedure – at the other he preaches the simple homily of love.

A similar pincer movement worked for Ben Cohen and Jerry Greenfield. They faced a complex problem: finding a way to raise capital for a new plant without compromising their socially responsible values. They looked at the problem from a variety of angles before arriving at a solution that was so elegantly simple, no one had ever thought of it before: selling stock only to people in their home state.

Flattening the organisation

Simplexity applies to the organisations as well. Wacky companies tend to have simple, flat organisations with few (if any) layers of management, decentralised power, and lean teams. They look simple, but can be highly complex as individuals within them take on an unusual amount of responsibility, form and disband project-based teams, and fulfil multiple roles. These simplex structures tend to be fast, flexible and able to do more with less. They also make the most of the talent available by giving employees the freedom to make decisions and act on them quickly, and to do what it takes to get the job done.

At Southwest Airlines, control, ownership and responsibility belong to those closest to the action. There is a structure and a hierarchy (though a flat one, with only about four layers of management) but people are free to work around it when they need to.

Says Herb Kelleher: 'We've tried to create an environment where people are able to, in effect, bypass even the fairly lean structures that we have so that they don't have to convene a meeting of the sages in order to get something done. In many cases, they can just go ahead and do it on their own. They can take individual responsibility for it and know that they will not be crucified if it doesn't work out. Our leanness requires people to be comfortable in making their own decisions and undertaking their own efforts.'[23]

A lean team is often a function of a tight budget, but it does have advantages of its own. It doesn't allow room for bureaucracy and empire building, and it frees (or requires) people to use the full extent of their talents.

In late 1992, Jet Propulsion Laboratory (JPL), a US aeronautics company, took a call from NASA, asking if they could arrange a mission to Mars. The time and budget limitations were tight for any project – unthinkable for something as ambitious as what NASA had in mind. 'We were being asked to do a major NASA mission for the cost of a Hollywood movie,' writes JPL's flight systems manager Brian Muirhead in a book on the project. 'Well, at least our ending will be better,' we joked. 'We also had to do the job in three years, which was about half the time of earlier missions.'[24]

Says Muirhead: 'Because our constraints were so challenging, they drove innovation. They drove the creativity of the team. We knew we had to find different new ways to do business, and that was exciting.' The constraints drove innovation in both developing new technology (much of the existing technology was too expensive) and in fast-tracking talented people. 'We talked about being only "one deep" because we ran so lean. But I remember Cindy Oda, a member of the operations team, commenting, "It's better to be understaffed than overstaffed. Being understaffed, you're a little uncomfortable and people get more creative. They find other ways to do what they're asked to do."'

'The Pathfinder project gave people an opportunity to grow professionally and personally,' says Muirhead. 'Someone would see a job that needed to be done and would say, "I can do that." You always got better employees this way. They became more versatile, more valuable to the next project, because they had broader experience. And they were personally much more motivated. We gave people the opportunity to take on additional responsibilities, to show themselves capable, and they did the rest.'

Other wacky companies have also found that keeping structures and procedures streamlined makes it easier, and quicker, to make decisions and get things done. A high level of consensus between leaders and employees means that new ideas can be tried out rapidly.

Virgin's Richard Branson explains why leaner companies tend to be more innovative: 'People who leave companies with formal structures don't leave because of salaries. If they come up with a good idea, they're told to wait until the next meeting. Then they're told they have to make another presentation to another group, then another. Then the board takes it on advisement. And he's gone off to another company. With Virgin, we make decisions on the phone. If you've got a good idea and I like it, you can get on with it.'[25]

There are drawbacks to having a flat organisation as well. As Ben & Jerry's employees noted in their 1997 employee survey, the company's four to five layer organisation leaves little room to grow. As info queen Mitch Curren notes about the survey results: 'Job satisfaction was higher than the national average, but there was dissatisfaction with the chances for advancement.'

Because it refused to grow, the University National Bank and Trust had little to offer employees in terms of advancement, so CEO Carl Schmitt started what he called his 'bank within a bank' programme. Each of these mini-banks was headed by a senior vice president with three to four people on a team. Every team had its own customer list, oversaw its own portfolio of loans, and sent out correspondence on its own letterhead. 'It provided a sense of ownership without diluting our strategy of limiting growth,' says Schmitt.[26]

Julian Richer of Richer Sounds has also found a way to help employees who feel a need to grow and take on more responsibility in the flat structure. He gives them two jobs. Richer maintains that this is not simply an easy way to cut costs. He sees it as a way to keep his employees fulfilled. For example, successful shop managers are often associate directors. On one level, they are responsible for the continued success of their own store. But on another level they assume a different role – that of an area supervisor. In this capacity they will travel to other shops and check that procedures are up to scratch. The first area of responsibility enhances the second. Their role as associate director is complemented by their role as store manager. They never lose touch with the nitty-gritty of the retailing at store level.

Dis-organising the organisation

Another problem with flat organisations, though, is that, with shorter chains of command, managers have larger spans of control – each member of the reduced management team has more to do, and more people to manage, leaving them little time for long-term responsibilities like coaching their direct reports. Flatter pyramids are still pyramids, and organisations, especially those that haven't fully empowered their front line people, are still struggling with the shape.

Some wacky leaders decided that it would make more sense to create structures that more closely fit the markets they operate in. Many have abandoned the pyramid altogether and looked to the natural world for more adaptable structures.

The amoeba

The amoeba, for example, has an inbuilt mechanism that tells it when it needs to split into smaller units. Semco CEO Ricardo Semler coined this term for his way of growing large by continually hiving off new units.

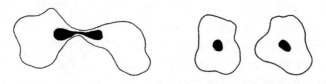

Figure 3.2 The amoeba

Early on in his career, Semler experimented with a variety of systems. He knew he didn't want a function-based system because these tend to reward risk-averse behaviour and encourage empire building.

He dismantled the old Semco hierarchy as much as he could, stripping away (and sacking) several levels of management, eliminating a host of titles and freeing up rigid career paths. Whatever structure Semler tried, though, it always seemed to revert to a function-based system. Eventually, thanks in part to reports from an employee he sent away to investigate practices in other parts of the world, Semler came up with the 'amoeba approach'.

'Our problems – the meetings that ran too long, the power struggles between groups of managers, the impossibility of making everyone in a plant feel like they were part of something, the alienation I saw all around Semco – weren't going to go away by themselves. They were rooted in bigness, the cure for which was simple. We would divide ourselves like an amoeba, and prosper,' he wrote. 'Factories that had become too large for their own good should be broken into units small enough to ensure that the people who worked in them would feel human again.'[27] Within these small units, employees can innovate constructively because they have intimate knowledge of the processes they are involved with and they know each other well enough to discuss things freely.

Richard Branson, whose Virgin empire now includes, at last count, just over 200 companies, operates according to the same principle. 'I keep them spinning off,' he says. 'Each company has to stand on its own two feet, as if they are their own companies. Employees have a stake in their success. They feel – and are – crucial to their company, because they are one in fifty or a hundred or several hundred instead of tens of thousands.'[28] 'Outside accountants would immediately look at our 200 buildings, 200 switchboards, and all that comes with them and say, "You're bleeding money!" But I say, "Look at what you get!" People who have worked for small companies and then big companies will tell you that it's not as much fun. In a small company, you can create a different type of energy. People feel cared for.'

A recent US study backs this up. A November 1995 Inc./Gallup survey of American workers asked randomly selected working adults throughout the United States about their jobs, their workplaces, and their job security, posing such questions as: Are you worried about losing your job? Does the stress of work cause you to behave badly with your family? Does your management do what's necessary to make your company a great place to work? Those who worked for small companies were consistently more satisfied on a whole range of constructs: in opportunities to grow, in feeling important, in having the tools they need, in using their potential, and in management doing what's necessary to make the company a great place to work.[29]

How small, then, is small? Intriguingly, in our sample, the 'just right' size – which is always measured in numbers of employees rather than sales or customer numbers – generally comes out about the same: between 150 and 200 people. And this works whether you're running a conventional company, a wacky one, a political faction or a communal village in the bush.

Plant size at Gore is fixed at no more than 200 associates. That's been company policy since the day Bill Gore walked through the plant and discovered he didn't know everyone. As so many other organisations have discovered, 200 people is about the size that enables everyone to know everyone else by name, skills and reputation. Jim Buckley wonders if even that is too many. 'Groups smaller than that are better. Once you get beyond 150 you get the negative aspects, like empire building and not everyone knows everyone.'

According to the New Scientist: 'Sociologists have known since the 1950s that there is a critical threshold in the region of 150 to 200, with larger companies suffering a disproportionate amount of absenteeism and sickness. Armies keep units between 130 and 200. The Hutterites, a communal living religious group, regard 150 as the maximum size for their communities . . . they find that when there are more than about 150 individuals, they cannot control the behaviour of the members by peer pressure alone.'[30] Looking at it another way, it's the community size below which no two members could conceal an extra-marital affair.

The blueberry pancake

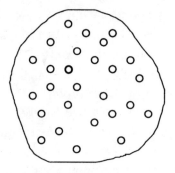

Figure 3.3 The blueberry pancake

The small unit principle also applies to multi-site, multi-unit and even multinational corporations. Those in our sample preferred to grow out, rather than up, and push power out to their operational reaches.

This is the case at VeriFone, a powerful multinational with thousands of employees on five continents, and only a small rented office building serving as a nominal headquarters. VeriFone's former CEO Hatim Tyabji calls this structure the blueberry pancake. 'All blueberries are created equally. Each blueberry is a location, they're held together by the virtual binary network (VeriFone's worldwide computer system). It doesn't emanate from the big blueberry at headquarters.'

There are a lot of blueberry pancakes in our sample. US-based power plant company AES has 6,000 employees working on four continents, yet no corporate departments for human resources, operations, purchasing, or legal affairs. Fewer than 30 people work at its Arlington, Virginia, headquarters.

IKEA, which now sells furniture through shops in 28 countries, may have its heart in the Swedish hinterland, but no one would say it has a headquarters there. That, says Sven Kulldorf, purchasing manager for IKEA Sweden, is because 'we never use the word headquarters. It is an ugly word within IKEA. First of all, we try to keep it as small as possible. And secondly, we have the stores. That's where the music is played and we call it service. Ninety per cent of what we do is to provide service and the other ten is providing guidelines. So head office, we don't use that word at IKEA.'

The blueberries at Finnish cleaning company SOL are the front line managers – 135 supervisors each heading up a team of up to 50 cleaners. These people have the power to hire, fire, run their own budget and negotiate deals with customers. This devolution of power allowed, by the end of 1997, 23 satellite offices to develop across Finland. The satellites, called studios, operate like mini SOLs, each responsible for its own costs and profits.

Hal Rosenbluth, CEO of travel services company Rosenbluth International, also operates a blueberry, but he's based his model on the family farm. 'What I'm beginning to see,' says Rosenbluth, 'is that the family farm is the most efficient type of unit I've ever run across, because everybody on the farm has to be fully functional and multifaceted.'[31] They have to be, because in farming, as in other businesses, people are up against thin margins, tough competition, and sudden changes in the environment over which the farmer has no control. So Rosenbluth broke his company into more than 100 business units, each serving specific regions and clients. Corporate headquarters supplies them with what they need, but doesn't make decisions for them.

Acer CEO Stan Shih has created what he calls a 'global federation of companies'. Acer is broken into five highly autonomous business units that are publicly traded. Shih plans to give more investors a chance to buy a piece of Acer by launching 18 other such public companies over the next five years, selling shares to local investors, and giving employees a chance to run their own show. Shih called it his 'disintegration business plan', though the aim was to vault Acer from a $2 billion to an $8 billion company by the year 2000.

Shih has broken with the traditional Asian model of autocratic, centralised control. Instead, he is spreading out the power as his company grows, creating a kind of CEO factory. In 1990, he announced he would create 100 general managers by 1997 – employees who run businesses, own Acer stock, take risks and act like owners. He met his goal and said that over the next two years he'll train another 200. The key to his success: his decentralised structure allows division managers to act and feel like owners – 'In our businesses, opportunities are popping up everywhere, so it's important for our managers to act like entrepreneurs.'[32]

The boundariless organisation

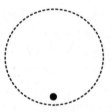

Figure 3.4 The boundariless organisation

The boundariless organisation is one where the boundary between it and its customers and/or suppliers has become indistinct and variable, often defined only by who pays the employee's salary. What matters is the smooth management of the processes around the borders. Information technology outsourcing, where staff continue to work in the same company, but for a different employer, is a classic example, when managed well. Wacky companies such as St. Luke's, The Lane Group, and ?What If! spend much of their efforts ensuring that they are as near boundariless with their customers as they can be.

In some cases, it is the clients who want to break down the boundaries. IDEO, the largest industrial product design company in the world, is so famous for its innovations that other companies just want to get closer to it. Companies hoping to catch the innovation bug include the Korean electronics conglomerate Samsung, which has created a joint design laboratory with IDEO in Palo Alto, California, and Steelcase, a US office furniture company which has taken an equity holding in the company. Both hope to learn the secrets of sustaining an innovation culture.

In most cases, though, the suppliers are the suitors, as at Lane Group, a British transportation company, where customer contracts provide for such a level of customer/supplier partnership you half expect someone to toss a bouquet. The marriage, or 'symbiotic partnership', as Lane Group managing director Rebecca Jenkins likes to call it, provides an almost shocking level of co-operation between the two parties. Jenkins even allows customers to view the books and conduct on-site environmental audits. As Jenkins says: 'We say to clients we want a real partnership. We want to become your logistics department.'

The partnership contract establishes basic performance indicators such as cost per unit and percentage of on-time deliveries, but also includes some unusual criteria, including how often the Lane Group is expected to come up with new ideas for the partner. The contract even establishes what the Lane Group's profit margin should be. The margin is set at the beginning of the relationship, and can then only be increased if the Lane Group reduces its costs. As Rebecca Jenkins says, 'It's about putting our money where our mouth is.'

The weighting of each component varies according to the client's own priorities. The Body Shop contract, for example, indicates that 40 per cent of the Lane Group's bonus depends on their making suggestions that lead to cost savings for the client. By 1998, Lane had earned the full 40 per cent bonus for three years running. The Body Shop has also imposed a set of environmental targets for the Lane Group and runs an environmental audit on the Lane Group's operations every year.

'We also,' says Jenkins, 'share all the financials. Anyone within the [client's] company can access any figures they want.'

Isn't there a risk involved? Doesn't such openness tempt the client to squeeze more cost savings? 'Partnership isn't about being squeezed,' says Jenkins. 'The relationship has to be much more than that. We expect these companies to be honest with us about their long-term strategy and we expect to play a part in that strategy. But it only works if all our employees buy into the partnership.'

A Lane Group partnership also involves having a Lane Group contract manager, administrative assistants and drivers all working at the clients' premises. This on-site work is a litmus test of the client partnership. These employees 'combine the culture of the client with Lane Group values,' Jenkins says.

It doesn't always work: 'We've walked away from business where the ethos of the other company wasn't really one of partnership.' In one case, for example, Jenkins felt the company was unable to 'get close to the client'. The client, it seemed, was only interested in the cheapest solution, and not in the partnership. So, though short-listed for the contract, the Lane Group took itself out of the running.

Intimacy with a few clients is relatively easy to encompass. With big numbers, it becomes more difficult. Yet Moses Znaimer seeks to create intimacy with the city of Toronto. The Canadian TV mogul has created a successful TV station by destroying the boundaries between the studio and the audience.

Znaimer is the founder of Toronto's Citytv, which has more than 600 employees, revenues of more than \$200 million and a consistently large percentage of the Toronto market. Znaimer is reaching out too, buying up stations as far away as Argentina.[33] Znaimer's philosophy is to get rid of the barriers that hide TV studios away in guarded suburban locations and the mindset that has them create artificial programmes with fake scenery and settings. He creates real TV, in real time, reflecting local reality – and it's cheap, too.

'The first task,' he says, 'is to escape the studio.' Citytv's studios aren't tucked away in the suburbs. Instead, they're among the street fronts of the busiest part of Toronto. Znaimer has built a studio with no sets or scenery. Instead, according to *Fast Company*, the building is equipped with 35 'hydrants', or camera and microphone outlets, all linked with miles of cable. Any corner of the building can be on-air within minutes. Anything can happen, anywhere, anytime, and find itself part of the broadcast. 'What we do, every one of us, constitutes the performance,' explains Znaimer. 'You don't have to choreograph it, because it's constantly there. Except in television, you never see it. You only see the static, artificial final product.'

A music show is filmed at street level in front of storefront windows – the street traffic adds to the show, and passers by can stop and watch. News isn't packaged for television – it's broadcast live as it happens from the streets. Shows can tabulate 20,000 calls an hour to do an instant public opinion poll, with results discussed as they come in. One daily news show allows people to e-mail questions and opinions for real-time interaction. There's even an electronic soapbox. Each week a thousand participants pay one dollar each for two minutes of video time – with all proceeds going to charity. If a video clip happens to touch on a local issue under discussion, it can instantly find its way into a newscast.

Inside Citytv studios, there are no walls or barriers, and nobody pays much attention to the clock. Says Znaimer: 'There are more people in here after two in the morning than at ten in the morning.' It's not unusual for Znaimer himself to be among them.

Chemical soup organisations

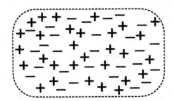

Figure 3.5 Chemical soup organisations

Chemical soup organisations are typically project-based. People generally have no permanent managers, but instead shift from project team to project team. The organisation constantly combines and recombines into new internal shapes to meet project needs. Personal success is defined not by title, but by the importance of the projects to which you are assigned, or invited, to work on. It can be both exciting and unnerving to work in this kind of atmosphere.

Lars Kolind, CEO of Danish hearing-aid manufacturer Oticon, dismantled a structure that had been in place since 1904 to create what he calls a spaghetti organisation – an organisation that liberates the individual by dis-organising the organisation. Coming on board to a troubled company in 1988, Kolind, who's also known as the king of chaos, saw an opportunity to reinvent Oticon along more radical lines. Kolind believed that the rules and structure of formal organisations stifled the contribution of individuals. His vision was to break that structure down, to allow each worker to behave like an individual within the company, and each project to operate like independent businesses.

Now at Oticon, team projects form the backbone of the company's internal free market economy. Any individual who comes up with a good idea can try to assemble a team and head that team as a project leader. The project leader has to compete for resources with other projects that others are attempting to get off the ground. The result is a form of natural selection, with the most successful projects winning out over the rest. Project owners are members of the company's management team. They help support projects and give advice where necessary, though their role is largely hands-off. At times there are more than a hundred project teams on the go, forming and disbanding as tasks are started and completed. Individuals invariably contribute to more than one project at a time. Hence the term 'spaghetti organisation' – a chaotic network of project teams.

At Oticon's headquarters just north of Copenhagen, employees carry their office with them wherever they go. Well, actually, they push them around the hardwood floor. Desks are no longer allocated; instead workers use the nearest available workstation, rolling their personal mobile carts and carrying their mobile phones to wherever they need to be in the building. Each cart can hold about 30 hanging folders. Staff don't need any more as paper is highly restricted. By getting rid of office furniture and forcing people to move around, banning paper and discouraging the use of e-mail, Oticon has forced people to start talking to one another again.

Getting people 'walking, talking and acting', builds respect, breaks down barriers, reinforces the lack of hierarchy and discourages territorial disagreements, says Kolind. The question of someone using your office, desk or computer simply does not arise if you have no office, desk or computer. The system (or lack of) also prevents inter-departmental rivalries. It's easier to respect colleagues if you can see what they are doing every day.

Dis-organisation also generates efficiency at high-tech fabric makers W. L. Gore and Associates, where 7,000 employees (called associates) generate sales of $1.4 billion, with no bosses, departments or job titles. The late Bill Gore's philosophy involved releasing workers from traditional corporate structures and getting things done through natural leadership and natural lines of communications. He called the system a lattice structure. The name was a play on the idea of the corporate ladder that young executives of his generation were expected to fight their way up in mid-century America.

The lattice structure was based on the natural underground lattice, or grapevine, that occurs in every organisation but is largely ignored in most workplaces. 'It's where the news spreads like lightning, where people can go around the organisation to get things done,' said Gore. The system is based, too, on Gore's belief in 'natural leadership by natural followership' – the idea that leaders need to earn their authority, and should be chosen by the people who follow them.[34]

So, at Gore, everyone is self-managing and free to interact directly with everyone else in the system. There are leaders, but their leadership is achieved only by persuading others to follow them, rather than by assigned authority. The work is done by multi-disciplined teams which come together for each project and work collaboratively, as needed, with other teams throughout Gore. The teams are clustered into plants, each with no more than 200 people, organised around technologies and market opportunities.

Other tenets of the lattice structure include:

- no fixed or assigned authority (associates have sponsors, not bosses, and no job titles)
- objectives established by consensus, and set by those who must fulfil them
- direct person-to-person communication
- tasks and functions organised by commitments
- lots of cross-level and cross-functional contact, which allows multidisciplinary teams to spring up as needed.

It also sounds, with its reliance on natural leadership and group imposed discipline, like the sort of anarchy explored in Golding's novel Lord of the Flies. It's not. As Bill Gore once told a researcher: 'You ask me how it works. The answer is, it works, every which way.' He also said: 'I'm told from time to time that lattice organisation can't meet a crisis well because it takes too long to reach a consensus when there are no bosses. But this isn't true. Actually, a lattice, by its very nature, works particularly well in a crisis. A lot of useless effort is avoided because there is no rigid management hierarchy to conquer before you can attack a problem.'[35]

Jim Buckley, a manufacturing leader in Gore's fabrics division, has been with the company since 1974. He explains how the lattice structure functions: 'We have top people here just as you would in a hierarchical company, though typically our top people operate more as a team. Everyone else works in teams. There are many little hierarchies in individual teams and there are leaders, though if you walked into the plant, you couldn't tell who the leader was. Leadership of each team evolves from the group – the person whom the team members choose as leader. I can go to people in other teams for help but I let my leader know. Teams form up around a problem or an opportunity. Some teams are short term, some in manufacturing are life-long careers.'

Gore associate Terri Kelly explains how each leader has to persuade people to join their projects: 'Although I'm a business leader for military fabrics, I'm a leader only if there are people who are willing to follow me. A project doesn't move forward unless people buy into it. You cultivate followership by selling yourself, articulating your ideas, and developing a reputation for seeing things through.'[36]

'It's a case of trying to spread leadership through the organisation. It's a way of task teams coming together to solve problems regardless of where they are in the hierarchy. They come to the task as equals and because they have something to offer,' adds Buckley.

Teams work, says Buckley, because: 'When eight to ten people are working on the same thing, they know each other, and can count on each other. They know each other's skills and weaknesses, and can trust each other. In that case, you don't need job titles, hierarchies and organisational charts because people know what you know and know what you can do. It's the concept of a community, of people who know and respect each other so you can get away from the trappings of command and control structures. If you see something that needs to be done, you do it, you don't not do it because it's not your job.'

Small groups, can, by contrast, inspire innovation, says Buckley. 'We've had a nice string of new products. The structure gives us a lot of agility, and we can develop teams quickly and we work cross-functionally all the time.'

Customers don't all like it, though. Some find a lack of continuity can be frustrating as they feel they don't know whom they are supposed to deal with. Others just find the lack of titles hard to get used to. The situation did present something of a challenge for the hapless journalist (one of the authors) hoping to arrange an interview with a manager. 'We haven't got any,' said the title-less person in charge of such things. Buckley concedes that, 'For customers and other people outside the company, you need titles. Titles are used so outsiders know who to talk to, though they're not used internally.'

Newcomers, too, sometimes have trouble figuring out who does what in a company without an organisational chart. Says Buckley: 'It can sometimes be difficult for newer people to learn how to network, and some people have trouble getting used to not being told what to do. Others complain they can't see their growth plan or career path. There is a career path at Gore but it's not as obvious as in other companies.'

Chemical soup organisations are based on a fine balance between competition and co-operation – where teams co-operate with each other, but compete for resources, so that the most worthy projects rise to the top.

Dee Hock had a similar vision when he designed the credit card organisation Visa. His organisational design was based on the way he saw things work in the natural world, where, as in chemical soup companies, groups within the organisation push forward, by a combination of competition and co-operation.

Visa, though one of the most recognised brands in the world, is little known as an organisation. That's because it's not so much a company as a loose federation of independent financial institutions. Each member issues its own cards and competes for customers with the other members. Yet these members have to co-operate with each other. For the system to work, participating merchants must be able to take any Visa card issued by any bank, anywhere.

To reconcile that tension, Hock and his colleagues set up a system based on free market economics. For example, instead of trying to enforce co-operation by restricting what the members can do, the Visa bylaws encourage them to compete and innovate as much as possible. 'Members are free to create, price, market, and service their own products under the Visa name,' explains Hock. 'At the same time, in a narrow band of activity essential to the success of the whole, they engage in the most intense co-operation.'[37] This harmonious blend of co-operation and competition is what allowed the system to expand world-wide in the face of different currencies, languages, legal codes, customs, cultures, and political philosophies.

This system of encouraging as much competition and initiative as possible throughout the organisation 'chaos' while building in mechanisms for co-operation 'order' Hock later dubbed the 'chaordic' organisation.

Chaos and tension had to be part of the equation: no one way of doing business, dictated from headquarters, could possibly have worked. 'It was beyond the power of reason to design an organisation to deal with such complexity,' says Hock, 'and beyond the reach of the imagination to perceive all the conditions it would encounter.' Instead, he says, 'The organisation had to be based on biological concepts to evolve, in effect, to invent and organise itself.'

Visa has been called 'a corporation whose product is co-ordination'. Hock calls it 'an enabling organisation'. He also sees it as living proof that a large organisation can be effective without being centralised and coercive: 'Visa has elements of Jeffersonian democracy, it has elements of the free market, of government franchising – almost every kind of organisation you can think about. But it's none of them. Like the body, the brain, and the biosphere, it's largely self-organising.'

It also works. Visa grew phenomenally during the 1970s, from a few hundred members to tens of thousands. And it did so more or less smoothly, without dissolving into fiefdoms and turf wars. By the early 1980s, the Visa system had surpassed MasterCard as the largest in the world and had begun to fulfil Hock's vision of a universal currency, transcending national boundaries.

Hock was convinced that the command-and-control model of organisation that had grown up to support the industrial revolution had got out of hand. Command-and-control organisations, he says, 'were not only archaic and increasingly irrelevant. They were becoming a public menace, antithetical to the human spirit and destructive of the biosphere. I was convinced we were on the brink of an epidemic of institutional failure.'

The star organisation

Figure 3.6 The star organisation

Star organisations have elements of both boundariless and chemical soup companies.

They have a small number of customers and organise their activities specifically around those customers. So each 'arm' of the star has its own shape, specific to the needs of the customer it serves.

The Words Group, a £4 million, 45-employee UK design, marketing and public relations company has used technology to become completely boundariless. By linking its intranet to an external network for clients, it has opened all its internal data to customers. Clients can look in on the status of their projects, and on the work being done for them, whenever they feel like it and without their counterparts at the Words Group even being aware they're looking.

'Clients will be able to see anything they like at any time,' says Words Group executive June Dawson. They'll even be able to view their PR agents' diaries and contact reports.[38] It's like working in a goldfish bowl, and that's exactly what the Words Group calls their project.

The big saving to both the Words Group and its clients will be in time. Time that is now spent preparing activity reports for clients – an estimated 20 per cent of the average PR agent's day – can now be spent on productive PR work. Word staff will be actually doing the work, rather than reporting on it, and, says Dawson, 'monthly meetings will be spent discussing issues and plans, rather than going through past actions'.

Clients, well aware that PR people have been known to pad the odd time sheet, are unanimously positive about the goldfish bowl. It's they, after all, who pay for time spent preparing activity reports.

The in-house response has been more mixed. Says Dawson: 'It's going to be rather like a chef working in full view of the diners. Many staff will feel as if they are working under a microscope the whole time. Anyone who tends to leave everything until the last minute will be very uncomfortable to be viewed in this way. I'm sure that some will want to leave. On the other hand it will work well for those who are consistent in their work and confident in their performance, which will be to our benefit.'

Coincidentally, open kitchens have become popular in restaurants of late. They're also catching on among other professional service providers. Dawson expects Words' open book advantage to last only a year or two, until competitors adopt the same practice.

Among them is London's St. Luke's Advertising. Unlike most advertising agencies, who'd rather clients didn't muck with the creative process, St. Luke's try to involve the client more closely. St. Luke's internal structure makes this easy. While other agencies operate in a linear way – St. Luke's founder Andy Law likens it to a relay race with the baton passed from client to account manager to creative and so on – St. Luke's operates in what he describes as 'a chaotic, anarchic non-linear system'.

Each team operates in a chemical soup manner – forming and disbanding according to projects; and each works in a boundariless way with clients. St. Luke's has even given over part of its building to clients in the form of theme brand rooms, reflecting each client's business. The campaign room for the teen-targeted Boots No. 17 make-up range, for example, features posters of pop-stars on lurid pink walls, with bunk beds for creative types in need of a nap. A room decked out with sliding glass doors, train seats and ticket office posters is for the Eurostar account; the matt-black room with music turntable, samplers and speakers is for Radio 1. And the high street shoe-shop? Clarks' shoes of course. These rooms aren't just for St. Luke's use either. 'Clients become members of the club,' says Law. 'They can use their room whenever they wish. With or without us.'

GSD&M, an Austin, Texas, advertising agency with 300 employees and a client list that includes Wal-Mart and Southwest Airlines, uses the same concept in their war rooms. The team, among them the people who thought of painting a Southwest plane to look like Shamu the Killer Whale, operate out of 30 war rooms in the offices they call Idea City.

Each war room has everything the team needs to focus on a client's business. There are red phones, exclusively for calls to and from the client, on the tables and the client's financial information, analyses and newspaper clippings on the walls. The rooms are also stocked with the client's products, those of its competitors, and other things the client's customers might own. In the Chili's Bar & Grill war room, for example, there's a booth with menus and a 'Please wait to be seated' sign.

'War rooms raise the intensity level and give us a mental edge,' says GSD&M president and co-founder Roy Spence. 'They remind us to keep our eye on the prize.'[39]

'The war room creates a sort of cocoon,' says James Martin, 33, vice president and director of marketplace planning (GSD&M's research function). 'It's not just decorated with stuff. The paraphernalia is a form of information. And having that information around you helps you put ideas together.'[40]

According to Inc. magazine, the agency has seen billings grow nearly six-fold in the past decade and boasts a 90 per cent client-retention rate.

The virtual organisation

If you come into the office one day and find your desk, chair, computer, and walls have gone, one of the following has happened – you've:

(a) lost your job
(b) entered an alternative universe
(c) got a new CEO who likes to do things differently.

Figure 3.7 The virtual organisation

A virtual organisation can have elements of both chemical soup and boundariless organisations, but its main feature is that it has little or no physical presence. It operates outside of time and space, allowing teams to form and disband as need be in a chemical soup manner, or work closely with customers, as in a boundariless organisation.

In 1976, ad agency CEO Jay Chiat abolished formal offices and introduced open plan cubicles, even for top management. In 1994, after an inspiration that came to him on a ski slope, he disposed of the cubicles, as well as the desks, phones, terminals and filing cabinets. He's been known, ever since, as the man who invented the virtual office.

Staff at Chiat/Day (now TBWA Chiat/Day) can check out the portable phones and laptops they need from central dispensaries, then plug into any available work station (laptop data ports are set about every 30 feet, even in the cafeteria/rec-room). Or, better yet, they can leave and go where the work is – at a project meeting or at a client's office. Chiat's reasoning? The office was outmoded. It had become, he told *Inc. Technology* magazine, 'an archaic space that you used to just store all your stuff, very little of which had anything to do with what you did.'[41]

'The work space has become a storage bin for obsolete reports and personal effects,' Chiat wrote in *Adweek* just before his California office went virtual. 'True, it was comfortable. But it was rarely used for anything but a filing drawer and a place for a computer and phone. It was pretty obvious that you didn't have to go to the office to make phone calls. Phones are everywhere. And computers have become increasingly powerful as they became smaller and more portable. So you can connect to the network from anywhere. If we work on projects, why not have project rooms – a place to interact, collaborate and hang out? Surrounding the project rooms will be private study carrels for people to use when they're not working directly with their team.'

'But what about the alienation that comes from having your own private space wrenched from you – as meagre as it was? Obviously, it has to be replaced with something more comfortable, nurturing, intimate and welcoming. So, we have designed a Club House. Think of every great club that you've belonged to, visited or couldn't get into. That's what this place will be, with every amenity we could think of to make our people want to come in, relax, do casual work, or to just hang out. And if you have to have a place for your dog pictures or stuff that you just can't get rid of, you'll have your very own – personalised with your picture – 3 ft × 18 in. × 18 in. locker. In what I might add is a very stylish, fun locker room.'[42]

Now staff at offices in Los Angeles, New York and Toronto work where they need to: at shared work stations, in the library, at clients' offices, at home or, as various visiting reporters have noticed, on the floor, in the corridors, and on their feet.

Paper is frowned upon in the virtual office. Files are no longer passed from person to person, instead information is posted on the computer system for anyone who needs it. Data 'drinking fountains' are terminals around the building where anyone can stop and check their e-mail. You'd be hard pressed to find a printer or photocopier at Chiat/Day. Most were removed, not being needed, so the theory goes, in a paperless office where old files had all been scanned into the system, stored, or tossed out.

Those who cling sentimentally to their piles of paper find there's nowhere to keep them. No one has an office, and beyond the locker room, no one (in theory) has any personal space. That means no personal stuff: no family photos, no award statuettes, no little plaques bearing tired office jokes. No pictures of your kids? 'That's what homes are for,' Chiat told Details magazine. 'The office is the office. It's about getting work done. If you can strip away all those little ego artefacts, you can really focus on the work.'[43]

Jay Chiat calls the structure team architecture. The idea, he told the *Financial Times* in 1994, was to encourage better interaction among co-workers and save money on overheads.[44]

Many staff find it does allow for better interaction, especially when working in the ad hoc, project-based teams common in the advertising industry. The virtual office makes it easy for multidisciplinary groups, pulled together to work on one project or one client, to physically work together, then regroup as needed for subsequent projects. And, laptops in the cafeteria notwithstanding, most staff do work that way, with their immediate project colleagues in what are called strategic business units – conference rooms furnished with a table, phones, computers and VCRs.

'We went to a team structure a long time ago,' explains Bob Kuperman, a senior executive in the LA office. 'But the architecture didn't reflect it. We didn't have project rooms, only war rooms of the sort a lot of agencies put together when they're pitching new business. Once we'd landed an account, everyone went back to their little hole. "Why do we work so well on the pitches, then revert to our old behaviour?" That's the question we were asking.'[45]

As for overheads, it's pretty clear that less real estate costs less money. According to *Inc. Technology*, alternative workspaces like Chiat/Day's have allowed some companies to cut in half the 200 square feet per worker used by most office workers. Savings in pricey locations like New York and Los Angeles can be substantial.[46] In Manhattan, Chiat/Day's old office housed 150 employees in 98,000 square feet. The new offices accommodate the same number on one floor a third that size. Some argue that the brave new office is nothing more than thinly disguised downsizing. The New York office had, after all, recently lost two major accounts (American Express in 1992 and Reebok in 1993).[47]

There were gripes in LA as well. According to *Detail*'s Buchanan, the first days of unassigned seats, when the 300 head office staff returned from their Christmas holiday, were chaos. There weren't enough phones, workstations, or laptops to go around. The only saving grace was an earthquake two weeks later. Chiat/Day, with its remote technology, was able to function, after a fashion, while the rest of the city shut down. As things settled down, some found they liked the virtual office, and found that the increase in face-to-face interaction sparked more ideas – the lifeblood of an ad agency.

Some have found, though, that they are now more firmly chained to their portable high-tech gear than they ever were to a desk. The radio phones and beepers that every staff member carries reach everywhere in the building – including the elevators and the washrooms. Oh, and say goodbye to nine to five: some now call the agency Chiat/Day and Night. Virtual work, staff have discovered, is ever with you.

Others felt uncomfortable with the lack of personal space. Said one executive who left: 'Humans need to nest a little bit, no matter how progressive the atmosphere.'[48] 'Nobody could be totally comfortable at first,' says Chiat. 'But I equate it to going to the shrink. For the first year, at least, you go in feeling pretty good and you come out after that fifty minutes feeling pretty bad. And then one day it changes.'[49]

And, for practical reasons, not everyone has gone virtual. Creative people in the Los Angeles office, for example, simply need larger computer screens for their work; and administrative assistants need to be where they can be found.

'When you are in an exciting, creative idea- and service-intensive business, the question is, 'Where does my work end and my life begin?' asks Jay Chiat. 'It's not likely that I will stop having ideas at 5:30 or that I will only have good ideas in the office. That's how we got to the virtual office. It is very simply a resource, supplying all of the support systems our people need to maximise their individual potential and allow them to perform their tasks at the highest possible level. It's not about working at home. It's about understanding that our business is task- or project-driven.'[50]

Financially, at any rate, the virtual office appears to be paying off. According to one Internet report, Chiat/Day employees now work out of their homes, cars, or client offices so ably that revenues have increased. When 100 additional staffers were added to the Venice, California, office, no additional space was needed – a major corporate saving. TBWA Chiat/Day chairman Bill Tragos says that if more changes are needed, then they will happen. 'I don't approach it like a religion. People are more important than architecture.'[51]

Hatim Tyabji, former CEO of VeriFone, has taken the virtual model even further, creating what is probably the closest thing yet to a virtual, paperless, purely electronic corporation. Based in Redwood, California – to the extent that it can be based anywhere – this Hewlett-Packard subsidiary creates and supplies electronic payment systems and software.

The most intriguing thing about VeriFone, though, is that it operates in a completely electronic world. It has no paper, no secretaries, few offices, and little time for outmoded concepts like office hours and time zones. Its staff on four continents communicate almost entirely by e-mail, video and phone conferencing. It is, according to the company Web site, a company that 'operates continuously through traditional barriers of time and distance.' Tyabji calls it the 'culture of urgency'.

Most employees never see each other, even though they are free to communicate with anyone (or, if they feel like it, everyone) in the company, on any topic, at any time, via e-mail. That makes e-mail much more than an information network at VeriFone. It's also the company's social system, its grapevine, and the repository of its culture and values. It's quicker than other systems, and it's completely unregulated.

VeriFone has done away not just with time clocks but also with time zones. Its 3,300 staff move work electronically around the planet so that somebody, somewhere, in VeriFone is always at work. 'In a conventional company, where all the engineers are sitting in the same place, you'd have a tremendous amount of serial processing. First you write the code, then you test it, then you integrate it. Here, because our people are distributed around the world, everything works in parallel. Before they go to sleep, the boys in Bangalore upload code and ship it to, say, Dallas or Hawaii, let those guys work on it, and then start again the next morning in Bangalore. Allowing our projects to follow the sun is something that we have done consistently – and with devastating efficiency,' says Tyabji.[52] VeriFone staff have a great deal of freedom to set their own hours, and, while they don't all work the 24-hour day, time on and time off can be more blurred here than in more conventional organisations.

It certainly involves releasing control, admits Tyabji. VeriFone is, he says, 'not all that different from a country. It's a free society. Which means we trust you. Which means there are no rules. Which means we expect you to behave responsibly. As I think about the evolution of this company, it's almost like the evolution of a new democracy. People learn how to handle freedom. When we were younger, we had far more breakdowns in the social system than we have today. You don't think I was tempted to clamp down? Of course I was – it's very easy to revert to totalitarianism. But we stuck with it. And we are a much stronger company for it.'[53]

VeriFone has not rebelled against traditional social structures. It has, however, rebelled against traditional physical structures, and thus has, indirectly, undermined traditional hierarchies, or at least made them less relevant. The trappings of status have gone not because of any workers' revolution but simply because they're no longer necessary. Secretaries, receptionists and other gatekeepers to executive offices are gone. If a staffer wants a word with the chairman, he sends him and not his secretary an e-mail. With no offices, there are no physical symbols of status. Most executive perks, like clubs and cars, also become irrelevant when employees are scattered around the world. With fewer trappings of status, employees feel more equally treated – that sense of mutual respect translates readily to pride in the workplace.

Says Tyabji: 'Our model of business is becoming the norm. And people who laughed at us are now following. People thought we were a bunch of loonies, that it was some kind of social experiment, but now they see our track record and they're following us.'

One of the authors first identified most of these organisational shapes in the early 1990s, during workshops with managers from a wide variety of organisations. They still seem to be the most common of the flexible organisation structures. There are, however, other structures that haven't seen quite so much use yet.

The collapsed sphere

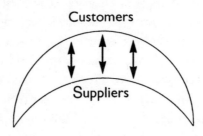

Figure 3.8 The collapsed sphere

Take, for example, the collapsed sphere – a shape described as one of nature's most common building blocks.[54] Imagine letting most of the air out of a beach ball and pushing one half inwards, until the internal surfaces are almost touching. Now think of the external curve of the resulting half-sphere as the customer interface, the interior curve as the supplier interface and the air space between as the organisational systems. The supply chain between customers, individual employees on the exterior surface and suppliers can be as small as the systems allow.

The systems that connect employees in a normal company invariably involve some form of hierarchy, because the organisation has to be able to exert some control over what people do. But what if those controls consisted of standard processes, by which employees can manage their own supply chain? The organisation then provides 'shape' in the context of common philosophy, branding and support systems the employees can call upon at need.

To some extent, this already happens with franchises and, in a limited way, with some of our wacky companies, such as Rosenbluth International with its family farm model detailed above.

Another is Lothian and Edinburgh Enterprise Ltd (LEEL), a public sector organisation promoting inward economic development in Scotland. LEEL has only two layers – six directors and 120 project managers. The directors are able to cope with such large spans of control – up to 30 people – by coaching project managers (any of whom may have responsibility for a project involving tens of millions of pounds sterling) when they need it and leaving them alone when they don't.

LEEL is near the ultimate in empowered, flat structures. Says CEO Des Bonnar: 'Project management for me is all about the director not lying awake at night, worrying about a project, because he or she knows that, if there is any worrying to do, you are doing it. If you have supervisors, you create a comfort zone that prevents learning. Every time you put another layer in, they've got to create a role for themselves.'

Communication in LEEL is mainly horizontal, both within and between teams. It isn't always easy to maintain the horizontal energy, however, especially as most of the communication systems are informal. At the beginning, says Bonnar, 'we used to have vertical departments, but the power structures and physical structures got in the way. Now we add value by making the lateral systems work, through cross-functional teams. People running projects are responsible for developing their own strategies and building their own teams around them.

'We used to have formal contracts between people, to specify what each should deliver. People didn't like it – they thought it was bureaucratic – so now it's only the very big projects where that happens. We break down the functional barriers in all sorts of ways. For example, if you make a presentation to the management, it won't be your director who responds to you on their behalf. That way, we prevent barons emerging.'

Working in LEEL is not a soft option. When everyone carries the can personally for major projects, it creates a high-pressure environment that isn't to everyone's taste. Few people who stay complain of the responsibility, however. Their main issues seem to lie in keeping the pressure on the management team to walk the talk even more than they already do – which makes it a tough environment for the directors, too.

Are there other, newer, more experimental organisational shapes? Almost certainly. Someone out there, undoubtedly from the wacky mould, is experimenting with some, or several, bizarre new organisational designs.

We can't be sure what they'll look like; all we can know is they will be like nothing we've seen so far. That's because wacky entrepreneurs do not start with existing structures and try to adapt them. They begin with their own, often half-formed ideas and build them into structures that work. This is true evolution at work.

THE BOTTOM LINE

▶ Structure follows philosophy.

▶ Flexibility and initiative are more important than systems or rules.

▶ Keep it simple, keep it small, cut the crap.

▶ There's no limit to the organisational shapes you can choose from.

NOTES

1. Ricardo Semler, Maverick, the Success Story Behind the World's Most Unusual Workplace (Warner Books, 1993).
2. Polly Labarre, 'This Organisation is Dis-organisation', in Fast Company, June/July 1996.
3. Robert Levering and Milton Moskowitz, The 100 Best Companies to Work for in America (Doubleday, New York, 1993).
4. Rob Walker, 'Back to the Farm', in Fast Company, February/March 1997.
5. Ricardo Semler, Maverick, 1993.
6. Ricardo Semler, Maverick, 1993.
7. Brenda Marks, 'The Underwear Makes the Man', in The Waterbury Republican-American, 10 November 1996.
8. Brian Dumaine, 'Asia's Wealth Creators Confront a New Reality', in Fortune, 8 December 1997.
9. Moira Petty, 'Heaven for Working Mothers' in The Times, 8 July 1998.
10. Robert Levering and Milton Moskowitz, The 100 Best Companies, 1993.
11. Jon Henley, 'Making Hard Work a Crime', in The Guardian, 16 June 1998.
12. Alex Markels 'Power to the People', Fast Company, February/March 1998.
13. Julian Richer, The Richer Way (Emap Business Communications, 1995).
14. Alex Markels, 'Power to the People', 1998.
15. Julian Richer, The Richer Way, 1995.
16. Elizabeth Conlin, 'Small Business: Second Thoughts on Growth', in Inc., March 1991.
17. Ricardo Semler, Maverick, 1993.

18. Tom Peters, *The Tom Peters Seminar, Crazy Times Call for Crazy Organisations* (Vintage, 1994).
19. Walter Goldsmith and David Clutterbuck, *The Winning Streak, Mark II* (Orion Business Books, 1997).
20. Ingvar Kamprad, *Testament of a Furniture Dealer* (IKEA, Almhult, 1976, revised 1992).
21. William G. Lee, 'A Conversation with Herb Kelleher', in *Organisational Dynamics*, Autumn 1994.
22. Marianne Detwiler, 'Wearing his Success on his Shorts', in *Entrepreneurial Edge*, Vol. 1, 1997.
23. Kevin Freiberg and Jackie Freiberg, *Nuts! Southwest Airlines' Crazy Recipe for Business and Personal Success* (Bard Press, Austin, Texas, 1996).
24. Brian Muirhead and Price Pritchett, *The Mars Pathfinder Approach to Faster-Better-Cheaper* (Pritchett and Associates, 1997) (www.pritchettonline.coml).
25. David Sheff, in *ASAP Forbes*, 24 February 1997.
26. Elizabeth Conlin, 'Small Business', 1991.
27. Ricardo Semler, *Maverick*, 1993.
28. David Sheff, *ASAP Forbes*, 1997.
29. Jeffrey L. Seglin, 'The Happiest Workers in the World' in *Inc. Special Issue: State of Small Business*, 1996.
30. Robin Dunbar, 'Why Gossip Is Good for You,' in *New Scientist*, 21 November 1992, pp. 28–31 (quoted in Tom Peters, *The Pursuit of Wow!*).
31. Rob Walker, 'Back to the Farm', in *Fast Company*, February/March 1997.
32. Brian Dumaine, 'Asia's Wealth Creators Confront a New Reality', in *Fortune*, 8 December 1997.
33. Christina Novicki, 'Don't Just Change the Channel. Change the Rules', in *Fast Company*, December 1996/January 1997.
34. F. Shipper and C. Manz, 'An Alternative Road to Empowerment', in *Organisational Dynamics*, June 1990.
35. F. Shipper and C. Manz, 'An Alternative Road to Empowerment', June 1990.
36. M. Kaplan, 'You Have No Boss', in *Fast Company*, October/November 1997.
37. M. Mitchell Waldrop, 'The Trillion Dollar Vision of Dee Hock', in *Fast Company*, October/November 1996.
38. David Summer Smith, 'Managing in a Goldfish Bowl', *Sunday Times*, May 1998.
39. John Case, 'Corporate Culture' in *Inc.*, November 1996.
40. Gina Imperato, 'Greetings from Idea City', in *Fast Company*, October/November 1997.
41. Joshua Macht, 'When the Walls Come Tumbling Down', in *Inc. Technology*, issue 2, 1995.
42. Jay Chiat, 'Welcome to the Club House in the Virtual Office: Office Atmosphere Changes at Advertising Agencies', in *Adweek*, 29 November 1993.
43. R. Buchanan, 'Brave New Work', in *Details*, February 1995.
44. M. Dickson, 'Dismantling the Office,' in *Financial Times*, 28 January 1994.
45. R. Buchanan, 'Brave New Work', 1995.

46. Joshua Macht, 'When the Walls Come Tumbling Down', 1995.
47. R. Buchanan, 'Brave New Work', 1995.
48. R. Buchanan, 'Brave New Work', 1995.
49. R. Buchanan, 'Brave New Work', 1995.
50. Jay Chiat, 'Welcome to the Club House', 1993.
51. J. Pendleton, 'A Virtual Office with Real Problems: Chiat/Day's Grand Experiment Reveals Pluses, Pitfalls', in MSNBC Online, January 1996.
52. W. Taylor, 'At VeriFone It's a Dog's Life (And They Love It!)', in Fast Company, November 1995.
53. W. Taylor, 'At VeriFone It's a Dog's Life', 1995.
54. Ian Stewart, Life's Other Secret: The New Mathematics of the Living World (Allen Lane/The Penguin Press, London, 1998).

4 The importance of having fun

'Weather at your destination is 50 degrees with some broken clouds, but they'll try to have them fixed before we arrive.' (Southwest Airlines in-flight announcement).

'We're the number one boxer short company in America and not because we spent a lot of money on advertising, but because we entertain people.' (Nicholas Graham, CEO, Joe Boxer).

In October 1987, in the days after one of this century's worst stock market crashes, New York's financial district was a dismal place to be. Only two people seemed to be enjoying themselves. Ben Cohen and Jerry Greenfield, two long-haired, blue-jeaned ice cream makers from Vermont, were handing out free scoops of ice cream to brokers on Wall Street. The flavours? Economic Crunch and That's Life.

These guys are so much fun their factory tours have become the biggest tourist attraction in the state of Vermont; they even have a committee to make sure everyone is having fun.

We've seen and heard about a lot of strange behaviour in our search for the world's wackiest companies. And it's not just the bosses who behave oddly. Witness also the aeronautics technicians who call themselves the seven dwarfs, the airline crew running 'find a hole in your sock' contests and sing-along safety announcements, the lawyers shooting hoops in the office (while their assistants dive to protect the computer monitors), the senior executives fiddling with their office race car sets, crayons and play dough, and the underwear designer – Joe Boxer, of course – shooting boxer shorts off a rocket and flying a planeload of journalists to Iceland for a frozen underpants toss. 'I'd like to co-brand with a country,' he muses.

These companies are all very silly. They're also profitable. And, yes, there is a connection:

- Travel services company Rosenbluth International was a small, unremarkable family firm until the founder's great-grandson, Hal Rosenbluth, came along, took to showing movies at lunch time and dressing up as a fish – and boosted billings from $40 million to $1.5 billion in less than ten years.

- At SOL, the whole work environment is relentlessly cheerful, with bright yellow décor, an office that looks like a playhouse, and the company logo, a bright yellow happy face, plastered on even the most serious documents. All this cheeriness has paid off – cheerful staff and happy customers have helped make SOL one of Europe's fastest growing and most profitable industrial cleaning companies.

- Springfield's CEO Jack Stack figures business is one big game. Why not – it's competitive, there are rules to follow and a score to keep, and people like to play once they know how. Stack has taught his employees the rules (everyone has financial training), posts the score, and keeps the whole workforce geared up for the game. And he's winning: Stack and his team turned a 1983 loss of $60,000 into a profit, in 1992, of $1.3 million on sales of $65 million. In nine years, the value of Springfield's stock multiplied 180 times, and its workforce grew six-fold.

- Richard Branson, one of the most successful businessmen in Britain, if not the world, reportedly runs his 200-odd companies at least part of the time from a hammock in the Caribbean, a pile of faxes on his lap. His secret? According to one Virgin employee, Branson sees everything as a game, and 'regards life as a cosmic version of Monopoly'.[1]

- At Odetics, a robotics firm located, appropriately, right across the street from Disneyland in Anaheim, California, employees proudly display the model of the space shuttle Challenger they made out of Budweiser cans. One office has a wooden dinosaur hanging from the ceiling. The company's fun committee, one of the country's oldest (it dates back to 1982), arranges Halloween pumpkin dances, carrot deliveries on

Valentine's Day, and contests in bubble-gum blowing
and telephone-booth stuffing. And watch out for
ODEX-I – that's the six-legged robot and company
mascot that wanders the office corridors.
- In just over 30 years an Italian family of fashion
designers grew their little shop into a 7,000 store
global network and one of the most famous brand
names in the world. The Benettons say it's all down to
their 'creative madness'. To celebrate, they posed for a
family portrait in a recent catalogue – all wearing
strait-jackets.

Is it profitable? Does it matter? Odetics co-founder Joel Slutzky
explains his philosophy: 'We feel that if it's not fun to get up in the
morning and go to work, then it doesn't matter what the profit and
loss statement looks like. And, in fact, we've found that there is a
tight linkage between how you feel about the company and how
you are going to do as far as growth and profitability and things like
that.'[2]

A number of academic studies back this up. The studies, held, for
the most part, in North America since 1989, have found links
between workplace humour and a whole range of positive
constructs. These include camaraderie, communication, group cohe-
siveness, creativity, motivation, stress relief, productivity, and a
leader's ability to effect change among followers.

Humour, it appears, is the management elixir of the nineties. As
one academic trio deadpanned: 'Humour is a concept that needs to
be taken more seriously in our field.'[3]

David Abramis, assistant professor of management and human
resources at the School of Business Administration at California State
University, Long Beach, was one of the first to study links between
fun and performance at work. In the late eighties he surveyed 341
California clerical workers, asking – basically – were they having fun
yet?[4]

He discovered that those who felt they were having fun at work
were, compared to people who didn't feel they were having fun:

- less anxious and depressed
- more satisfied with their jobs and with their lives in general
- more convinced that other people have fun at work
- more motivated by their work
- more creative at work
- better able to meet job demands and less likely to be absent or late for work.

A 1996 study has found an even more direct link between humour at work and hard business measures. John Sosik, an assistant management professor at Pennsylvania State University, Bruce Avolio, a management professor at the State University of New York at Binghamton, and Jane Howell from the University of Western Ontario found that humour can improve job performance – and even profits.[5]

In their study of 322 members of a Canadian financial institution, they found, says Sosik, that 'the use of humour was significantly and positively related to both individual and unit performance. One performance measure was a bottom line budget measure. And budget is measured in terms of dollars. So, yes, you certainly could say there's a link between the two.'

Most of the wacky leaders in our sample have always known that it pays to have fun. Sosik points to Sun Microsystems, a Mountain View, California-based software company. At Sun, the engineers' April Fools' Day pranks, which have in the past included building a workstation at the bottom of a shark tank and assembling a car in an office, now attract scores of photographers to see what they'll do next. CEO Scott McNealy arrived at work to find his engineers had built a golf hole in his office, complete with a green and water hazard. 'I don't know if it improved his game or not' (McNealy is said to be a passionate golfer), says Sosik, 'But it is exactly that kind of relationship with one's employees that can help to form bonds that improve performance.'[6]

Forming bonds is also the main motivation behind Southwest Airlines' manic behaviour. Southwest, with its sing-along safety announcements, impromptu parties and job interviews where candidates are asked to tell jokes, has to be one of the most fun-loving companies in the world.

All this silliness, though, serves a number of serious purposes, says Southwest's vice president, people, Libby Sartain: 'Humour helps communications, and it helps break down barriers. The environment here is not bureaucratic or élitist and humour helps foster that. If you see your vice president in a funny circumstance, it lets you know they're human and that they're approachable when there's something serious to deal with.'

The robot makers at Odetics have also found that fun, enjoyment and recreation can humanise an organisation. Odetics employees (just the people, though, not the robots) enjoy the use of a cinema, a weight room, a pool, and tennis and volleyball courts. Everyone gets generous time off and the company also sponsors programmes in stress management, acupressure and yoga.

Bill Prichard, Odetics' public relations manager and a member of the company's fun committee, sees these facilities as ways to increase communication and good employee relations. 'At the fitness centre, for example, everyone is in sweats pumping iron – from the janitor to company officers. There's free communication among the ranks, an openness that carries over into the office.'[7]

Sosik agrees. Humour, he says, can lead to 'increased morale and cohesion. People feel more open to communicate in a more trusting way. Build trust and you're able to get people motivated. They're happy to be there, and they come up with better ideas. It's so competitive out there, I think that's the key to survival.'

Fun helps recruit and retain employees

For many companies, especially high-tech firms, the key to survival is, increasingly, their ability to attract and retain the people they need.

And, to do that, they have to compete on fun; money, it seems, just doesn't cut it anymore. As one 1998 survey revealed, most high-tech employees rate an enjoyable work environment before salary in selecting a job.[8]

Stephen Brooks, director of Product Development at Vancouver's

Multiactive Software, is counting on this. His is one of many Canadian high-tech firms using fun as a last line of defence against the higher wages offered by American employers. They can't compete on pay, in this industry that absorbs talent faster than colleges can produce it, so they're competing for young programmers' hearts, minds and funny bones – stocking their office fridges with chocolate bars, replacing board room tables with foosball games, and designing offices that look more like frat houses than business units.

Electronics Arts Canada, which designs game software, has invested heavily in creating a fun workplace. Its C$55 million office complex, built in 1998, includes a football field, a basketball court, fitness facilities with instructors, several arcade rooms, and even an indoor roller hockey rink.

Workers at Seagate Software, another fast-growing Vancouver company, get an office ping pong table and the use of a nearby ski chalet; down the street at Multiactive, the boss picks up the Friday afternoon beer tab.

'One of the key parts to our recruiting is creating an office atmosphere where people have fun,' says Brooks. 'It makes up only a part of a person's decision to work here, but it's a huge part of keeping them here.'[9]

Employees in these industries get calls at least monthly from headhunters, offering salaries that, with the exchange rate, can work out at more than twice what Canadian employers pay. Most, though, aren't budging. Multiactive hasn't lost a programmer since it started four years ago. Seagate has doubled in size every year for the past few years. 'Someone will always pay more in the industry, and there's the dollar and tax issues, but if I'm connected to the people I work with, and I love the environment I work in, you're going to have to pay me tons of money to leave and offer me something similar,' said Helen Sheridan, director of human resources for Seagate Software.[10]

In Silicon Valley, where the competition for brain power is, if anything, even more intense, employers are also adding fun to their arsenal. At Sun Microsystems, picked by Fortune magazine as one of America's best employers in 1998, employee turnover is only two-thirds that of its competitors. Fun is what keeps them there. Says human resources manager Ken Ivares: 'Our goal is to keep them so busy having fun every day that they don't even listen when the headhunters call.'[11]

Among the winners is the Geek Squad, a Minneapolis-based computer installation and repair company where engineers wear clip-on ties and too-short black trousers, carry special agent badges, and drive 1950s cars, called geek mobiles, around to rescue office workers from their computer troubles. It's a clever gag on a number of levels, not least in its recognition that, when the system's down, Clark Kent is the real superhero. Much of the wackiness, says chief inspector and founder Robert Stephens, is designed not so much to get in the customers (they have plenty of those) but to attract the most talented geeks and nerds.

Stephens, a 29-year-old former lab technician, has been called on to offer his insights to such non-geeks as the Harvard Business School Alumni and readers of The Wall Street Journal. Says Stephens: 'One of the things I tell people is that the majority of marketing is not necessarily to bring in business, it's to bring in good people.'

When Stephens launched his company in 1993, he knew exactly whom he wanted to work with. 'I saw a sense of heroism in these geniuses with brilliant minds, but six days worth of food on their shirts and no social graces. They dedicate so much of their time specialising in one area, that everything else goes to pot. Most people like that disappear in basements of corporate America. I wanted to attract those people, the oddballs.

And, when people, especially brilliant odd-balls, are choosing a job, he adds, 'there's one thing more important than money and that's self-esteem. People want to feel they're part of something interesting and special.' Computer repair work is, says Stephens, 'just a few steps up the food chain from plumbing. The work is not glamorous, but the nature of the work is. Computers are at the core of all businesses and when they go down, there's nothing more important than getting them fixed.' 'Superheroes do exist and we're it. We're the real men in black. Staff really get into the drama and theatre of it.'

The Geek Squad, despite the intense competition for technical brains faced by all high-tech companies, has no staff turnover at all.

Fun sparks creativity and innovation

Many of our wacky offices are done up with off-beat, even silly, décor, like the ten-foot high Alice in Wonderland chairs at Joe Boxer's office, or the graffiti murals that Liisa Joronen commissioned for SOL City. Many are also stocked with toys and games, from racing cars to foosball tables to wads of play dough. These aren't for killing time (well, not entirely). Humour and a chance to play help people let off steam and keep their creative energy flowing through stressful times. It also tends to arise naturally in innovative, energetic environments.

Pathfinder, the group charged with landing a vehicle on Mars, was no exception. The seven employees who did the wiring called themselves the seven dwarfs, each with a relevant name (Grumpy did the quality control).

According to Doug Hall, who runs Richard Saunders International, one of America's leading creativity and new product idea consultants: 'Fun is fundamental. As our education increases, our imagination decreases. If you're laughing you're more likely to break all that education and come up with a wicked-good idea.'[12]

Anecdotal evidence, academic studies and observation of wacky companies, all indicate that fun, play and silliness can promote creativity and risk taking. This, in turn, suggests that there are hard business reasons for maintaining a wacky atmosphere.

Psychologist Alice Isen and her colleagues at the University of Maryland, for example, found that people who had just enjoyed a funny film solved problems more creatively. Similarly, Mary Ann Glyn, assistant professor of organisational behaviour at Yale University, discovered that people who see problems as games come up with more creative solutions than those who see the same problems as work.[13]

What is fun?

Fun (of the sort that makes for better workplaces) involves more than stunts and games in the office. It can involve treats, rewards and breaks from work; ideally though, as we've found in many of our wacky companies, the most fun is derived from the job itself.

Just about anything can be fun for somebody. Professor Abramis, in a study of California office workers, asked subjects to rate a variety of what most people would consider fun and non-fun work activities, from parties and awards to working alone, attending lectures and giving or receiving a performance appraisal, as 'fun' or 'not fun'. Though most people, not surprisingly, plumped for the parties, significantly, every one of the 55 activities was considered fun by at least a few people.

Fun at work, then, can involve a whole range of activities, including:

- recognition and rewards
- celebrations
- random acts of silliness
- symbols and rituals
- care for mental, spiritual and physical health
- freedom to behave like a human at work
- freedom to behave like a human outside of work.

Recognition and rewards

Every company looks for ways to motivate and energise its employees. The usual course is to offer rewards to individuals for specific achievements – reaching a sales target, say, or signing up new customers.

The highly competitive British music retailer Julian Richer, for example, has developed a detailed, almost Pavlovian award structure, with treats and prizes handed out little and often to keep his retail staff hopping. The rewards, like the use of two Bentleys and a Jaguar for winners of a sales contest, are off-beat and interesting. The system though, with its emphasis on internal competition, is fairly conventional.

Richer's other perks, such as the free use of holiday homes or invitations to meals at top restaurants, are more in keeping with the most wacky company's way of doing things, where rewards are used not so much to reward individuals, as to recognise long-term, team results, or simply to create the kind of atmosphere where fun can flourish.

Celebrations

Wacky reward systems are more likely to celebrate group achievements and offer unconditional thanks to everyone for being part of
the team. The most obvious – and popular – way to do this is to
throw a party. And wacky companies do party. It's been said of
Southwest Airlines, for example, that they could single handedly
keep the balloon industry afloat.

And, while conventional companies will begrudgingly mark
special events, such as a centenary or Christmas, wacky companies
need little excuse for a party.

Ben & Jerry's joy committee, for example, tries to throw an event
at least once a month to celebrate such little known holidays as Barry
Manilow's Birthday or National Clash Dressing Day. Dress Up Day,
where everyone gets to see just how funny their co-workers look in
suits, is also a favourite.

At Rosenbluth Travel, August is Associate Appreciation Month,
with Hawaiian Shirt Gonzo Friday, Rosenjeopardy Games, Hoagie
Day, and a formal party called Salmon-chanted evening (salmon is
the company symbol – it represents bucking against the tide).

Virgin CEO Richard Branson is also famous for his parties. From
the start, the Virgin business was run on a deliberate policy of
mixing business with pleasure. For years, the entire staff of the
record company, publishing company, and studio management team
would spend weekends away together at a country house hotel at the
company's expense. Any discussion of sales figures or business plans
was banned, but sport, sleep and vast quantities of food and drink
were de rigeur. Often the weekends finished up with a large bill and
a request not to return.

Despite its size, the social aspect of the business remains important
to this day. Branson still hosts a series of parties at his home each
year for all Virgin employees – everyone from senior managers to
airline crew, shop assistants and secretaries are lavishly entertained
with a fun fair, barbecues, bouncy castles, punting on the river and
other activities. It is a Virgin tradition, too, that Branson himself ends
up in the water at least a couple of times in the course of the
weekend. And, though things have toned down a bit from the sex,
drugs and rock 'n' roll days, outrageous things still happen at Virgin

parties. Apparently, Ivana Trump still hasn't forgiven Branson for hanging her upside down over a swimming pool.

Southwest's parties are a little more clean cut, but at least as frequent. Just about anything is an excuse for a party at Texan airline: new routes, a millionth customer, new planes, new facilities, impromptu parades and costume parties – even Elvis Presley's 58th birthday. 'Halloween is the funniest day we have at work,' says Southwest's vice president, people, Libby Sartain. 'Every plane, location and airport group dress up and, at headquarters, very little work goes on.' The people department, she says proudly, have won the 'most highly effective and blatantly obvious suck up to Herb' award for five years running. 'At the end of the day at Halloween I'm so exhausted from laughing I can hardly walk.'

Besides its usual roster of parties and events, Southwest also has a sort of fun swat team on hand. The E (for encouragement) team, a subgroup of the culture committee, will fly in to cheer up staff wherever morale needs a boost. 'They'll arrive unannounced and throw a party, maybe put on a barbecue and clean the staff's plane for them while they eat. It's just to let people know they're appreciated,' says Libby Sartain.

At Southwest, or any party-centred company, celebrations serve a number of purposes. They recognise and reward employees for their team efforts, foster pride in accomplishments, and create a sense of history and a body of shared company lore.

Random acts of silliness

What really makes a workplace fun, though, are not just the special events and celebrations (though these help) but the kind of atmosphere that allows people to laugh and let off steam as part of their daily work. Many of our wacky companies have, for example, exceptional employee facilities, with sports and recreational facilities on site, and treats like gourmet cafeteria food, free popcorn or company massage therapists.

At the very least, a wacky company has a good supply of toys. From basketball hoops to crayons, race car sets and wads of play dough, toys play a central role in many high performing companies.

It also seems that, the more intellectual capital required for a job, the more toys are lying around.

Squelchy stuff is especially effective. At strategy meetings, Geraldine Laybourne, CEO of children's TV network Nickelodeon, hands out wads of Gak – a kind of extra-gooey play dough that the company merchandises. 'You'd be surprised how relaxing it is to manipulate the stuff. People listen better and start sharing ideas,' she says.[14]

Crayons are good too. At travel services company Rosenbluth International, boss Hal Rosenbluth once gave out paper and crayons to about 100 associates (as he calls employees), and asked them to express what they felt about the company. Colouring within the lines was not required. Says Rosenbluth: 'It elicits feelings that aren't going to come out in a survey.' Rosenbluth also asked a group of senior managers to write down the names of every green vegetable they could think of. The idea was to demonstrate that nobody has all the answers.[15]

Rosenbluth, it appears, has tapped into the secret of silliness: you can get a lot more accomplished if you don't take yourself too seriously.

Symbols and rituals

Mike Warren, president of Alabama natural gas distributor Alagasco, figured this out too. When he joined the troubled utility in 1984, he wanted to discourage the rigid, conventional style of thinking he called the 'utility mind-set'. So he got himself a rubber dinosaur stamp. Any paper that came across his desk with pre-historic reasoning in it got the dinosaur stamp and was returned to sender. Employees enjoyed the idea enough to put together a 15-foot long paper maché dinosaur, which made the office rounds. In 1986, the union gave Warren the Dinosaur Killer of the Year award.[16]

Symbols and rituals – even, or perhaps especially, silly ones – can be more effective in bringing home a point or demonstrating company values than any amount of pontificating. Southwest has adopted the nuts they serve to passengers as their unofficial symbol; Rosenbluth's mascot is the salmon that swims upstream.

At garden equipment company Smith & Hawken, a pink pig,

symbolising a heavy workload, circulates around the office, landing on the desk of whoever has bitten off more than they can chew that day. Sympathy (and, with luck, practical help) moves with the pig.

And, while the company song may, mercifully, have never caught on in the West, some sports rituals are taking hold. Wal-Mart folks start the day with a shimmy and a cheer. Meetings are like pep rallies, with employees shouting out Wal-Mart cheerleading songs, and workspaces are plastered with homilies of happiness.

Even seriously non-wacky companies can use fun in similar ways. At IBM's Southern Trading Area Office, an elaborate ritual takes place whenever a salesperson closes a deal or gets a qualified lead. First, she smashes a massive gong, in the office for the purpose, so everyone knows about it. Then, at the mini racetrack also in the office, she moves the toy horse with her picture glued to the jockey's face out of the gate into the track. 'The idea is to get each salesperson "out of the gate" each day,' says Karen Donnelly, an executive in the Client Satisfaction Center. The sales leader for the day gets to pick one of her colleagues to play that morning's sales song on a tuba.[17]

The feel good factor: care for physical, mental and spiritual health

Some companies, rather than trying the gee up motivating techniques offered above, offer a selection of more easy-going treats designed to ease stress and smooth the creative flow.

Management at UK creativity consultancy ?What If! have, for example, implemented what they call 'The James Brown Principle' – a number of initiatives designed to make the staff, in the words of the song, 'feel good'.

These involve fun and games – like the office model racecar set – but also a range of health initiatives. The company supplies both a yoga teacher and a company slate at the local pub. Ben & Jerry's also subscribe to the feel good principle. They offer a range of alternative medical treatments – from alternative health therapies to three free pints of ice cream a day – and have also been known to bring in masseuses for sore production workers during hectic times.

Henry Bertolon, co-founder and CEO of NECX, a computer product distributor in Peabody, Massachusetts, was so concerned about his top team's 'feel good factor' he hired a psychologist to help them cope with the company's rapid growth. The consulting psychologist – Will Calmas, a psychologist with an MBA – meets with NECX's top eight to ten executives every Friday morning, with no agenda, but free permission to discuss things that managers aren't normally supposed to talk about: fear, hostility, frustration and secret desires.

'We focus on talking,' says the aptly named Calmas. 'Most of us have come from homes where we're taught, "Don't say anything if you can't say anything nice." We bring that attitude into the corporate world. But if you don't talk, you can't resolve anything.'[18] It is a bit touchy feely: at first, executives avoided the meetings, and two quit rather than join in. The main reason was fear – once Bertolon stressed that no one would be punished for revealing their darker thoughts, people began to open up.

The sessions seem to be working. In 1995, Calmas asked members of NECX's management team to rate themselves on things like helping each other and being approachable to staff. The average on the first test was 1.5 out of 10. A few years later, it was 7.5.

Meanwhile company revenues increased from $62 million in 1992 to almost $400 million in 1996; employee turnover fell from 42 to 20 per cent. 'Companies rarely commit to improving their people's emotional health,' says Bertolon. 'We want to be a billion-dollar company. But along the way, we're going to look out for our people.' Bertolon adds that well-adjusted people also cope better with change, and that's a critical skill in his fast-changing business.

Therapy might be just the thing for computer people, but it's hard to imagine, say, engineers or construction workers getting in touch with their inner feelings. Think again. In Britain at any rate, it turns out tough guys do share. In 1997, Birse Construction, one of the UK's largest civil engineering contractors, brought in a firm of industrial psychologists to run group therapy sessions, encouraging staff and managers to open up about their feelings and share childhood experiences. The idea was to humanise the culture that chairman Peter Birse felt had become overly aggressive. However, where therapy is normally used to reduce aberrant behaviour, Birse's objective was to encourage it.

It seemed to have worked. Birse hit the headlines in 1998 when Caerphilly Council, with which Birse had a legal dispute, complained to several government bodies that the contractor had mailed a pixie toadstool to their offices, followed by a fax with some verse by Nelson Mandela, and that six Birse employees showed up at a council meeting dressed as cartoon characters, led by Mr Blobby and Bugs Bunny. The council's chief executive Malgwyn Davies failed to see the funny side and protested that the actions amounted to harassment.

According to French, the gestures were meant to help Davies 'free himself from the institutional attitude' that had led to the dispute in the first place. 'I thought it might open up the channels of communication,' says French. 'People use these fairies to meditate, to relive stress. I thought it was all getting a bit stressful for him.'

All the efforts at Birse, from the therapy session to open communications, and reinventing the culture and principles, are meant to ease stress and create a more human (and humane) culture and to return the company to its more values-led roots.

Fast growth during the eighties had engendered an aggressive management style at Birse. Says French: 'the business had evolved into something we didn't want it to be. Slowly, imperceptibly, it was starting to operate in an aggressive and confrontational way. Suppliers were being squeezed. Customers weren't being treated with the honesty they deserved. There was fear in the workforce as the new style began to bite.'

Others in the industry and the media, and several employees who've left, thought that Birse management was completely bonkers. Says French: 'There was a time when people thought the world was flat. Back then anyone who said otherwise would have been ridiculed. What we're saying is maybe there's a better way to do business than being completely stressed out and fearful all the time.'

A lot of companies are asking this same question, and concluding that it's in their interest to help reduce that stress. Healthy, happy, well-adjusted employees, with good work/life balance, and a reasonable balance of sanity and madness, are demonstrably more productive, more loyal, and more likely to stick around.

So, along with the fun and celebrations to lighten up the workday, most wacky companies also make a concerted effort, through flexi-time and creative benefit packages, to help take some of the edge off life in general.

The freedom to be yourself at work

Good employers recognise that people have lives outside of work. Wacky employers, though, do that and more – they enable people to have a life at work, too.

Bruce Tulgan, founder of Rainmaker Thinking, Inc., a consultant in New Haven, Connecticut, wanted to know what makes a company 'cool' – a word synonymous enough, for our purposes, with 'wacky'. He interviewed more than 1,300 American workers aged 35 and under about their jobs, then searched his database for the keyword 'cool', to find out what they liked and wanted at work.[19]

What he discovered was that 'really cool companies don't just help employees manage their lives outside of work, they also allow employees to bring life into their work. How? By allowing them to express their individuality on the job through casual dress and personalised office décor, and by allowing them to play while at work.'

This, says Adrian Simpson, a UK consultant in new workplace practices, is the wave of the future. Traditionally, he says, 'there has been a trade-off. To compensate for not being myself I get job security, a company car, a pension etc. It's an unwritten deal, but it's not a natural way of behaving. And it's not a reality anymore.'

It's certainly not the reality at Dyson. UK designer James Dyson – whose slogan is: 'We should be human beings not business people' – hires mostly very young people, offers them challenging work and encourages them to be different as a matter of principle. Dyson calls it his 'anti-brilliance campaign'. 'Very few people can be brilliant. And they are over-valued. It's much more exciting to be a pioneer. Be a bit whacko and you shake people up. And we all need shaking up.'

Tolerance, openness and acceptance are also essential parts of the culture at Ben & Jerry's. According to Mitch Curren, Ben & Jerry's info queen: 'Employees are free to express themselves as individuals and to express their opinions. It wasn't until I actually got into the company that I really came to appreciate it, but this is a very, very open company where you can work and be yourself. I can't imagine any typical company making me feel this comfortable.'[20]

Southwest Airlines, whose recruitment advertisements specifically ask for people who 'colour outside the lines', hires people who don't fit other corporate moulds and lets them be themselves at work. Such tolerance is the quickest way to any non-conformist's heart. 'So many atmospheres in corporate America are oppressive, making you feel you have to check your brain and your sense of humour at reception before you go to your office. At Southwest, we allow people to be themselves,' says vice president, people, Libby Sartain.

The freedom to be yourself outside of work

That freedom to be yourself can, in some cases, extend far beyond the job.

Graduate recruits to ?What If!, for example, each receive a welcoming gift of £1,000 to spend on something they've never done before. Activities chosen so far include courses in massage and drawing, a stay at a health farm and a parachute jump.

At Rhino Foods, employees are encouraged to set and achieve goals, whether work-related or personal. Called the 'Wants Program', it involves training employees as wants co-ordinators. Employees then meet, alone, with their wants co-ordinator, once every quarter for an hour or so during working hours, to set goals and arrange plans for achieving them. Some aim for work-related goals, such as winning a promotion, but others aim for personal ambitions, like writing a book, buying a home, or learning a new sport.

The programme, which is optional, costs a fair bit in time, but Rhino management feels it is time and money well spent. If an employee achieves goals on a personal level, he or she can focus that much more on work and, says Marlene Dailey, director of HR, 'The more they understand that they create their own world, whether it's here or at home, the more confidence they have in their abilities. They're more likely to speak up and offer their ideas.'

Says Castle: 'If we can get people who are good at getting what they want, then we have a group of people who can be proactive about getting results either in their personal life or while they're here at work.'[21]

Fun for customers

Anyone who's ever flown Southwest Airlines, got a break dancing lesson while buying ice cream at Amy's Scoop Shop, or shopped anywhere the staff are genuinely enjoying themselves, knows that fun is contagious. If staff are having a good time, so will customers.

Richard Branson figured this out a long time ago. He told *Corporate Entertainment*: 'If you don't have a happy and highly motivated workforce, customer satisfaction goes out of the window, and if you don't have satisfied customers, you don't have a business.'[22]

So did SOL CEO Liisa Joronen: 'In a service business if you're not happy with yourself how can you make the customer happy?'[23]

Fun is a cheap way to gain publicity

Wacky companies get a lot more mileage than others from their marketing money.

As we detailed in Chapter 2, wacky companies don't spend a lot on market research, focus groups, segmentation, or targeting. And (with notable exceptions such as Benetton) they hardly ever buy advertising – partly because they don't have much faith in conventional marketing techniques, partly because they'd rather not spend the money.

What they do have is a powerful knack for publicity and an uncanny ability to get a lot of value from their marketing buck just by behaving really, really differently.

Most of Joe Boxer's stunts seem to have more to do with outrageous one-upmanship than with selling products. In 1995, for example, CEO Nicholas Graham launched a 6,000 square foot electronic billboard, or as he calls it, the world's largest e-mail, in Times Square. He's launched boxer shorts from a rocket, staged a wedding in Times Square and made enough cross dressing appearances to rival a female impersonator. In an effort to get media attention during New York's fashion week, Graham flew 150 journalists to Reykjavik for a fashion show with dancing sheep, a parachuting Santa, and his own confetti. It wasn't as easy as it looked: 'It's hard to get enough confetti in Iceland,' he reveals. Addressing the crowd of fashion writers in Reykjavik, he observed: 'I know a lot of us woke up this morning and thought, "Why am I in Iceland?"' The audience waited. 'Well I don't know.'

He knew all right. 'There are lots of different ways of buying advertising.' Graham told one garment trade journalist. 'There is the traditional way, and then there is this way.'[24]

His way certainly works. 'Finally this year we did some market research for the first time and we found out what we already know: very high brand awareness,' says Graham. 'Two hundred million Americans (75 to 76 per cent of the population) have heard of us. That's incredible for someone who's never really advertised. Our customers are fun seekers; they like to have fun.'

Why does Richard Branson dress up in wedding gowns, abseil down the side of stores, and fly about in balloons? Not because he's an exhibitionist (those close to him say he's quite shy), but because he knows what will make 'a back-page photo into a front-page one.'[25]

In 1985, Ben Cohen and Jerry Greenfield made a Cowmobile – a renovated mobile home that they took to the road to give out free scoops of ice cream across America, scooping a thousand cones a day. In a San Diego traffic jam, they just tossed tubs of ice cream out the window to cars in the next lane.

To promote a launch into Boston (their first big city market), the two ice cream moguls shut down production and drove all four employees to Boston, where they ran into office buildings and handed out ice cream to startled workers. Says Wendy Yoder, an employee on the Boston launch: 'People looked at us like we were on drugs.'[26]

Later, they turned a potentially negative story – stepping down of the founder – into a way to remind the world what fun guys they really are: The 'Yo! I Wanna be CEO' contest.

Sometimes, to get really good publicity, you have to be a little bit sneaky. Burton A. Burton (yes, that's his real name), CEO of the Casablanca Fan Company in City of Industry, California, always sponsored a float in the Rose Bowl parade, even during years when Casablanca was cutting its advertising budget. One year, according to

Inc. magazine, Burton designed a float with a Bengal tiger and trapeze artists, which, somehow, got stuck right next to the media grandstand. For nearly 20 minutes, the float filled TV screens while the reporters repeated the Casablanca name over and over. To this day, Burton – who also brings his pet boa constrictor to work, rides around his offices on an old bicycle and starts craps games at sales meetings – swears he doesn't know what happened.[27]

Special agents at the Geek Squad don't even have to bother with stunts. Their everyday working style is bizarre enough to attract all kinds of attention. 'We get a lot of press coverage and a lot of people ask our opinion on doing PR,' says chief inspector Robert Stephens. 'The funny thing is, we've never sent out any press releases at all. The word just kind of gets around.' Nor does the Geek Squad do much advertising.

'As brilliant as a lot of people say we are at marketing, we did it out of necessity. Advertising is expensive.' Instead, The Geek Squad use their inherent geekiness, and their theatrical way of working as their advertising. It works – the company is providing computer support to the Rolling Stones on tour and is becoming the long distance computer support of choice for many Hollywood stars. 'We have an article coming out in *Newsweek* – that's free advertising. Now we're almost at the point where we can afford advertising, but why would I want to do that?'

Don't try this at home – using fun to solve legal disputes

Malice in Dallas, the day in 1992 when Kelleher chose to settle a legal dispute with a televised arm wrestle, is just part of the Herb Lore that has built up around the company.

Set at Dallas's Sportatorium, and hyped with cheerleaders, the theme from *Rocky*, and plenty of media, Malice in Dallas had all the build up of the match of the decade. Actually it was just a friendly contest between Southwest Airlines, represented by Herb Kelleher, and Stevens Aviation, championed by chairman Kurt Herwald, to decide the rights to the slogan 'Plane Smart', which Stevens Aviation had been using before Southwest came up with it.

It was Herwald who proposed the arm wrestle, but Kelleher, a former lawyer, naturally, accepted the challenge. Herwald won, but graciously allowed Southwest to keep the slogan. When reporters asked Kelleher, as he was carried out on a stretcher, whether it had all been done for publicity, he responded with mock innocence: 'Why, I never even thought about it in those terms.'

According to an article on the company Web site: 'Malice in Dallas is now an epic, a story thousands of people inside and outside Southwest Airlines know almost by heart. This rambunctious alternative to a drawn-out, boring, lawyer-enriching, half-million courtroom battle was exactly the sort of antic that Americans have come to associate with their favourite maverick airline. Everybody won: the companies got great publicity, the media had a field day, and charity got $15,000. Everybody had a blast. Southwest's canny ability to perpetuate its image this way is a large factor in its name recognition and success.'

Fun adds value by turning an ordinary product or service into an experience

The notions of theatre as an important element of customer experience and of customer experience as a critical part of customer satisfaction have been around for quite a while. Japanese chefs, fairground hawkers and snake oil salesmen have all thought of it.

It is, however, becoming an increasingly important marketing trend. The authors of a 1998 *Harvard Business Review* article claim that customer experience will soon be the driver of competitive advantage, the way service was a decade ago.[28]

Now, according to Joseph Pine and James Gilmore, all kinds of businesses are selling experiences: hotels, airlines, shopping malls and restaurants. The most obvious are the 'eatertainers', like the Hard Rock Café and 'shoppertainers' like Niketown, Nike's retail complex.

The trend, also called 'Entertailing', comes as no surprise to Stanley Marcus, the 93-year-old former chairman of upscale US retailer Neiman-Marcus. As he told *Inc.* magazine in 1998: 'I imagine that if you were back in Jerusalem in 20 AD, you would have found some guy at the marketplace who had a snake in a basket. Maybe he'd let you stick your head in a basket and see it only if you bought something.'

Pine and Gilmore define experience marketing as what happens when 'a company intentionally uses services as the stage, and goods as props, to engage individual customers in a way that creates a memorable event.'

Joe Boxer's Nicholas Graham, for example, may sell underwear, but as far as he's concerned, he's in show biz. 'We don't just make boxer shorts – we're an entertainment company,' says Graham. 'I like to think of Joe Boxer as a global joke shop, graphic design studio, and entertainment extravaganza all in one.'[29] 'Our philosophy is that the brand is the amusement park and the products are the souvenirs.'[30]

Joe Boxer's product line has expanded to include jeans (a label instructs the wearer to place underwear on the inside), bed linens, watches (synchronised to fun time), ladies' and children's wear, and motor scooters. Underwear now accounts for only 45 per cent of sales. Graham has plans to expand the entertainment theme beyond underwear to TV sitcoms, movies and video games – all starring Joe Boxer. 'It's always been an entertainment-driven business,' he says. 'Our goal is to build an entertainment company. Disney already does that, but they make the movie first and then the underwear. We made the underwear first, now we'll make the movies.'[31]

The Joe Boxer experience doesn't come cheap. However, for many companies, the great thing about creating experience as a competitive advantage is that it doesn't have to cost very much.

That's what one Tel Aviv restaurateur figured, when he opened his fashionable Café Ke'ilu (or Café Pretend), where diners can enjoy the ultimate café experience, and see and be seen on the trendiest street in Tel Aviv. One thing they can't do is eat – management doesn't bother with food, it's usually no more than an afterthought in fashionable cafés anyway. Diners, however, do get a bill. According to the Jerusalem Post, even though they're served with empty plates and glasses, they still get a bill: about four dollars on weekdays and twice that on Fridays.

Southwest Airlines also creates a great passenger experience with virtually no amenities; what they can't offer in material comforts they make up for with fun, and, as a result, Southwest passengers usually have a great time without meals, reserved seating or other frills.

The same challenge faced BC Ferries. The deeply broke Canadian ferry service had, somehow, to tempt tourists to spend up to 33 hours on an old ferry, with no cabins, to travel to places no one has ever heard of, that connected with nowhere, where it was almost certain to rain. 'We started off with a white board,' says Marie Graf, the corporation's customer service manager. 'And asked, what are we going to do with this route to make people say "I want to go on this"?'

'I always believe that when you go someplace, you want to see it, you want to feel it, you want to touch it, and you want to take something back with you. That's what we tried to do,' says Graf. 'So we took what would normally be a BC Ferries route and made it a soft adventure cruise that would be guest-centred and participatory.' That means fun and games. The management team worked with native villages en-route to arrange shore excursions, salmon barbecues on deck replaced the usual school-dinner-style cafeteria meals, and the crew pitched in with deck golf, bingo, and – in a self-deprecatory reference to most cruise ship facilities – an inflated paddling pool. They even wrote special sea shanties for the occasion.

The most significant feature in creating an experience, though, was the way crew members were actively encouraged to socialise with passengers. Says BC Ferries executive Ross Harris: 'Traditionally a BC Ferries crew is stand-offish. We've tried to break down that barrier; we gave crew time in their workday to socialise with passengers.'

Was it hard for staff to be sociable? 'Yes it was,' says Graf. 'One of our engineers, Tom Truscott, when asked if he'd be interested in calling bingo said no. He tried it once, though, and he's been calling bingo ever since. We're giving staff the opportunity to try different things.' Most crew get into the swing of it. Crew members, officers and even head office executives who just happened to be on board take turns at entertaining passengers with wildlife spotting tips, historical anecdotes, and lame jokes over the open mike style PA system. Marie Graf, for example, reads out passages from local history books whenever she's on board.

Captains, too, have got into the freewheeling spirit of things. They'll stop the ship to let kayakers slip off into the water, or take detours round islands to show off a favourite beach. Some have even been known to change course to follow a pod of killer whales.

'Captains are given a level of flexibility because we are trying to enhance customers' experience,' says Graf.

A lot of things about the route – including the fun and humour, the crew who seem to genuinely enjoy hard work and customer interaction, the *esprit de corps*, and the way both staff and passengers make a virtue of necessity by so relishing their cheap and cheerful surroundings – are reminiscent of Southwest Airlines.

Intriguingly, though, Graf, a leading member of the team that helped create this ambiance, had never heard of Southwest. The BC Ferries team came up with this style out of circumstances, necessity and imagination, without looking to see how it was done elsewhere. They copied nothing and imitated no one.

Another ground breaker in the experience economy is IKEA – one of the first retailers to make shopping at its stores more of an experience than a chore. When founder Ingvar Kamprad started IKEA in Sweden's rural Small Land, it was not easy to encourage people to visit stores that might take them several hours to reach. The solution was simple. Make a trip to an IKEA store more of a trip – make it a day out, with a restaurant and play areas for children. The concept started with the first store in Almhult, where IKEA installed a crêche and other kids' facilities. Today, especially at weekends, you will often find the children being amused by clowns or other entertainers. The restaurants, too, with prices kept low enough to ensure that customers with young families can afford to eat there and not have to bring sandwiches, also make the trip more of an event than a chore. Frequent shoppers can also get cheaper petrol thanks to a deal IKEA has struck with local suppliers.

British hi-fi retailer Richer Sounds takes a similar tack, with free hot drinks, lollipops, umbrellas, and car windscreen stickers pleading for mercy from traffic wardens. A 'no doors on shops' policy means easy access for all.

IKEA's and Richer's products add to their draw, of course, but even commodity retailers can benefit from a little entertaining. Record chain Sanity, for example, has grown to be Australia's largest music retailer by providing the kind of shopping environment its young customers want. They want it so bad, they'll pay full price at Sanity for a CD they could get for 20 per cent less elsewhere. When the Titanic Soundtrack was the top selling CD in Australia, a lot of chains sold it for under AU$25; Sanity retailed it at AU$29.95. Sanity sold more copies than anyone else in the country.

Brett Blundy, the founder of Sanity and managing director of its parent company, Brazin, told *Australia's Business Review Weekly*: 'There is nothing magical about what we do. We've grown by providing good customer service, ensuring we always have the products our customers want, and offering the right store environment.'

Brazin is too modest. In reality there is a certain amount of magic involved: Sanity, 'has created an environment that its customers like,' says Sudeep Gohil, a director of the youth marketing consultancy, Vertigo Communications Group. 'It has also positioned itself, through the look of its stores, the staff it employs and the products it stocks, as an authority.'

Sanity, according to Denis Handlin, chairman and chief executive officer of Sony Music Entertainment Australia, is a 'consumer magnet'. 'It has developed a great culture and kids see it as an exciting, hip destination. It has good staff, and a thematic, consistent approach to marketing.'

At *Amy's Scoop Shops*, a seven-store chain in Austin and Houston, Texas, there's a lot more than ice cream on offer. Here, scoopers really perform – juggling with their serving spoons and tossing scoops of ice cream to one another behind the counter. They give freebies to any customer willing to perform right back, with a song, a dance or a little poem. They have cone-eating contests, dress-up days, theme nights, and a lot of leeway in running their stores.

One night shift team, to deal with the problem of customers arriving at closing time, applied tough love. Wednesday nights were lock in nights – any customer still in the store after closing time was not permitted to leave until they'd learned to do the Time Warp dance – demonstrated by staff from the freezer tops. This didn't reduce the numbers arriving at closing time – in fact word got round and numbers boomed – but it did boost sales and add to Amy's reputation for fun.

It makes sense to be silly in an ice cream parlour. People like that sort of thing. What they don't want is silliness in important places, like, say, financial institutions.

Except in Palo Alto. The most popular bank in that California town had an alien space ship crashing through the wall and a stage with a vintage vaudeville curtain behind the tellers. Until a corporate buyout in 1996, the bank offered free shoe shines and decorated its courier trucks with images of bank executives cheating at poker and forging cash.

Carl Schmitt, a former state banking inspector, had seen enough boring banks in his career. He wanted to create a fun bank. He called his one-branch community bank the University National Bank and Trust, mostly so he could use the UNBT initials to promote his idea of an UN-Bank. Customers loved it. Even though UNBT couldn't offer the full services and multi-branch banking of the big banks, it could offer personalised service, irreverence and fun.

That's what the British king of irreverence, Richard Branson, was counting on when he entered the UK financial services market. It was hard to imagine anything more incongruous than the one-time hippy entrepreneur talking about pensions and investment plans. Yet, once it became clear that Branson and his team were serious, nothing seemed more natural – Virgin, with its impeccable street cred, offering young people an alternative to the stuffy bankers and insurance companies and providing a no-nonsense approach to financial services. Pensions could now, thanks to Branson, be sexy and fun.

And it's not just consumers who like the experience concept. Even business buyers like to be entertained.

Trade shows have always been places for business to business marketers to show their theatrical side, and displays are becoming increasingly radical and interactive. Or, in some cases tasteless. Few of those present will forget the conference where Sun Microsystems CEO Scott McNealy tried to get his dog, Network, to raise a leg over cardboard fire hydrants emblazoned with competitors' names.

Increasingly, though, led by companies like the Geek Squad, even business to business suppliers are injecting fun into humdrum daily transactions. And why not? Everyone wants a positive experience when they purchase a service, no matter how practical. 'When someone shows up at your house or office, besides not smelling bad, you want them to be nice. You want a nice experience,' says Geek Squad chief inspector Robert Stephens.

'We're not that different from Disney, because we're delivering an experience,' he says. 'The difference between us and Disney is that they construct the experience first; the reason we're doing this is to make our jobs more interesting – it's our chance to be rock stars.'

Having someone pull up in a 1950s roadster dressed like the Man from Uncle and flash a special agent badge has got to take some of the edge off a hard disk crash. It's not quite Disneyland, but it's as close as you can get in the midst of an office crisis. But, stresses Stephens, at the end of the day, it's not the entertainment that customers pay for, and it's not the entertainment that's behind the squad's revenues doubling, and even tripling, every year since their launch in 1993: 'I don't think we'd get away with driving old vehicles and carrying police badges, if we weren't as good as we are. We're the best, we're good at what we do. It's not just fluff. They're not paying for a Broadway show, they're paying to get their computer problems solved.'

Other master problem solvers, equally talented at creating hip experiences for clients, are the growing bands of creativity and new product consultants. Doug Hall of Richard Saunders International, for example, keeps people shut away in his mansion surrounded by toys and music while he coaches them through generating ideas.

?What If!, a North London consultancy that helps its clients solve marketing problems and dream up new products, finds it helpful to immerse clients in the consumers' experience. On one occasion, for example, a client that made snack products aimed at lower income people couldn't understand why their products weren't selling. The project team at ?What If! gave each board member 80p and sent them out to buy lunch. 'They were horrified at how little they could get for that much,' says ?What If! consultant Kristina Hunt. 'But that's how much your typical customer has to spend,' we said. 'You've got to cater for their budgets.'

Another technique is called 'the street'. The company has a special arrangement with people living in certain streets in London. 'We take clients there and say "knock on any door in this street, and the people who live here will let you into their homes",' explains Hunt. '"You can see how they use your products and hear what they think of them." It's very powerful because they see with their own eyes.'

Wacky companies are good at theatre and good at creating interesting, involving customer experiences, but they also recognise that the customer experience is most powerful when it is a reflection of the *employee* experience. Staff in theme parks take off their silly costumes when they are not on show; people in wacky companies put them on. Genuine wackiness relates not to how you behave when you are on show, but how you behave behind the scenes.

How to create a culture of fun

How can companies encourage fun at work?

According to humour researcher John Sosik, 'they need to create a culture that supports it, and that starts with leader setting an example. Study companies like Ben & Jerry's, Southwest Airlines and Sun Microsystems where people aren't afraid to make mistakes, where they're not afraid to be innovative, where people don't perceive the workplace as a place where they hang up their brains when they walk in the door. There's a new style of leadership that's empowering people, that's fostering a culture where you're not afraid to have fun and enjoy what you're doing.'

Set a fun example

The most effective fun is usually led from the top. Only when leaders are big enough to make fools of themselves (intentionally, that is) will subordinates feel comfortable with off-beat behaviour. Our wackiest leaders are those willing to make themselves objects of fun to serve a purpose.

Some, like Southwest's Libby Sartain, say their bosses have no ego. It's more likely that their egos are big enough to do such things as dressing in costumes to entertain their employees or generate publicity for their companies.

Drag seems to be a common costume of choice. Ben & Jerry's erstwhile CEO Chuck Lacey is probably best remembered for pouring his six foot eight inch bulk into a brief tutu for a staff party. The bearded Richard Branson wore a tasteful satin wedding gown and veil to promote the launch of yet another new enterprise – Virgin Bride, a wedding planning venture. He told reporters at the time that the inspiration came from a business plan proposed by one of his flight attendants; others suspect he just couldn't resist the pun.

At one of Rosenbluth's Live the Spirit weekends (a culture boosting company-wide get-together held every other year), CEO Hal Rosenbluth entered the arena dancing down the middle aisle dressed in a salmon costume (salmon is the company mascot and symbol – it means bucking the tide) while playing a saxophone with the song 'He's a Rebel' blaring through loudspeakers. When he hopped on stage, whipped off his salmon head and asked, 'is this any way to run a travel company?', 2,600 associates and clients roared back, 'Yes!' The other executives finished the weekend by dressing as rock stars and lip-synching to hit tunes.

There is, though, a fine line to be walked when managing with humour. According to Sosik, managers who use humour also tend to use a style called transformational leadership. This is the open, consultative style preferred by wacky managers, as opposed to the traditional command and control style. Transformational leaders seek to raise performance by being supportive, building teams and putting the interests of the group ahead of their own.

Sosik and his colleagues found that a transformational style, combined with humour, had a positive effect on overall unit performance. Surprisingly, though, the more humour such a leader used, the lower their staff rated them as individual managers. Explains Sosik: 'When a leader uses a transformational leadership style and mixes it with humour, that raises overall unit performance. But the manager is doing it at his or her expense.' He or she is seen as less effective.

Sosik's research team didn't look at the type of humour used, but did observe that transformational leaders sometimes use self-deprecatory humour. 'Ronald Reagan used humour effectively,' says Sosik. 'He always used jokes that were pointed at himself; he used a folksy, homey kind of humour that brought himself down to people's level. It's a good way of raising trust and making a person seem more approachable. Others will feel they have something in common with the leader. They can see they were in their shoes in the past and because of perseverance got where they are today. People want to emulate them and that's how you get extra effort out of followers. If you don't have trust, you're not going to get any performance out of followers.'

Sosik notes that humour can also have some negative effects on individual performance. For example, followers may see the use of humour around setting goals and target objectives as inconsistent with the seriousness surrounding the goal-setting process.

Humour may also be seen as distracting the leader away from attending to employees' individual needs. 'Some people might perceive it as a waste of time,' Sosik says. 'Some might be bored by humour, or it may be the wrong type of humour – what may be funny in one culture may not be funny in another culture.'

Can humour interfere with productive work? 'There's a time and a place,' says Sosik. 'We're not suggesting that managers try to be [a comedian like] Jay Leno or Jerry Seinfield. When used strategically, when [for example] there's a stalemate or people are taking themselves too seriously, it can be effective. We need to understand more when it's appropriate. Really good leaders are good at knowing when it's effective. Even Herb Kelleher said he doesn't use it all the time.'

'It's probably not appropriate when you're new. It's better when there's a base level of trust and prior history when [employees] know where you're coming from. It's not the best way to enter a new relationship.'

And, of course, there's always a need for sensitivity in humour. So the story goes, one manager, at a goodbye lunch for a downsized employee, said, 'This is fun, we really ought to do it more often.'

Hire fun people

At Amy's Scoop Shops, the application form is a plain white paper bag. The tradition arose when a store manager ran out of application forms, but the idea stuck. Now applicants are challenged to demonstrate their creativity and sense of humour by doing what they can with the bag. Some have attached balloons, plastered the bag with images of their accomplishments, or drawn cartoons and board games. One made a pop up Jack in the Bag, another inscribed hers with the 'Amysburg Address'. Says CEO Amy Miller: 'An applicant who produces 'something unusual from a white paper bag tends to be an amusing person who would fit in with our environment'.[32]

At Southwest Airlines, humour is a job requirement, and the company seeks out this attribute in recruits with job ads promising 'pants optional workplaces', and asking for applicants who 'colour outside the lines'. Says CEO Herb Kelleher: 'We look for attitudes; people with a sense of humour who don't take themselves too seriously. We'll train you on whatever it is you have to do, but the one thing Southwest cannot change in people is inherent attitudes.'[33]

Southwest's rigorous selection process, explains vice president, people, Libby Sartain, starts with a group interview for 25 to 30 applicants. 'You can tell from there who has a sense of humour, simply from how they interact and who laughs at others' jokes,' she says. 'We then invite people we think will fit in for interviews with three people for an hour each, and ask behavioural based questions, like: "Tell me a situation where you turned an unhappy customer into a happy one." We might ask, "When have you used your sense of humour to alleviate a difficult situation?", but we rarely have to do that. We can usually tell by then who has a sense of humour.'

People go to a lot of trouble to prove that they're silly enough for Southwest. Would-be employees have sent in applications filled out in crayon, delivered in cereal boxes, mounted on top of pizzas, packaged with confetti and noisemakers, and even done up as labels on bottles of Wild Turkey (Kelleher's favourite whisky).

Libby Sartain remembers her wackiest applicant: 'There was a young man in a suit in a lawn chair in front of the building with a sign that read: "Will work for peanuts". We had him in for interviews and offered him a job, but it turns out he wanted, oh, chocolate covered macadamia nuts or something.' (He chose another employer offering a higher starting salary.)

US unemployment has been very low for several years, and many industries, including airlines, are finding it hard to get staff. 'We're not lowering our standards, but we're having to work harder to find the best people. We won't compromise, but we will leave positions vacant if necessary,' says Sartain. 'It's kind of like a religion to us, having the right people.'

Make fun a priority – put someone in charge and give it a budget

Wacky companies don't necessarily spend a lot of money on their fun, but they do make it a priority and earmark money for it. They are also less likely than conventional companies to cut the entertainment budget when times get tight.

Julian Richer of Richer Sounds, for example, treats employees to holidays no more lavish than youth hostelling trips, and has generated one of the UK's most successful suggestion schemes by providing a drinks allowance and encouraging staff to discuss work at the pub after hours.

Sprint Paranet, a network services company in Houston, Texas, even has a full-time director of fun on the payroll. Director of fun Mona Cabler, has a cute title but a tough job, boosting team spirit and morale in a company where most staff work off-site with clients. 'Fun and work are mutually reinforcing,' she says. 'When companies say they're employee-centred, they usually mean centred on helping employees achieve the company's goals. We emphasise helping individuals achieve their personal goals. My role helps combat the corporate mind-set that says you don't mix work with pleasure. Besides, we hire non-stop, and having a director of fun is a great recruiting tool.'[34]

At Ben & Jerry's, 'If it's not fun, why do it', has been part of the company credo from the beginning. In reality, though, making ice cream is a lot less fun than eating it. As Lager puts it, the factory work can be 'mentally and physically gruelling. What you'd expect in a small business grappling with the implications of explosive growth.' In 1988, at the peak of the company's growth, one manager described the factory as a 'sweatshop in a pastoral setting.'[35]

That was about the time that Jerry Greenfield walked into a heated meeting about short production capacity and announced that the real problem at the plant was a troubling shortage of joy, and that he'd be launching a joy committee to deal with it.

Peter Lind, Ben & Jerry's head of research and development and Grand Poobah of the joy committee explained to *Psychology Today* that, before the official launch of the joy committee, 'Jerry Greenfield spread joy on an irregular yet constant basis.'[36]

The committee, now called the Joy Gang and made up of

volunteers from various departments, besides throwing parties, is empowered to hand out 'joy grants' of up to $500 to buy things, such as cocoa machines or stereos, to bring everyday joy to a particular department. They'll also throw surprise guerrilla-style joy events as needed, or come to work in drag if need be.

Rhino Foods, a Burlington, Vermont, dessert manufacturer, and a neighbour and supplier to Ben & Jerry's, also has a standing fun committee. According to *Personnel Journal*, an important part of the committee's role is to find fun ways to diffuse tension in the workplace. One year, after a particularly trying new product start up, the director of operations donned a complete ice hockey goalie kit and invited staff to toss leftover frozen cheesecake at him. 'We work pretty hard and have a lot of pressure to grow the company,' says Marlene Dailey, director of HR. 'Increasing sales and product requires a ton of teamwork. So the fun committee does little things that make a big difference.'

Rhino employee Stephen Mayo agrees. 'I can be honest, I'm not wild about working,' he says. 'But working at Rhino, I can get out of bed, and I don't have the work knots. I look forward to being here the time I need to be here. It's unlike any company I've ever worked for. And Ted [Castle] knows I'll be here until I retire. As long as the company needs what I'm giving it and it's giving me what I need, I'll be here without a doubt.'[37]

Remember that fun is a necessary, but not a sufficient, condition for job satisfaction

Dress-up days in the salt mine are not going to boost morale in the long term. Fun can only have a positive effect on performance if it is part of a balanced diet of respect, trust and decent working conditions.

According to David Abramis, a humour researcher at California State University, 'We found [in a study of clerical workers] that, while fun and satisfaction are positively related, and both contribute to productivity, they are clearly different. Statistics aside, many comments confirmed this, such as, "My job is satisfying . . . but I wouldn't say it's any fun."'

Abramis concludes that it's possible for someone to be satisfied with a job but not have much fun, or have fun without being satisfied. 'The difference may be that fun is emotional and immediate – a matter of excitement, play and humour. Job satisfaction seems more thoughtful and long term, related to matters like security, pay and working conditions.'

THE BOTTOM LINE

▶ People are a lot more likely to commit to your business if they expect to have fun – and that applies to both customers and employees.

▶ Fun starts at the top – boring leaders create boring environments.

▶ Craziness makes more and better headlines than sanity. Why pay for promotions and advertising when you can get it for free?

▶ Fun works better when you work at it. The more effort people put into having fun, the more they and the company get out of it.

NOTES

1. Des Dearlove, 'Business the Richard Branson Way' (Capstone, 1998).
2. Robert Levering and Milton Moskowitz, The 100 Best Companies to Work for in America (Doubleday, New York, 1993).
3. Bruce Avolio, Jane Howell and John Sosik, 'Examining How Using Humor Moderates the Impact of Leadership Style on Performance' (unpublished).
4. David J. Abramis, 'All Work and No Play Isn't Even Good for Work', in Psychology Today, March 1989.
5. Bruce Avolio, Jane Howell and John Sosik, 'Examining How Using Humor'.
6. Dave Ivey, 'Study Says Humor in the Workplace can Boost the Bottom Line', Detroit News/ Associated Press, 2 September 1996.
7. David J. Abramis, 'All Work and No Play', 1989.
8. KPMG and the Canadian Advanced Technology Association Alliance.

9. Catherine Porter, 'For a Real Good Time, Join a High Tech Firm', in *Vancouver Sun*, 1 August 1998.
10. Catherine Porter, 'For a Real Good Time', 1998.
11. Anne Fisher. 'The 100 Best Companies to Work for in America', in *Fortune*, 12 January 1998.
12. John Grossmann, 'Jump Start Your Business', in *Inc.*, May 1997.
13. David J. Abramis, 'All Work and No Play', 1989.
14. J. Fierman, 'Winning Ideas From Maverick Managers', in *Fortune*, 6 February 1995.
15. Robert Levering and Milton Moskowitz, *The 100 Best Companies*, 1993.
16. Robert Levering and Milton Moskowitz, *The 100 Best Companies*, 1993.
17. Matt Weinstein, *Managing to Have Fun* (Simon & Shuster, New York, 1996).
18. Scott Kirsner, 'Want to Grow? Hire a Shrink!', in *Fast Company*, December 1997/January 1998.
19. Shari Caudron, 'Be Cool! Cultivating a Cool Culture Gives HR a Staffing Boost', in *Workforce*, April 1998, pp. 50–61.
20. Jennifer J. Laabs, 'Ben & Jerry's Caring Capitalism', in *Personnel Journal*, November 1992.
21. Gillian Flynn, 'Why Rhino Won't Wait 'Til Tomorrow', in *Personnel Journal*, July 1996.
22. *Virgin Corporate Entertainment* magazine.
23. Gina Imperato, 'Dirty Business, Bright Ideas', in *Fast Company*, February/March 1997.
24. Michael Marlow, 'Joe Boxer has Plans from Jeans to TV Screens', in *DNR*, 14 April 1997.
25. *The Man who Has Won it All – Except the Lottery* (Review of Branson autobiography) in *Daily Telegraph*, 24 August 1998.
26. Fred Lager, *Ben & Jerry's: The Inside Scoop – How Two Real Guys Built a Business with a Social Conscience and a Sense of Humor* (Crown Publishers, New York, 1994).
27. J. Hyatt, 'My Favorite Company', in *inc.*, April 1989.
28. B. Joseph Pine II and James H. Gilmore, 'Welcome to the Experience Economy', in *Harvard Business Review*, July–August 1998.
29. Joe Boxer Web site (www.Joeboxer.com)
30. E. Trinidad, 'Make 'em Laugh', in *HB Body Fashions*, January 1997.
31. Marianne Detwiler, 'Wearing his Success on his Shorts', in *Entrepreneurial Edge*, Vol. 1, 1997.
32. John Case, 'Corporate Culture', in *Inc.*, November 1996.
33. Kevin Freiberg and Jackie Freiberg, *Nuts!*, 1998.
34. Lisa Chadderdon, 'Job Titles of the Future – Director of Fun', in *Fast Company*, December 1997/January 1998.
35. Fred Lager, *Ben & Jerry's*, 1994.
36. David J. Abramis, 'All Work and No Play', 1989.
37. Gillian Flynn, 'Why Rhino Won't Wait 'Til Tomorrow', in *Personnel Journal*, July 1996.

5 The hard underside

> 'This is not a love fest. It's a business. Nobody loves me but my wife.' (Former VeriFone CEO, Hatim Tyabji)
>
> 'We're not different than other companies – we have to make money.' (W. L. Gore associate, Jim Buckley)
>
> 'At the end of the day, are we still trying to sell more stuff? The answer is yes.' (St. Luke's co-founder, David Abraham)
>
> 'If we were all madcaps and merry clowns, this company wouldn't last a day. High morale comes as a result of knowing what you're in business to do.' (Odetics CEO, Joel Slutzky)[1]

Just because these companies are wacky doesn't mean they don't subscribe to business disciplines. In fact, discipline is one of their most common characteristics.

Wacky companies, as we've established in earlier chapters, often have a great sense of fun, high flexibility and little in the way of formal structure. They do, however, have a strong overriding culture and philosophy providing framework and guidance.

The results? Managers of wacky companies don't have to keep telling, motivating – or coercing – people to do things, and are free to concentrate on the disciplines that matter.

Looking past the fun and games and unorthodox structures of these companies, what we saw again and again were managers and employees who knew which details mattered and went to great lengths to get them right. They ignored the details that didn't matter.

Southwest Airlines, for example, despite its outward appearance of wacko silliness, runs a very tight ship. Cost and time controls, including its teams' ability to turn planes around in under 20 minutes, are at the very heart of its success – it's this tight discipline that enables the airline to make a profit at rock bottom fares.

And inside the wackiest leader, behind the craziest polka dot ties, the ballerina costumes, the outrageous stunts and the deceptively relaxed manner, beats the heart of a cost accountant. Joe Boxer's

Nicholas Graham, for example, observed one interviewer, 'would like to be perceived as a leader, who flies by the seat of his pants. In reality, his mission is cool and calculated. He knows his industry, his competition, his customers and his strategic partners. Most of all, he knows how to plan and execute a marketing campaign that captures the attention of potential customers and etches in their minds – and wallets – the brand name, Joe Boxer.'[2]

In other words, he's a lot smarter than he looks in his fire engine red suit and polka dot tie. And he can say 'bottom line' without sniggering. Graham sounded very businesslike when he told *Entrepreneurial Edge*: 'I am very aware of the fact that our retailers are our investors. We have to make them money and the bottom line is a return on investment in our product. We have to give that to them. So, I manipulate what the market wants, or what I like, and try to work it out.'

Richard Branson is known as an exceptionally tough negotiator – even to the point of creating bitter enemies out of people who have lost out in negotiations with him. (He is also a master at turning such situations to publicity advantage – his reconciliation with Tubular Bells creator Mike Oldfield and 'private' apology drew thousands of pages of press coverage.)

Ahmet Ertegun, the founder of Atlantic Records, nicknamed Branson 'the baby-faced killer' because of his tenacious negotiating skills. Branson's biographer Mick Brown recalls that even arch-rival British Airways chairman Lord King admits he made the mistake of underestimating Branson because of his pullover and grin.[3]

Grocery store chain Whole Foods has a soft and cozy, Birkenstock and granola image. Its business though, is decidedly hard-nosed. 'There's this notion that you can't be touchy-feely and serious,' says co-founder and CEO John Mackey. 'We don't fit the stereotypes. There's plenty of managerial edge in this company – the culture creates it.'[4]

Competitors and observers tend to underestimate the eco-centric Patagonia for the same reason. Says CEO Kris McDivitt: 'Because we have chosen to run this company differently, people are suspect of its capacity for success.' Yet, she stresses, 'Patagonia has made a profit every year for 20 years including 1991 [the year it made mass redundancies]. This is a record that no other company in its industry can match.'[5]

And, in Finland, happy go lucky SOL is, in reality, firmly rooted in the disciplines of total quality management. Joseph Juran, the American management expert and one of the founding fathers of the quality movement, was so impressed that he invited CEO Liisa Joronen to sit on a panel of experts to discuss the future of business. Joronen is a respected business leader in Helsinki and is regularly asked to join the boards of other Finnish companies.

What do they control and how?

Costs

Employees of wacky companies may have fun at work, but they don't spend a lot of money doing it. Southwest Airline's employees, for example, will go to great lengths to control costs in their areas. Their pilots have a reputation among air traffic controllers, as 'requesters' because they often ask for landing patterns that will save them a few minutes of flying time.

Setting up its headquarters, SOL used an industrial building, rather than a normal office building and purchased residential instead of office furniture. This cut the costs of setting up the office by two-thirds.

Ben Cohen and Jerry Greenfield, the two cheapskates who initially bought one five-dollar ice cream making course between them, never forgot their penny-pinching roots. Former CEO Fred Lager took great pride in cutting waste: banning Post It note purchases, keeping pens and pencils under lock and key, and handing out Fred Awards for innovations in cheapness.

These actions in themselves probably had little effect on the bottom line, he concedes, but they did 'encourage a cost-cutting mentality that kept everyone focused on the impact our individual and collective actions had on the bottom line. And, since employees split up five per cent of the pre-tax profits each year, they had a personal incentive to approach their jobs with an owner's perspective.'[6]

Cost consciousness has to be led from the top – it couldn't possibly work otherwise. CEOs of wacky companies are always the head cheapskates, setting examples by living and working frugally themselves. Their actions may make little difference in the ultimate bottom line, but that's not the point, by flying coach and living modestly, these leaders let employees know that they're not being asked to make any more sacrifices than their leader. If they look like eccentrics in the process, so much the better.

Ingvar Kamprad, Swedish founder of the 5.8 billion pound home-furnishing empire IKEA, is a notorious kroner-pincher. On business trips he takes public transport, flies economy and shares hotel rooms with his sons to save money. At the office, he wears work shirts, writes memos on paper napkins, and carries his documents in a plastic bag.

No one at IKEA is allowed to fly first class; Anders Moberg, Kamprad's second in command, also flies economy and won't take taxis when public transport is available. As IKEA Sweden executive Sven Kulldorf said in an interview: 'I was in Asia last week and then Sunday evening I flew to Singapore and on Monday morning there was a board meeting. One could say that, from a very theoretical point of view, it would have been better for me to fly business class, but we don't do that. Everybody flies economy.'

VeriFoners, too, always travel coach class. The edict applies to everyone, unless they use their own frequent flyer miles to upgrade, even the CEO. Says Tyabji: 'When someone says "You want me to go to South Africa on the back of the bus?" When they see that I do the same thing, that's moral authority. [With that] people will follow you to the ends of the earth.'

According to the 100 Best Companies to Work for in America, Wal-Mart executives, who are expected to travel a great deal in their jobs, often sleep two in a room at Holiday Inns, and, says founder Sam Walton, 'eat at family restaurants when we have time to eat'.

Walton, in his autobiography, muses: 'I wonder if a lot of . . . companies wouldn't do just as well if their executives lived a little more like real folks. Many people think it's crazy of me to fly coach whenever I go on a commercial flight, and maybe I do overdo it a little bit. But I feel like it's up to me as a leader to set an example. It's not fair for me to ride one way and ask everybody else to ride another way. The minute you do that, you start building resentment and your whole team idea begins to strain at the seams.'

And, contrary to the image of the successful entrepreneur, most of our wacky CEOs lead simple, unglamorous lives at home − further evidence that they're not motivated by money. Richard Branson may have treated himself to a private island in the Caribbean (now owned by the Virgin group), but generally avoids flash − he has little interest in luxury or high fashion and wears whatever clothes his wife, Joan, buys for him.

Acer's Stan Shih lives with his mom, his wife and three kids and buys clothes on discount. Liisa Joronen rides her yellow bicycle to work most days and, on a bluff overlooking the Pacific, Patagonia's Chouinard is building a house made from recycled materials. It has no storage space as he doesn't intend to own anything he doesn't absolutely need. The only flashy member of our cast is Softbank CEO Masayoshi Son, whose ostentatious guarded mansion would look more at home in Beverley Hills than low-key Tokyo.

These people may be cost conscious, but they're not cheap. According to Harvard Business School professor John P. Kotter, cheapness is for those with less imagination. 'Cheap is trying to get your prices down by nibbling costs off everything,' he says. 'If you're selling paper plates, you make them thinner. You hire people at minimum wage. Mindless stuff. But customers will eventually see the cheapness of it all. They'll notice that the paper plates don't work as well. They'll get tired of going into a grungy store with surly personnel, and they'll simply say to heck with it if they have an alternative. They'll shop at Wal-Mart.'[7]

Productivity

Smart operators, like the companies in our sample, keep their costs and prices down, not by being cheap, but by being productive − by getting the most from people, equipment and capital. Most have lean structures and do more with less, with minimal management and more hands at the sharp end. Their productivity measures almost always outrank those of their competitors.

This irritates the competition no end, when feisty little banks like UNBT − the one with the alien space ship crashing through its wall −

boasts average assets per employee that are 21 per cent higher than its competitors' and a profit margin that's 17 per cent fatter.

Or when IKEA sells goods priced 20 to 30 per cent below rivals', and still makes twice the margin. The secret? According to industry analysts, it's some kind of IKEA magic that turns over twice the industry average per square metre of shop space.[8]

Not even IKEA though, can beat the retailing productivity of UK hi-fi salesman Julian Richer. According to the *Guinness Book of Records*, Richer Sounds, between 1992 and 1998, produced the highest sales per square foot of any retailer in the world.

The real irritant, though, is Southwest Airlines. It's the only US airline to have shown a profit every year since 1973, and its net profit margins, averaging over five per cent since 1991, are the highest in the industry – despite offering fares low enough to compete with ground transport.[9]

Southwest consistently beats every productivity measure in the industry. It serves 2,400 customers per employee; its nearest competitor serves half that number. It takes 84 Southwest employees per aircraft to operate the business; others need from 111 to 160 employees per aircraft. Perhaps most famously, Southwest staff can turn around an airplane (meaning land, unload, clean, cater, refuel, and reload it) in less than 20 minutes.

How do they do it? With a million little efficiencies, with a hard working, motivated, cost-conscious staff, and efficient, streamlined systems. It's very simple, but it's not easy.

Libby Sartain, Southwest's vice president, people, explains how it works: 'We work harder than most people. We pay comparable salaries and benefits to other airlines, but we keep costs low by using our equipment more productively. Other airlines sit on the tarmac for 45 minutes to an hour. At Southwest, our pilots, rampers and flight attendants unload 137 people and their luggage, clean and cater the plane, load up another 137 people and take off again in under 20 minutes. The pilots and the flight attendants clean the plane. Our people don't get breaks.'

As a result, a typical Southwest plane is used 11.5 hours a day, versus 8.6 hours a day by other carriers. And because planes only make money when they fly, this translates into profitability.

And, while much of Southwest's enviable productivity is probably driven by the sheer will of its employees, systems, all designed to keep planes in the air, come into it as well.

Following the rules of simplexity (as described in Chapter 3, Dismantling the Organisation) Southwest reaps myriad savings in time and money by flying only one type of airplane (the Boeing 737). Besides getting bulk deals from Boeing, this streamlines training, crew scheduling and turnaround procedures.

Other efficiencies include:

- Avoiding congested airports. Where there's a quicker and more convenient, if less glamorous, airport, Southwest will use it.
- Flying short haul, point to point, rather than using hub and spoke system. This way, Southwest manages about twice as many flights per day per gate as the industry average.
- Not linking with other airlines. Southwest staff don't work as hard as they do just to sit on the ground waiting for other airlines' delayed flights.

Hard, productive work is the unglamorous secret behind Southwest's success. It applies to many other wacky companies as well.

The approximately 350 Patagoniacs working in Ventura, California, wear shorts and T-shirts, run or bike to work, enjoy on-site childcare, home-cooked vegetarian meals, generous salaries and benefits, access to the latest equipment for their favourite sports, and an employee education budget that equals that of research or promotion. Staff turnover is only about 10 per cent.

Says Patagonia's Setnicka: 'Journalists come in here and see people sitting around wearing flip flops, with their feet on their desks and surfboards leaning up against the wall. It may appear casual, but in actuality people are working very hard. We expect so much of ourselves we sometimes get our own work/life balance out of whack.'

Expectations run high at VeriFone, too, says former CEO Hatim Tyabji. 'We are very clear about the quid pro quo of life at VeriFone. The quid pro quo, in return for all the freedom we offer, is a tremendous emphasis on accountability. We expect you to perform and we expect you to deliver the goods. I don't care if you don't come to the office or if you take long lunch breaks. We don't have any system for lunch breaks. It's bullshit. You perform, you can do anything you want. You don't perform, you're out.'[10]

At W. L. Gore, the workplace is co-operative with no bosses and no fixed authority. This does not mean it's soft though – just the opposite. 'It's not a place that people can hide. If you're not pulling your weight, people will know it. If people aren't contributing, people know about it,' says Gore associate Jim Buckley, a manufacturing leader in Gore's fabrics division.

Debts

A distinctive feature of many long-lived wacky companies is a conservative balance sheet. Most have been able to finance their expansion from their own pockets. This limits their risk and – this is important for wacky entrepreneurs – means they don't have to answer to bankers.

Southwest, for example, keeps a very conservative balance sheet and, as a result, isn't as weakened by debt as some other airlines. According to Gary Kelly, Southwest's vice president and chief financial officer: 'Our target is to do at least 50 per cent of our capital spending with internally generated funds.'[11] Standard and Poor's gives Southwest an A– credit rating, the highest in the US airline industry.

Nicholas Graham of Joe Boxer says he has never borrowed money to expand his company, and IKEA's stores generate so much cash (about $43 million a year in revenues and $3 million a year in cash) that the chain is able to finance expansion from its own earnings.

Richard Branson, too, has learned to expand his empire without trips to the bank. Most of his companies are held in partnership. As he told Forbes magazine, the powerful Virgin brand name means that 'we're at the point that we can get 100 per cent of the funding we need for most ventures from external sources and yet keep complete control. We're back in the record business as of last November [1996] with a new label, V2; $100 million has been put up by investors in exchange for 30 per cent of the company, but we have complete control and no financial commitment at all.[12]

Product and service standards

Most of our wacky companies are indifferent to market research — they don't care much about people who aren't customers. They care very much, though, about people who are, and can be pernickety in the extreme about product and service standards.

At SOL, with its loose-knit company structure, accountability is essential to keep the organisation from unravelling. Performance measuring is the counter-weight by which CEO Liisa Joronen balances the autonomy she allows her staff with the high service standards she demands for her customers. Joronen measures frequently and often, and most measures focus on customer satisfaction. 'The more we free our people from rules,' she says, 'the more we need good measurements.'[13]

When the company wins a new contract, the salesperson and the new customer work together to establish performance benchmarks. The customer then uses these criteria to assess the performance of the cleaning team each month. Instead of numbers, though, assessments use happy faces: a laugh, a smile, a straight face, a frown or tears. The target for the company is at least 90 per cent smiles. Cleaners carry a 'quality passport' updated monthly and detailing their performance as determined by customer surveys. Joseph Juran, one of the founding fathers of the total quality movement, describes SOL as 'the future of quality'.

The company intranet is also used as a tool to hone customer performance. The sales database tracks SOL's existing customers and key accounts and provides critical information about them: which employee last contacted them, the reason for that contact, and promises made to the customer.

At Richer Sounds, customers fill out forms grading the service they received whenever they made a purchase. For every 'excellent' an employee is given he or she receives five pounds — even if the purchase amounted to less than that.

A mystery shopper also visits stores anonymously, compiling a detailed report on service standards that refers to individual employees by name. Nothing unusual in that, except that while normally this kind of measurement would be unpopular with staff, at Richer Sounds, a positive assessment by the mystery shopper can net the staffer in question a jackpot of £100.

At Dyson, product quality is jealously guarded. All final assembly is done by hand and every new employee – as the former trade minister Richard Needham discovered when he joined the company as a non-executive director – spends their first day assembling one of the companies vacuum cleaners. Familiarity with the product, Dyson believes, means that employees are more committed to the company, and to product quality.

Ben Cohen also expects ice cream testers to show some personal commitment. The Ben & Jerry's co-founder is famous for sending test batches back to the lab hundreds of times, and would rather retool the production equipment than compromise on chunk size. A man who suffers for his art, he insists that there is only one way to really understand ice cream: 'You've got to eat through the pint to experience how the chunks and swirls combine. I get very concerned when we have all these people in research and development who are really skinny.'[14]

Customers

If there's one group most business people would dearly love to control, it's their customers. Some wacky companies do. And why not? Since customers can have such an unpleasant effect on service standards, profitability and employee morale, it only makes sense to be selective about who you'll serve.

Carl Schmitt, founder of the University National Bank and Trust (UNBT), had to be picky about his customers. As a purposely small bank, he only had room for so many and, because UNBT committed to a high level of service for its customers, it didn't have time for fleeting relationships.

'We don't want one-stop customers,' said Schmitt. Every customer had to open a minimum-balance checking account, and went through a rigorous credit check before being offered a place on one of UNBT's customer training seminars. 'If we have your chequing account, then you're not as likely to go across the street for a higher certificate of deposit rate,' Schmitt says.[15]

Values-based UK advertising agency St. Luke's is prepared to lose business if it sees a client's behaviour or products as unethical. Similarly, if it feels unable to enter a constructive dialogue with a client it will pass up the opportunity to increase billings at the cost of ethical compromise. In the past, St. Luke's declined multi-million dollar business for tobacco advertising. More recently, it turned down an account with a bio-tech company because the client refused to discuss issues associated with genetic engineering.

Herb Kelleher at Southwest Airlines provides some of the best customer service in the airline industry, but he's adamant that the customer is not always right. 'I think that's one of the biggest betrayals of employees a boss can possibly commit. The customer is sometimes wrong. We don't carry those sorts of customers. We write to them and say "Fly somebody else. Don't abuse our people."'[16]

Patagonia's Yvon Chouinard would rather not sell to most of his customers, but, as a manufacturer of consumer goods, he has little choice in the matter. In a statement to the editors of The 100 Best Companies to Work for in America, he railed: 'I look at 250 million people in America, and I say 125 million of them are full of shit and they're doing everything wrong. They are leading this country down a suicide path and they are destroying the place. I don't want those people to buy my stuff; I don't want to sell anything to those people. I want to piss off 50 per cent of the people in America, and the other 50 per cent are going to be absolute rabid, loyal customers. That is enough for me. I really believe that if you're not making enemies, you're not trying hard enough.'

Chouinard, though, just doesn't seem able to offend people no matter how hard he tries. Shortly after Patagonia had (with Ben & Jerry's) taken out an ad opposing America's involvement in the 1991 Gulf War, George Bush showed up on the cover of People magazine wearing a Patagonia jacket.

Sohan Singh, proprietor of a small grocery in Burmantofts, a district of Leeds, has had enough of badly behaved customers. He's banned them all from his premises because, he says, they are rude and noisy. The shop's patrons must peer through the window to decide what they want before ringing a bell to be served through a small hatch in the door.

Singh says he was forced to take drastic action after fighting a losing battle against bad manners. First, he banned smoking, then the use of coarse language, then baby strollers, then pets, and finally, customers. 'People were abusing the system by smoking cigarettes or pushing prams,' Singh says. 'People would come in expecting supermarket prices, but we cannot afford that. Then they get abusive over a few extra pennies.' The threat of lost revenue has not deterred him. 'I have lost business,' he admits, 'but I cannot say how much. I am a man of principles, and I stand by my decision.'[17]

Who enforces discipline?

Wacky leaders set standards, mostly through example, but they let employees exert their own controls – on themselves, on their co-workers, and even on their superiors. These controls work, and tend to be consistent, because everyone is working to the same basic set of values.

Employees themselves

Most controls are self-enforcing, as employees generally agree with them and want to see the company succeed.

About a quarter of Semco staff set their own salaries, each with a self-set element of risk. Individuals agree to risk a smaller or larger proportion of their salary in return for a potential bonus if the company does well. In the good years they win; in the bad years they help keep costs down. There is also the added benefit that their salary does not stick out if the company is looking to reduce costs by shedding staff. This applies equally as a restraint to setting unduly high salaries.

At SOL, where no records are kept of hours worked, anything from 10 to 50 per cent of salary for cleaning staff varies according to how closely they meet various targets they've set themselves. If an employee misses the target for an area, he or she only loses that element of the total bonus available.

Co-workers

At Whole Foods, a US grocery chain structured along autonomous team lines, standards are maintained by competition among the teams. Each of the 43 autonomously run stores competes with the others on pre-set measures of quality, service and profitability. And it's not just friendly competition either – the results of the game affect every employee's bonuses and chances for promotion.

'Whole Foods is a social system,' CEO John Mackey told *Fast Company* magazine. 'It's not a hierarchy. We don't have lots of rules handed down from headquarters in Austin. We have lots of self-examination going on. Peer pressure substitutes for bureaucracy. Peer pressure enlists loyalty in ways that bureaucracy doesn't.'

Team members also approve all new hires. Managers may recommend someone, but no one is hired until they've completed a trial period and been approved by at least two-thirds of their team mates.

According to Mackey, rejecting new hires can be proof of a team's effectiveness. 'They're saying, "This person isn't good enough to be on our team." They're standing up to the leader, taking ownership of their team, saying, "Go back and try again."'

Store manager Ron Megahan says, 'I'm not the one you need to impress. It's your fellow team members. And they will be as tough as they can be, because ultimately [the hiring decision] will be a reflection on them.'[18]

At Gore, it's also your peers you need to impress – especially as it's your co-workers who set your pay. Gore associate Jim Buckley explains: 'We pay based on contributions. We have a leadership team for each function. They benchmark with other companies, and determine what fair market pay is for various jobs. They go to each team and ask each member to rank, anonymously, the input of other team members. The team chooses a few people as benchmarks and pays them the going rate; those above and below them in team rankings are paid proportionately more or less. The perceptions across the team are very consistent. People aren't dumb. They know who's pulling their weight.

'Our objective is to be externally competitive and internally fair. It's fair that people who contribute more, whether through talent, experience or hard work, earn more money. We ask for team members' perception of contribution, past present and potential,' says Buckley. 'The more senior people are usually perceived as higher contributors – we consider it a problem if they're not – though there are no automatic increases for seniority.'

Controlling the boss

AC Nielsen boss Nicholas Trivisonno knows that happy employees mean happy customers. Each year, his 20,000 employees fill out anonymous job satisfaction questionnaires. If the number claiming to be happy in their work falls short, then, according to The Times of London, the senior managers, including the chairman, see 25 per cent lopped off their annual bonus.

This is part of Neilsen's dramatic turnaround. Split off from Dun & Bradstreet in 1996, AC Neilsen is again an independent firm. Trivisonno is working hard to restore the morale, reputation, and profits that declined during the previous several years. So far, new technology and efforts to keep staff happy have helped double profits almost immediately. Shares gained 60 per cent in a year.[19]

Many of our wacky companies ask employees to appraise their bosses. Ben & Jerry's employees rate their superiors annually, and at Semco, subordinates complete a multiple choice assessment twice a year. The form, filled out anonymously, is used to determine the competence of the management. Any manager scoring less than 70 per cent will be under pressure to improve or find another position.

Employees at Semco are also involved in the hiring process, whether it's for a subordinate, colleague or supervisor. Anyone up for promotion, too, must first undergo a group interview conducted by their prospective subordinates.

Says Semler: 'We didn't believe Semco had to perpetuate a system in which a person is hired, who impresses his future boss but does not have the respect of his subordinates. Nor did we understand why we should keep a supervisor who wasn't well regarded by those who were supposed to follow him.'

External audits

Because they have higher ideals and higher standards for themselves, wacky companies tend to be more self-critical than others and will have their operations audited in ways that other companies would never dream of.

Patagonia has run tough environmental audits on its operations since 1991, and the Body Shop spends about $100,000 a year screening suppliers to enforce its animal-testing ban.[20]

Robotics company Odetics conducts an annual associates' survey. Every year they use a fresh set of questions, and CEO Joel Slutzky responds to each signed survey individually.

Whole Foods conducts an annual morale survey asking tough questions about employee attitudes toward the company. It also asks about fears and frustrations and about how closely staff believe the company is adhering to its values. The results, like almost everything at Whole Foods, are posted for all employees to see. The company describes the results of the morale survey in its annual report to shareholders, revealing such dirty laundry as various regions' dissatisfaction with the company's health insurance changes, worries about excessive inter-team competition, and even low confidence in their leadership.

Ben & Jerry's run a social audit to check how well its social mission is being met, and it's no PR exercise. The company has a history of being very hard on itself, as this self-effacing passage from the company's 1990 Annual Report demonstrates: 'Ben & Jerry's has yet to print nutritional information on packaging of its original super-premium ice cream; it has no paid parental leave policy; and it has only one minority in a senior management position. In the case of energy, due to inadequate record keeping the company is unable to report on energy conservation actions. Relations with franchises have improved; even so, the company's communications with franchisees about the social mission have been uneven.'

The company is also highly critical of itself as an employer. In 1994, Liz Bankowski, Ben & Jerry's director of social missions and a member of its board of directors, wrote to the authors of The 100 Best Companies to Work for in America, asking to have Ben & Jerry's removed from the listing. The book, she wrote, 'makes Ben & Jerry's sound like a fun place to work, makes it sound like we've all had just one jolly year. Well, it would be a total lie if I told you that this was a fun year for us. Business was good. But fun? No. We are not one of the most innovative companies when it comes to internal systems. We have too much to learn ourselves to be put in the position of getting calls from businesses throughout the country asking us how to create a great work environment. Ben and Jerry and I were absolutely clear about this: we did not feel that we deserved to be held up as an example of a great place to work.'

AES, the power plant company, conducts an annual values audit – surveying employees to determine how well they think the company is practising what it preaches. Employees are asked how well descriptors like 'friendly', 'arrogant', 'growing too fast', or 'taking on too much risk' describe the company. They are also asked whether they agree with such statements as: 'We work because the work is fun, fulfilling, and exciting and when it stops being that way we will change what or how we do things,' or 'We do not try to get the most out of a deal at the cost of being unfair to a customer, supplier, or related party.' The results are seen as a performance indicator and affect top executives' salaries and benefits.

According to Fast Company magazine, in 1992, workers at one US plant falsified emissions reports, saying they feared for their jobs otherwise. AES managers discovered this, reported it, and paid the $125,000 fine. Still, the co-founders took personal responsibility for the values breakdown, issued a public apology and reduced their own bonuses by 65 and 85 per cent respectively. Again, in 1996, after a number of plant accidents, AES executives reduced their own bonuses by nearly 10 per cent.

Says co-founder Dennis Bakke, 'mistakes are inevitable. But that doesn't mean we abandon our values. We're going to continue to strive to live by them, even though we're going to fail sometimes.'[21]

THE BOTTOM LINE

▶ Who needs controls or systems when everyone exerts self-discipline? Enforcement is everybody's business.

▶ It's better to discipline your customers than your employees.

▶ Never, never be beholden to a bank.

NOTES

1. Shari Caudron, 'Keeping Spirits up When Times are Down', in *Personnel Journal*, August 1996.
2. Marianne Detwiler, 'Wearing his Success on his Shorts', in *Entrepreneurial Edge*, Vol. 1, 1997.
3. Mick Brown, *Richard Branson, The Authorised Biography* (Headline, 1998).
4. Charles Fishman, 'Whole Foods is All Teams', in *Fast Company*, April/ May 1996.
5. Robert Levering and Milton Moskowitz, *The 100 Best Companies to Work for in America* (Doubleday, New York, 1993).
6. Fred Lager, *Ben & Jerry's: The Inside Scoop — How Two Real Guys Built a Business with a Social Conscience and a Sense of Humor* (Crown Publishers, New York, 1994).
7. Marc Ballon, 'The Cheapest CEO in America', in *Inc.*, October 1997.
8. IKEA's New Game Plan', in *Business Week*, 26 September 1997.
9. Kevin Freiberg and Jackie Freiberg, *Nuts! Southwest Airlines' Crazy Recipe for Business and Personal Success* (Orion Business, 1998).
10. J. Kutler, 'VeriFone's Unconventional Chief', in *American Banker*, 20 April 1995.
11. Kevin Freiberg and Jackie Freiberg, *Nuts!*, 1996.
12. David Sheff, 'Interview with Richard Branson', in *ASAP Forbes*, 24 February, 1997.
13. Gina Imperato, 'Dirty Business, Bright Ideas', in *Fast Company*, February/ March 1997.
14. Cole Morton, 'Cookie Dough Dynamos', in *Independent on Sunday*, 15 February 1998.
15. Elizabeth Conlin, 'Small Business: Second Thoughts on Growth', in *Inc.*, March 1991.
16. Tom Peters, 'Personal Glimpses,' in *Reader's Digest*, July 1995.
17. Stuart Miller, in *Guardian*, reprinted in *World Press Review*, April 1998.
18. Charles Fishman, 'Whole Foods is All Teams'.
19. Jon Ashworth, 'Research Boss Who Finds it Pays to Keep the Staff Happy', in *The Times*, 14 April 1998.
20. Anne Murphy, 'The Seven (Almost) Deadly Sins of High-Minded Entrepreneurs, in *Inc.*, July 1994.
21. Alex Markels, 'Power to the People,' in *Fast Company*, February/March 1998.

6 Wacky companies need wacky leaders

'Leadership is the art of having people do what you want them
to do and go in a direction that you set, willingly or unwillingly.
Willingly is leadership. Unwillingly is coercion.' (US Marine
Corps Commander, Major-General Michael Williams)[1]

'I like owning my own business. It gives me the freedom to dress
as a goofball.' (Joe Boxer CEO, Nicholas Graham)[2]

'Hubris? What's that? Get me a dictionary!' (Richard Branson)[3]

'I know I will have succeeded when I am no longer
needed.' (Former VeriFone CEO, Hatim Tyabji)[4]

If you've been served drinks by a stewardess wearing lipstick, high
heels and a beard on any other flight, you've probably been working
too hard. If you're on Virgin Airlines you've just met the boss.
Richard Branson has been known to dress up as a stewardess, as a
bunny rabbit, as Spiderman – anything to get the front-page photos
he relies on to keep the Virgin name front and centre.

Branson, who once bet a plane load of employees he would ski
down a Swiss mountain naked – then did it anyway when no one
took him up on the dare – can seem a little odd, but he's not the
oddest. Rosenbluth International's Hal Rosenbluth, for example, has
been known to dress as a fish (the company's unofficial mascot is a
salmon) and Southwest Airline's Herb Kelleher favours Easter Bunny
outfits. SOL's Liisa Joronen is a familiar sight riding around Helsinki
on her yellow bicycle, and Quad/Graphics' Harry Quadracci will
always be remembered for once arriving at his company Christmas
party riding an elephant.

WOW Toys founder Nadim Ednan-Laperouse, who admits to
Branson-like aspirations, has appeared in the business pages of The
Times posing, fully clothed, playing with his toys in the bath.

In 1993, Luciano Benetton, president of the Italian clothing
company of the same name, posed naked for a series of ads
promoting a Red Cross clothing drive. A strategically placed caption,

'I want my clothes back' helped bring in 460,000 kilos of donated clothes for various international charities – and generated reams of press for the company.

In a different league altogether is Vladimir Stehlik, CEO of Poldi Steel in the Czech Republic. Stehlik has been known to give interviews in his underwear and get workers' attention by firing a pistol on the factory floor. More recently, he's been running his company from prison, having been arrested for fraud.

The founders of wacky companies are typically wackier than any part of their business. They're unconventional, eccentric and, usually, oddly dressed. But that's just what's in front of the curtain. Their employees, rivals, customers, friends, critics, even their spouses, tell us that behind the wacko torn jeans and tutu costumes these people are driven, focused, and uncompromising. They are also, in most cases, highly energetic people with strict value systems who inspire fierce loyalty in their followers, largely because they would never ask anyone to do anything they're not willing to do themselves. They are also sensitive listeners, well attuned to how people working for them are applying the principles that make the organisation different.

Where did these people come from?

Most of our wacky leaders had minimal experience of big business, though their pre-entrepreneurial careers make for some interesting biographies: Joe Boxer's Nicholas Graham was a lead singer in a punk band, and Patagonia's Yvon Chouinard was a vagabond, rock climber and blacksmith. For many, their wacky business was the first and only job they've ever had.

Their education varies widely, as do their family backgrounds, experience in business, age and social class, but basically, our wacky leaders boil down to three broad types.

The outsiders

These people are misfits. Some brought their tough childhood values to the workplace; others were just too strange to land a regular job. Most are white, male, educated and middle class, and thus able to side-step any major barriers to the business world. Each was, however, an outsider, with no formal training, industry experience or connections. And being outsiders, whether or not it was apparent to others, meant they had more to prove. Their inexperience also meant they had nothing to unlearn and were thus free to try radical new ways of doing things. That's how Branson's empire got its name – a co-worker on his first venture, Student magazine, suggested 'Virgin' because, she said, 'We're complete virgins at business.'[5]

Ingvar Kamprad, the founder of IKEA, grew up on the wrong side of the fjord, in the bitter and harsh conditions of Small Land, Sweden, during the great depression. His experiences of hard work, Spartan values, thrift and frugality shaped a philosophy that now affects every aspect of the company he developed.

Masayoshi Son, president of Softbank Corporation, is known for breathing a breath of fresh entrepreneurial air into a Japanese high-tech industry dominated by big corporations. Some call him the Bill Gates of Japan. Son was an outsider as a student at Berkeley, but he was also an outsider at home in Japan – the son of Korean parents, he grew up poor on the Japanese island of Kyushu. A Korean name and background confers little advantage in ethnically homogeneous Japan.

Patagonia's Yvon Chouinard came from a French Canadian family in Maine and didn't learn English until he was seven years old. He has, possibly as a result, preferred solitary pursuits to this day.

Paul Hawken first went into business in 1966 with Erewhon, one of the first natural food companies in the US. Like so many successful entrepreneurs, Hawken set up a stall for himself because he thought he was unemployable. A high school vocational counsellor had convinced him that no one would hire him, not even the post office.[6]

Ben Cohen and Jerry Greenfield first met in 1964, as two chubby 13-year-olds in a grade nine gym class. 'We were both nerdy kind of guys,' says Greenfield. 'We were not cool, we were not popular. We were fat, smart kids.'[7] After a few draft-evading tries at college and, in Cohen's case, an impressive record of getting himself sacked and an aptitude test that revealed 'unresolved conflicts with authority', the two went into business together. Ben Cohen, like so many others in our sample, would have made a bad employee.

Joe Boxer's Nicholas Graham, who claims to have gone into the underwear business because he 'needed some underwear', has the kind of CV that would mark him as unemployable in the real world. Born in 1958, in Calgary, Canada, he was expelled from high school before spending five years in Europe (mostly in the UK). He picked up some graphic design training along the way before moving to San Francisco in the early eighties and landing a job as the lead singer of a high-energy punk band. He's also Canadian – a background he shares with many of America's leading comics. 'We have a perspective on America that's not as American as the Americans. We don't take it so seriously.'

Nadim Ednan-Laperouse, the 33-year-old founder of the enormously successful WOW Toys, told the UK's *Express* newspaper (23 March 1998) that teachers at Pimlico Comprehensive reckoned he was a bit of a dunce. 'They thought I was a bit of a daydreamer, not very academic and wouldn't go very far,' he says.

The rebels

Some of our leaders were born to run businesses – they just didn't do it the way their families expected them to. Ricardo Semler, Liisa Joronen and Hal Rosenbluth were all genetic blips in business dynasties – each went into their respective family businesses, but not with the family mind-set.

SOL founder Liisa Joronen was a member of the powerful Finnish industrialist family, the Lindstroms. She had sought to apply her ideas about management within the family conglomerate, but this met with resistance from her father. Eventually an arrangement was arrived at allowing Joronen to buy out the cleaning and waste management part of the business and operate it independently.

Joronen's rebelliousness started at an early age. 'At school I was sent out of the classroom,' she recalls. (Though she went on to study economics at Helsinki University.) 'I have always been a rebel,' she says. 'Not in a hard way, but against the mainstream.'

Later, as chief executive of her family's national laundry chain, she questioned everything. She asked why 'when workers come to work they have to shut off their brains', and why managers (and she knew many personally) seemed incapable of doing things for themselves at work, like making coffee, that they could manage perfectly well at home. Hiving off her own business allowed her to change everything. 'For me evolution isn't enough; I want constant revolution,' she says.

Ricardo Semler originally joined his family's business, Semco, as his father's intended successor. But it was not long before Semler junior realised that his laid-back non-authoritarian approach to life was bound to lead him into conflict with his father's traditional methods. Semler, at just 21, was far younger than most of the managers he fired when he took over the reins.

Sun Microsystems' Scott McNealy, the ivy league practical joker who became CEO when he was only 30 years old, didn't join a family business, but did have it in his blood. His father was a vice chairman of American Motors, and he attended Harvard and the Stanford Business School (though it took him three tries to be accepted at the latter) before taking his first job in a tank factory. In Silicon Valley, where most leaders, including Steve Jobs and Bill Gates, are college drop-outs, this background marks McNealy out as something of an odd-ball.

And he certainly is an odd-ball, having made a name for himself with his famous April Fools' Day pranks and mottoes like 'Kick butt, have fun'. McNealy has, says Sun engineer Jakob Nielsen, 'almost institutionalised the notion of corporate rebel, like somebody who can go off and do something really off on a tangent'.[8]

Richard Branson, the son of a barrister, also came from an upper middle-class background, but left school at 16 to run his magazine Student full time. His headmaster's parting words, as Branson recalls in his autobiography, were, 'Congratulations, Branson. I predict you will go to prison or become a millionaire.' He was right on both counts – the prison was a brief spell after a failed customs ruse.[9]

Poldi Steel's revolver-wielding CEO Vladimir Stehlik has also done prison time and is now running his business from a Czech jail following fraud charges. Then there's Ho Kwon Ping, head of the vast Ah Chang International Group and of Singapore Power, the country's newly privatised utility.

In 1977, while a reporter for the Far Eastern Economic Review in Singapore, Ho, who was also a student at the time and something of a left-leaning Ho Chi Minh fan, was arrested and detained for a month under the country's Internal Security Act for writing pro-Communist political articles. He'd already been suspended from Stanford University for challenging the faculty on racial and other issues.

Ho went on to take the reigns of his family business, the Ah Chang International Group, an Asia-wide corporation with interests in property, hotel development, argo-industry, construction, trading, and specialised engineering. Since taking over his family business interests, Ho has expanded it to a conglomerate with an estimated revenue, in 1994, of some US$222 million.

By 1995, Ho had come full circle. That year, the very government that had imprisoned him two decades before entrusted him with privatising Singapore's public utilities. As a businessman, he's been described as affable, far-sighted − he saw opportunities in Thai tourism long before his rivals did − and well connected. Despite his jail time, he's very much a part of the Singapore establishment. No longer a radical, Ho finds vent for his political beliefs through extensive civic and philanthropic work, working on a range of issues from protecting the environment to promoting the use of Mandarin.

He's also something of a practical joker, and pretension is a favourite target. In Ho's conference room, there's an easel supporting what looks like a Rembrandt original. It's actually a laser-crafted copy worth about $2,000. Ho had it made, he told *Asia Inc.*, in the heyday of Japanese art-buying to fool collectors who didn't know as much about art as they thought. 'We did this to show them up,' he chuckles. 'It actually worked a few times.'

Ho has always been a rebel in a society with little room for rebelliousness. He feels, despite the prison time, that bucking convention has its rewards − for the individual, and for the nation. As he explained in a 1994 address to the National University of Singapore: 'Creativity often rewards the non-conformist, the iconoclast, the generalist who treats life not as a linear fast track to success, but as a forest of rich discoveries that one can meander through, creating one's own trail. The nation's soul will be shaped by those who are less obviously successful but are willing to take risks: artistic, career or intellectual.'[10]

The visionaries

All of our wacky leaders are visionaries to some extent. One group, though, including leaders like Softbank's Son, VeriFone's Tyabji, Jay Chiat, Citytv's Znaimer and, from a different angle, Yvon Chouinard, stand out in this regard.

What drives these people, more than a chance to make money or create jobs for themselves, is the opportunity to be at the cutting edge of technological, and thus social, change. It is often said of these leaders – in retrospect – that they could see the future. That's because they took a hand in creating it.

'Bill Gore was ahead of his time. He could see into the future,' says Jim Buckley, an associate hired by Gore himself in 1974. 'Every company today is trying to become global. Bill's second and third plants were overseas. He was organising joint ventures in Japan when "Made in Japan" was synonymous with tacky. He had a strong personality and was very, very smart. And he was a very ethical person; his belief in people was very strong.'

Masayoshi Son, president and CEO of Softbank Corporation, was a college student in California in the seventies. Even then, he could see that personal computers would be the wave of the future: 'I was convinced that the trend that had just begun in the US would hit Japan shortly thereafter,' he said.[11]

While still an undergraduate, Son designed a pocket translator that went on to become the prototype for Sharp's Wizard pocket organisers. On his return to Japan, he founded Softbank. Now Japan's leading PC software distributor and its largest computer book and magazine publisher, it has 16 subsidiaries and sales in 1996 of US$1.5 billion. Son sees his company playing a central role in the next technological revolution. 'Our company mission is to become the infrastructure provider for the digital information industry.'[12]

VeriFone's Hatim Tyabji probably speaks for most of these leaders when he reveals that his overriding motivation is, 'an opportunity to see my own footprint in the sand, a chance to create a new industry and a new culture and a new way of doing things.'

The folk heroes

Creating new industries and new culture has on occasion promoted some leaders to a fourth category: the wacky leader as folk hero.

Stan Shih, founder and chairman of computer manufacturer Acer, is, for example, something of a folk hero in Taiwan. Revered by many as a visionary, his popularity, according to the *Financial Times*, verges on cult status. A self-made man, he built Acer from a tiny chip distributor into one of the world's five largest manufacturers of PCs, and has inspired a generation of high-tech entrepreneurs. His company is the crown jewel of the government's made-in-Taiwan campaign to promote the island's industry. So highly is he esteemed that Lee Teng-hui, Taiwan's president, once considered inviting him to become premier.[13]

Richard Branson, Ben Cohen, Anita Roddick and others have also gained (and to some extent, created for themselves) a celebrity status that takes them well beyond the business pages. When a BBC Radio poll asked 1,200 listeners who'd they choose to rewrite the Ten Commandments, Branson scored fourth, after Mother Teresa, the Pope and the Archbishop of Canterbury.[14]

Some court it – as Herb Kelleher, Richard Branson and Ben Cohen have all done to help promote their businesses. Some, such as Hatim Tyabji, steer well clear of celebrity. 'One thing I will absolutely not have is a cult of personality,' he told *American Banker*. And he certainly doesn't want any adoration, as he said in an interview: 'This is not a love fest. It's a business, and I brought in the business. Nobody loves me but my wife.'

How did wacky leaders develop their business beliefs and knowledge?

Most of our wacky leaders were self-taught. We were hard pressed to find any who had been to business school. And of those who'd learned on the job in large corporations, most opted not to apply anything they'd learned there.

Howard Putnam, a former United Airlines vice president who served as Southwest's president and CEO from 1978 to 1981, was once asked, 'What was the greatest thing you ever did for Southwest

Airlines?' Putnam responded: 'I didn't implement anything I learned at United.'[15]

Their formal training and education runs the gamut from high school drop-outs like Nicholas Graham and Richard Branson, to multiple degree holders like Hatim Tyabji (who holds graduate degrees in electrical engineering and international finance) and Liisa Joronen, whose degrees in sociology, philosophy and education were all put to interesting use at SOL.

Many showed entrepreneurial flair from an early age. Branson was a millionaire by the time he was 23. Other self-taught wonder kids include Sausage Software's Steve Outtrim, who found himself at the head of a multi-million dollar operation when he was only 23, and Richer Sound's Julian Richer, who decided at the age of 12 that he would be a millionaire. At 14 he was buying and selling hi-fi equipment through the *Exchange and Mart*, and at 17, while still studying for A-levels, had three people working for him on commission.

Ricardo Semler was only a moderate scholar but showed considerable leadership potential at school – he was class president and captain of the athletics team. He also showed an early talent for business, running a school snack stand and inviting sweet and drinks companies to compete as suppliers. He invested his profits in the stock market and took his fellow students on holiday with the proceeds.

Some of these people are real, live Horatio Alger stories. The cliché about the poor boy flogging newspapers on a street corner who grew up to become a media mogul, for example, is not as far fetched as it sounds. Both IKEA's Kamprad and Virgin's Branson started selling magazines as teenagers.

Observing good practice

Our wacky leaders are anything but copycats – but they know good practice when they see it – and most found it in places where others wouldn't think to look.

Acer CEO Stan Shih, unlike most of his peers in Taiwan's high-tech industry, did not study or work abroad. Instead, he got his business training at his mother's grocery store. There, as a small boy, he discovered that stationery offered a high margin but lower turnover, while duck eggs, though slim in margin, turned over cash every day. 'I made more money selling eggs than stationery,' he says.[16]

For IKEA's Ingvar Kamprad, it was the hard work, ingenuity and resourcefulness he saw during his rural childhood that he worked into his winning business philosophy.

Joe Boxer's Nicholas Graham learned about showmanship during his days in a punk band. 'That's when I found out that performing is really so much fun. I really loved it. And that was when we would stay up until four in the morning and make $10.'[17]

If wacky leaders do copy a basic approach, they make it their own.

Observing bad practice

Many of our wacky leaders had a lot of experience at the top rungs of big business – most of which they do not want to repeat.

Lars Kolind, the brains behind the remarkable turnaround at Oticon, speaks for many when he says, 'I was inspired by frustrations in former jobs. Management seldom made a positive contribution to the development of businesses: too much control, too little spirit, joy and inspiration.'

Many wacky leaders started their careers as fast-tracking young executives, but, for the same reasons, just couldn't settle into the corporate groove.

As a young man, Dee Hock, the founder of Visa, walked away from fast-track jobs at three separate financial companies. Each time he quit in frustration at the way command and control, hierarchical, rules-bound systems were stifling creativity and initiative – and in the process, making the company too rigid to respond to new challenges and opportunities.

MOS Burger founder, Satoshi Sakurada, had a similar experience, though, in the context of Japanese culture at the time, somewhat more radical. Though Sakurada was all set for a lifetime career with Nikko Securities, the role of a loyal salaryman just didn't sit right with him. In 1962, while on an assignment in Los Angeles, he tasted his first hamburger, and was thereafter lost to the corporate world.

'After returning to Japan I went through a restless phase,' he says.

'I quit my job, even though it was with a major company, and afterward changed jobs again several times. I couldn't seem to find a company that fit with my management philosophy.'[18]

Bill Gore also left the corporate world for philosophical reasons. During the 1950s, as an engineer with chemical giant DuPont, Gore worked on the development of a Teflon-like material called PTFE; a product he believed (correctly as it turned out) had great and undeveloped potential. Du Pont wasn't interested in pursuing the invention, but Gore's belief in the product, and perhaps the belief that he could do better on his own, inspired him to quit his corporate job and set up production with his wife Vieve, in his basement. Gore also took with him his experiences with a conventional 1950s American corporate environment, and a great many opinions about what did and didn't work, all of which provided fuel for his radical new workplace design.

We also have the narrow-mindedness of big business to thank for James Dyson's off-beat work style and innovative designs. While developing his dual cyclone cleaner – now a market leader in the UK – Dyson tried to get backing from a number of leading manufacturers. One multinational company, he says, would only agree to meet him if he signed over the rights to anything he might reveal to them in advance. Another wanted to license the product but refused to put anything in writing, saying that he would have to 'trust' them.

Dyson sensibly declined both offers, but his brush with the corporate world gave him important insights into the management culture that prevails in large companies. He was determined that his own firm would be different. Dyson's operation is now determinedly anti-corporate: neckties and memos are banned, and hierarchy and status are frowned upon. Dyson also makes a point of hiring people right out of university, before they've had a chance to adopt a corporate mind-set.

Trial and error

Most of our wacky leaders had minimal experience in the business they launched. Even those with corporate backgrounds chose, on the whole, sectors far removed from the industries they'd worked in.

Richard Branson, for example, boned up on the complexities of the airline business while he ran it, and he's done the same with all the other industries he's been in. 'I knew nothing about the airline business, financial service industry, soft drink business, any of them – until I started,' he says. 'I've never read [a business book] and never took a course in management. I've been fortunate to learn by experience, by making mistakes, by trying. I've learned every day by doing things different and new. It's what has kept it fascinating – that it is so many different businesses. And every one of them helps me with the last one, from the record business to the airline business and now life insurance and credit cards and banking – learning, learning, learning, learning.'[19]

Acer's Stan Shih knows a thing or two about learning. His company, now the world's third largest PC maker, nearly went bankrupt in the eighties. More recently, a flawed expansion into America created a loss of $141 million – Taiwan's biggest corporate loss on record.[20] The company bounced back quickly, though. As he writes in his autobiography *Me Too is Not My Style*: 'I would not be surprised if I am the CEO in Taiwan who has paid the highest tuition in learning those lessons.'[21]

Ben Cohen and Jerry Greenfield, makers of some of America's most popular ice cream, started out knowing little about ice cream that they couldn't learn from eating it. They also learned about business the hard way. Describing themselves as 'unencumbered by experience,'[22] the two learned, among other things, that cash flow improves enormously when you don't pay bills, and that putting candy bars in the cash deposit bags helps compensate bank staff for the extra work involved in reconciling the account. Two months after opening, Cohen and Greenfield put a sign on the door, reading: 'We're closed today so we can figure out if we're making any money.'[23] (They weren't.)

Ignorance appears to have been, if not bliss, at least effective, for many inexperienced entrepreneurs. Andy Nulman, the 38-year-old CEO of Montreal's Just for Laughs Festival, parlayed a two-day local event into the world's biggest comedy festival, employing over 400 people and bringing over half a million spectators. The non-profit event even pays its own way. How did he do it? 'I hate to toss a scud missile into the Harvard Business School,' (the bearded, blue-jeaned and earringed Nulman doesn't look the violent type). 'But basically it all boiled down to not knowing what we were doing. Often the new and better ideas come from those who don't know the rules.'[24]

Leading with values and wisdom

What sets wacky leaders apart from the norm isn't just what they have and haven't learned, but how they apply their knowledge.

One way of looking at it is through how they exert their influence on the organisation. Think of it as a two-dimensional diagram. On one axis is a spectrum from *intuitive wisdom* (a deep-seated, personal understanding of what makes things tick) and *received wisdom* (the lore of textbook, business school courses, sometimes more akin to common knowledge). On the other axis is a spectrum from personal values and beliefs to corporate vision and values.

The professional manager, replete with accountancy qualifications and maybe an MBA as well, tends to fall into the bottom right corner of the matrix. The professionals have to rely on systems and constructs, on the intellectual approach, because they lack the creativity and nerve to do anything else. People in their organisations rarely feel passionate about the vision and values, even if they seek to apply them. To them, values are a means to an end, rather than a starting point. Similarly, departing too far from received wisdom is perceived as too risky – these bean-counters need to operate within their comfort zone.

A few business leaders, such as Lee Iacocca at Chrysler, or Jack

Figure 6.1 Values and wisdom

Welch at General Electric – who's been quoted as saying that effective managers 'have to operate on the lunatic fringe' – emerge with the breadth of vision and creativity to challenge conventional wisdom and steer against the trend. These intrapreneurs stimulate radical change in the corporations they lead, but they are still essentially corporate animals, operating from within the accepted structure rather than from outside it. They change the way the company functions, but their aim is to make it do the same things better, rather than do different things entirely. They fit more or less comfortably into the top right corner.

In the bottom left corner congregate the many leaders who feel uncomfortable with the values of the traditional business world, but lack the courage or insight to change it. They may follow the latest management fad, perhaps be in the vanguard of applying it, but they cannot articulate strongly enough why this is the way to go, nor can they capture the imagination of the masses behind the big idea. Ricardo Semler and others among our wacky sample started here, trying to apply their values by experimenting with available business theory. When they discovered that there were no theories available for what they wanted to do, they set out on their own – abandoning received wisdom and moving up to the top left corner.

It's here that most of our wacky leaders gather. They have a perception of business reality that is built almost entirely on personal experience, observation and experimentation, and they do what they do because it is important to them. They march to their own drummer, oblivious to the advice of more cautious advisers.

Most people think they're mad, but theirs is a structured, productive sort of madness, and unlike most crazies, wacky leaders are aware of their own madness. VeriFone's Hatim Tyabji, for example, once described himself as 'lucidly crazy'. 'That means having the conviction to do things that most conventional people would consider crazy. I don't care what people think – I do what I believe is right.'

'In 1987, when I told the board that we were going to run the company as a virtual company without any paper correspondence, they told me that's not the way things are done in Silicon Valley. My response was: I'm going to do it anyway. The board (the whole board) thought I was loony tunes. I did it anyway.' How could he do it without the board's support? Because his belief in what was right was stronger then their doubts.

Besides, more often than not, their crazy ideas pan out. Tyabji's certainly did, and as Ben & Jerry's Fred Lager observes, 'A lot of Ben [Cohen's] seemingly whacked-out ideas weren't so wacky, once they were implemented. Ben's entrepreneurial drive pushed the organisation beyond its perceived limits, but without him, "impossible" projects that more traditional managers were often too quick to dismiss would never have been attempted. Beyond the sales and profits that these ideas generated, they were what gave the business its identity and made it unique compared with our more corporate competitors. He was forever fascinated by what was new and different about the business, which, in turn, was what had fuelled our growth.'[25]

Wacky leaders are different because they give themselves permission to be. That is something that few professional managers can ever do – not least because their whole career has been about fitting in. Even the few exceptions, such as Sir John Harvey-Jones at ICI, typically only ever make it to the top right corner of the matrix.

If you intend to become a wacky leader, you will need to:

- abandon the normal corporate world before it warps your soul
- abandon all the principles anyone else in business taught you and seek your own, from first principles
- have the guts and self-belief to insist on doing things your own way, no matter what anyone else tells you, and in spite of the initial failures that may come your way.

Leadership style

There are as many leadership styles as there are wacky leaders. These people are, after all, originals. They do have some common features, though. For starters, they all communicate through humour and play, whether to large audiences or small. To put it another way, they take their values seriously, but not themselves. It is this willingness to demonstrate the values at their own expense that lends many of them charisma and prompts them to such outrageous behaviour.

For Quad/Graphics CEO Harry Quadracci, clowns are his role models: 'Clowns are a perfect symbol of Quad/Graphics' philosophy of management, because, unlike so many others, they are not wedded to conventional wisdom. They retain their childlike ability to be surprised, and the flexibility to adapt to, or even thrive on, change,' he says.[26]

Observers also note how rare, and welcome, such style is in big business today. As one University National Bank and Trust board member – George G. Parker, professor of management for Stanford's Graduate School of Business – said of the bank's founder, Carl Schmitt: 'Carl is a nut. He's fun to work with . . . He's colourful, buoyant, a real freethinker, which you don't see too much of in this business.'[27]

Some would say there's a little too much wackiness in the computer industry, but, as former Sun Microsystems treasurer Thomas J. Meredith (now vice president for finance at Dell) said of Scott McNealy: 'His humour and ability to raise a crowd to its feet is in many respects exactly what you need in CEOs and leaders of today's industry'.[28]

Scott McNealy has a reputation for stunts that verge on the tasteless, but they do get his company the attention it needs. 'Just think about it,' says a spokesperson for a competing firm. 'Sun sells Unix, a boring techie thing. You think if not for McNealy they'd be so successful and have so much name recognition?'[29]

Similarly, men's underwear is unlikely to have got quite so much attention without the antics of Nicholas Graham and his alter ego Joe Boxer. 'He's a showman and a marketer, and he passionately believes in his brand,' says one customer, Bloomingdale's CEO Michael Gould. 'Nick's a success because he's an original,' adds Fern Mallis, head of the Council of Fashion Designers of America. 'This is not brain surgery. Nick brings a new attitude, a new accessibility to things. With Nick involved, it's a lot of fun.'[30]

They're not all charismatic. Stan Shih, CEO of Acer, is so personally nondescript even his wife, Carolyn, has called him 'interestingly boring'. In Shih's book Me Too is Not My Style, Mrs Shih writes that her husband takes very seriously the conferences that others regard as merely social gatherings, and is 'forever poring over large stacks of documents when in his car or on the plane'.

Energetic

Shih may not have the charisma, but he does have the relentless energy common among wacky CEOs.

And it can be contagious. Scott McNealy's special gift, says former sales vice president Carol A. Bartz, is to energise his people. 'Energy comes right out of his pores,' she says.[31]

The same can be said of Southwest's Herb Kelleher. Though he was 67 years old in 1998, he still hadn't opted for anything like semi-retirement. 'Herb works harder than anybody,' says Southwest's vice president, people, Libby Sartain. 'He's on the job, 12 hours a day, seven days a week.'

Richard Branson is also a real dynamo, despite his laid-back, shuffling appearance. While the other young people working on his first venture, a magazine called Student, happily got stoned at lunch hour, the teenage Branson was working the phones, drumming up business. Today, writes his biographer Mick Brown, a big part of Branson's success is his passion and energy: 'He is passionate about what he does, and determined not to waste a single moment. He has enormous energy, and is completely single-minded and ferociously competitive.'[32]

Former VeriFone CEO Hatim Tyabji was, until his retirement in early 1998, on the road 80 per cent of the time, travelling up to 400,000 air miles and making about 200 customer calls a year. Among the many bits of Hatim lore circulating around VeriFone's modems is the one about Tyabji, hopelessly ensnared in a Paris traffic jam, commandeering a motorcycle to reach a client meeting on time. This sort of thing seems reasonable to Tyabji: 'To me, that is the essence of leadership,' he says. 'Leadership is an ongoing, non-stop, continuous process.'[33]

Inspiring

It also takes a certain amount of guts, and an ability to inspire followers. Scott McNealy's vice president, Ed Zander, says his boss has both. 'Scott has an incredible ability that I haven't seen in this industry much – to stay the course, to stay with things even in the darkest hour.' This approach helps McNealy inspire loyalty among his followers. 'He will, inside the company, instil a sense of, "We're going to go take this hill. We may have some casualties, but we're going to go take it",' says Zander.[34]

Wacky leaders inspire their followers. They also tend to attract people who share their enthusiasms and beliefs, so they hang on to employees longer, find it easier to implement changes in strategy, and have fewer communications problems than their competitors.

They can do this because they make good role models. They act as living examples of their management philosophies, and never ask any employee to do anything they're not prepared to do themselves. They may change with the times, experiment and take the occasional wrong turn but, overall, they can be relied on to practise what they preach.

Or simply practise without preaching. Says VeriFone's Hatim Tyabji: 'When it is very clear, internally and externally, that you march to a "do as I do", not a "do as I say" culture, you engender moral authority.'

Accessible

They also make sure the loyalty runs both ways. Wacky leaders are consistently supportive of their employees and make themselves available to them.

Julian Richer makes a point of spending five to ten minutes talking to each member of staff whenever he visits a store, and every year in the run up to Christmas, the company's peak sales period, he travels around the country spending a day working alongside staff at each of his stores. Richer also gives his staff his home phone number and tells them to ring him if they have a problem.

So does Richard Branson. In his monthly letter to his 5,000 airline staff, the Virgin CEO includes his home address and phone number. As a result, he says, he gets about 40 letters a day, and they are answered (though not necessarily by Branson personally). 'People don't necessarily call, but they know they could.'[35]

Anyone at VeriFone could e-mail former CEO Hatim Tyabji, and get an answer within 24 hours. 'There's no such thing as too busy,' he says. 'If it's important enough, you have the time.'

Most wacky leaders make time for their employees. They're rarely seen in their office (if they even have one). Instead, they prefer to spend their time out and about – mostly with employees and, to a lesser degree, with customers. They manage by walking around – or, in some cases, by flying, ballooning, surfing or cycling around.

At IKEA, both Ingvar Kamprad and his heir apparent Anders Moberg make a point of staying in touch with shop staff and customers; popping, often unannounced, into stores and asking startled clerks what's moving. 'If you aren't interested in customers you can never be in retail,' says Sweden purchasing manager Sven Kulldorf. 'If you don't understand what the customer wants then you can never run a retail operation. You must be out there, otherwise you are blocked. You lose track and you lose touch. Being close to the customer means you know their needs.'

Southwest's Herb Kelleher prefers to hang out with employees. According to vice president, people, Libby Sartain, 'He spends a lot of time in the field getting to know employees. He has an uncanny ability to remember people's names and can probably call half of his 26,000 staff by their first names. The other half he hasn't met yet because they've just been hired in the last year,' she says.

Yvon Chouinard, by contrast, has a management style some describe as 'MBA' or 'management by absence'. He spends up to eight months a year away from the company, hiking, fishing and skiing in exotic locales. This, says, former CEO Kris McDivitt, doesn't mean he's not working. 'People are so myopic about work. Are you saying he's not working because he's not here sitting at a desk beating the shit out of people? When Yvon's gone, he's working. He's got product with him, and he always comes home with new ideas.'[36]

'McDivitt,' reports Inc., 'launches into a sermonette on how her boss's global trekking has resulted in reforestation projects in Chile and includes relationship-cementing ski trips with dealers in Japan, and chance encounters with mountain climbers offering valuable feedback on equipment. "Do you know what that's worth? It's like gold," she says. "It's all about how you form relationships with people."'[37]

Says current public affairs director Lu Setnicka: 'Yvon calls himself the "outside man". He's out testing new products and coming up with ideas. He's not at all involved in the day-to-day management of the company, but when he comes back from a three-week fishing trip in South America, we'll all pick his brains.'

One place you won't find these leaders is at their desk hunched over a computer. A lot of them, like Jay Chiat, have banned offices and desks for everyone, CEO included, and many, like Chouinard, refuse to use computers. Richard Branson, who plans to be the first to offer Internet services on transatlantic flights, never learned how to use a computer. Branson, who keeps his appointments in a paper diary and scribbles notes in a notebook or on his hand, told *Forbes*: 'I can't use a computer. If I'd been brought up in the computer world, I would. But I'm too old to change.' Branson was born in 1950. 'I know the power of technology and respect it. Even if I don't have the time to spend hours on-line, I have people who do. I make sure we're on the cutting edge,' he says.

Detail minded

People like Branson have clear, if unconventional, views about what is and isn't important. They will be indifferent to some tasks, like using computers, but obsessive about tiny details in the areas that matter to them.

Ben Cohen, for example, is known as something of a flavour dictator. Says Mitch Curren: 'He knew what was good and what wasn't. He would often send a recipe back to the drawing board hundreds of times so we got it right.' 'You never have the ice cream that you want. The ultimate is always beyond your grasp,' says Cohen.[38] He and Greenfield still try out recipes by hand at home before submitting them to R&D.

Ingvar Kamprad has involved himself in every detail of IKEA's growth and expansion, down to the recipe for the Swedish meatballs that are served at every outlet's restaurant.

Julian Richer has been known to carry a notepad wherever he goes, jotting down ideas as they occur to him while he travels around the country visiting various parts of his business.

And, despite his youthful humour, Sun Microsystems' Scott

McNealy is widely respected for his uncommon attention to the dry financial side of his business. As Lawrence J. Ellison, CEO of software company Oracle Systems, told *Business Week*: 'There are two things I think of about Scott. One is passionate leadership, and the other is his rigorous financial management. And that's uncommon to find in one person. Usually, the financial guys aren't so outspokenly passionate, and all leaders are not detail-oriented.'[39]

Uncompromising

These people are driven, uncompromising, focused, determined, energetic and eccentric. Is it any wonder, they are, on occasion also described as 'hard to work with', 'difficult' or 'a pain in the ass'?

Many of our wacky leaders have a hard edge to them. Underlying their fun-loving, people-first leadership styles, are high expectations of their employees and a core set of uncompromising standards. Some even call it fanaticism.

Hatim Tyabji, for one, sets high standards. 'We run a tough minded business and we run tough reviews,' he says. 'People respect you when you're honest with them, when things don't go right they're told, and there's praise when things go well. People resonate to fairness.'

Patagonia's Yvon Chouinard takes a similar approach. Kevin Sweeney, the company's former director of public affairs, lauds Chouinard as a wonderful teacher but says, 'He can be pretty rigorous if you don't meet the standard. He'll come back at you.'[40]

Nor is Chouinard what you might call a happy-go-lucky guy. While other wacky entrepreneurs imbue humour and joy into what they do, Chouinard seems driven by a bleak pessimism, a dire world-view, and even a low opinion of many of his customers. His reaction to an honorary Yale doctorate in humane letters was, 'I don't even like humans. I like trees.'[41]

Julian Richer is also known as a demanding taskmaster, though his method is more public. Once a month, staff at Richer Sounds sit down on a Saturday to watch their CEO rally the troops via video. Besides informing them of company news, Richer also uses the video to single out anyone he believes is guilty of stupidity or bad behaviour. Richer, it seems, has little confidence in his ability to hold an audience – he puts a code word in the video to ensure everyone watches the whole thing.

The most contradictory of all these personalities is that of Ben & Jerry's Ben Cohen. Says former CEO Fred Lager, 'For all that he brought to the company, working with Ben was, in plain English, a pain in the ass. Contrary to his laid-back public image, Ben was a taskmaster and a perfectionist who held everyone to incredibly high standards. He rarely passed out praise and was always focused on what was wrong or had fallen through the cracks. Despite the button he'd take to wearing [it read "Question Authority"] he didn't mean his authority.'

Cohen, says Lager, often didn't acknowledge other points of view, partly, he reasons, because Cohen had had first-hand experience with every job in the company, and he was a quick study on anything affecting the business. 'Still, Ben's management style was at odds with how he wanted the company to treat its employees. His intent was that Ben & Jerry's would be a business that conveyed love, support, and respect to those who worked there.'

He was also as hard on himself as he was on anybody else. 'He readily acknowledged his shortcomings as a manager, and was remorseful that he couldn't improve. "I don't work well in groups," he'd say . . . In all, Cohen is a bundle of contradictions: He preached slow growth to maintain the company's culture, but kept coming up with new projects, products and markets to enter. He wanted to create a loving, caring workplace, but was a hard and critical taskmaster.'

He also had unrealistic expectations about how fast things could be done, and could almost be relied on to change his mind about most decisions. 'Operating in a last-minute, crisis mode was the norm if it was something in which Ben was involved, and as a result, the organisation was in a constant state of turmoil,' writes Lager. 'He often came up with last minute suggestions that could send projects quickly spiralling back to square one. Because of being second-guessed all the time people were reluctant to proceed with anything until they had Ben's input. Since he was away from the plant so often, succumbing to that temptation would have had a paralysing effect on the company . . . "Ben is Ben" was the saying most managers used to explain the phenomena, which essentially meant that you should just expect him to change his mind or come up with some seemingly whacked-out idea, and not be surprised when he did.' A large part of both Lager's and Greenfield's jobs were to insulate the other employees from Cohen. 'Someone suggested I keep a copy of Ben's schedule and show up half an hour after he did to mend fences,' wrote Lager.

Exceptional leaders often forget they are dealing with ordinary people, and are shocked to discover that they are, in fact, getting ordinary performance. As Ben Cohen discovered early on, you have to allow some room for human flaws. In the early days at the first gas station location, he relates in his book,[42] Cohen calculated that the company should be able to make a profit at the prices set — providing employees scooped precisely the same sized cones each time. Try as they might, employees could not achieve this level of robotic precision, and Cohen was eventually, and reluctantly, persuaded to raise his prices enough to squeeze in a little margin.

Jay Chiat's personality was, similarly, an incalculable factor in the success of Chiat/Day. According to *Adweek* reporter Greg Farrell: 'While the creative teams made the ads that earned Chiat/Day its enfant terrible status, it was Chiat's dogged insistence on raising the bar that made them stars — or broke them. His agency's motto of many years has been "Good enough is not enough," and Chiat always has applied that to the work.'[43]

For a 1993 article marking the agency's 25th anniversary (and prematurely musing on life post-Chiat), Farrell interviewed a number of former agency employees about working with Jay Chiat. The picture they paint is of a strong-willed, autocratic perfectionist, who inspires fierce loyalty in others: 'If you were going to last there, you'd have to be a certain kind of person,' says Mike Shine, who worked at Chiat's New York office in the late eighties. 'You'd need a thick skin, because he wasn't going to sugar-coat. If you go into this not used to having your work ripped, you won't feel good about yourself unless you can take the criticism.'

'Every time Jay walked into the room, he put the fear of God into everyone,' adds Michael Smith, a former Chiat/Day creative director. 'He has a way of pushing people around him. He was the father everyone wants to please. I had run-ins with Jay, when he was angry or frustrated. But where he's coming from is, "Is this the best we can do?" It was never abusive, never about you. It was about the work.'

It was the virtual office concept that really brought out Chiat's despotic side. In 1994, he banned all personal space and belongings from Chiat/Day's offices in Venice, New York and Toronto. 'I'm a total hard ass about it,' he says. 'You're not going to make changes if you have a committee decide what's best for the office. We had a bunch of committees. All they did was confuse the issue. You've got to manage the denial, you can't manage by permissiveness, because if you permit this (he points to a pile of papers) stuff happens. They come in and squat and they'll be there for three, four weeks. It's kind of a homeless pattern, you know – they set up under a bridge, and pretty soon they have all their things around them.'[44]

Chiat's attitude to running the virtual office matched his approach to most things: there's no point doing something if you're not prepared to go all the way, and it really doesn't matter what anyone else thinks.

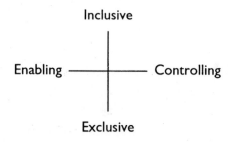

Figure 6.2 Styles of leadership

A useful way of exploring leadership style is the model in figure 6.2, which defines how leaders approach the task of influencing others. Wacky leaders can be found operating in all these styles. Leadership styles tend to be dispersed around two axes:

• the inclusive/exclusive axis measures how closely
  leaders involve others in their dreams and ideas
• the enabling/controlling axis measures whether they see
  their role as making things happen or letting things
  happen.

Inclusive/enabling

In this quadrant we find highly empowered companies, such as SOL, Semco and Whole Foods, where employees have bought into the leader's vision and are given the freedom and discretion to find the best way to fulfil it.

Richard Branson also runs his empire this way. 'I rely on others in every aspect of this company,' he says. It's a big reason why people like to work here. If a company is doing well, they may not hear from me for some time. If they need my helping hand – fire-fighting – I'm here and they know it. We actually do have a rare board meeting, but they're an excuse to get together. We don't need them. Communication is much less formal and it works fine.'[45]

These leaders also tend to use what is known as a transformational style of leadership. Transformational leaders seek to raise performance by treating workers as individuals, inspiring them to work together, and putting the interests of the group ahead of their own. 'They're kind of like Gandhi, though from an organisational perspective we don't see too much of that,' says John Sosik, an assistant management professor at Pennsylvania State University.

Southwest's Herb Kelleher, for example, is a typical transformational leader. Vice president, people, Libby Sartain, who's worked closely with Kelleher since 1988, describes him as 'brilliant and big hearted. He's compassionate and loving. He wants the best for everyone, and he has an incredible sense of humour. You have to give him credit for creating the company, but he wouldn't take it. He's got no ego, he's unassuming, and makes fun of himself.'

'Herb will also make tough decisions when he needs to,' she adds. 'But, unlike others, he'll give you an extra chance or two. He won't take one look at you and say "you screwed up I don't like you anymore".'

And, despite the celebrity status and personality cults that have built up around some wacky entrepreneurs, it is this inclusive, enabling style that appears to have the most impact on performance. A 1998 American study determined that a CEO's personality traits alone have little connection to a company's financial returns. Instead, the real determinate of success was how well the CEO fostered healthy group dynamics among his or her immediate subordinates. The study found that the most effective CEOs were open with information and receptive to ideas and criticism from their subordinates.

As one of the study's authors, Randall Peterson of the Johnson School of Management at Cornell University, told the *Independent on Sunday*: 'Disney's Michael Eisner and Coke's Roberto Goizueta had strong, consistent and clear visions for their companies, but they were also open to criticism and made successful adjustments when advised their case had altered.'

'Our findings suggest that the CEO's personality plays an important role when it is able to mesh with or foster similar strong values among the senior management group which reports directly to him,' he adds. 'In today's steadily less hierarchical and more flattened organisation, having personality traits that enable you to manage and operate in teams will be essential for executives in profitable and growing companies.'[46]

Inclusive/controlling

This is an odd balance, where the leader will gather others' opinions but enforce the final say.

British retailer Julian Richer exemplifies this management style. His company, Richer Sounds, has a great deal of upward communication systems, including one of Britain's most successful suggestion schemes, yet his staff are highly controlled, with a Pavlovian system of small, frequent rewards and punishments, such as fines and public humiliation, for poor performance.

Richer is convinced that a well-managed organisation can use strong central control and empowerment at the same time. In practice, this means that employees are free to make their own decisions, as long as they fit within Richer's framework. 'I think there are usually two ways of doing something,' says Richer, 'a right way and a wrong way.'[47]

Richer is careful to add that it is important to build upward communication into the system. This helps to identify whether the central control is oppressive or wrong.

Exclusive/enabling

These CEOs lead with a clear vision, but they let their employees decide how to implement it.

Acer's Stan Shih, for example, has a powerful vision to create a globally dominant computer company yet, to accomplish that vision, he uses an enabling, transformational leadership style – a style so unusual in Asian companies that it makes some of his colleagues uneasy. Shih describes his management model as collective entrepreneurship. He says, 'I do not like my colleagues to be yes-men. Neither do I like the idea of being treated as a boss.'[48]

Patagonia is driven by Yvon Chouinard's forceful beliefs, and while there is little give and take at the vision level, on the implementation side, Chouinard seems rather laissez faire.

Similarly, Hatim Tyabji ran VeriFone according to his own strict philosophy and 'moral authority'. However, the company's unusual operations, with its free flow of e-mail and rapid time frames, made a command and control style impractical even if that had been Tyabji's style.

Exclusive/controlling

Some of our socially responsible companies, despite their messages of peace and love, actually fall into this unfashionable quadrant.

Leaders like Ben Cohen and Paul Hawken can become so focused on outside achievements and social goals that they have little room for others' ideas about either the vision or the implementation of it.

Being socially progressive does not mean being internally democratic, explains former CEO Fred Lager: 'Inadvertently we'd created the expectation that we would solicit everyone's input before making any decision. In an article in the March 1989 Daily Plant (Ben & Jerry's in-house magazine) I made it clear that wasn't going to be the case. "The company is not and never has been a model of democracy." Even on issues on which we did solicit widespread input, having a voice did not equate to having a vote ... In some areas, having a values-led organisation precluded participation in decision making. Ben's vision for the business, for example, was far ahead of the direction our staff might have chosen by consensus or head counting. For the most part the social mission, in particular that part of it which could be construed as the company's political agenda, was not really open to debate.'[49]

At Ben & Jerry's, says Mitch Curren 'There's never been an atmosphere where, by making a suggestion it just happens. But we do have an atmosphere where people at the top do listen.'

Patagonia is no bastion of workplace democracy either. With only two shareholders (Mr and Mrs Chouinard) and no outside directors, Patagonia can be insular, argues one Inc. reporter: 'In the Patagonia culture, which espouses egalitarianism, true power, in fact, devolves to a small élite: Chouinard, his wife, Malinda, and (former) CEO Kris McDivitt. Over the years, professional managers have come to manage the growth – and left, often exasperated. Chouinard has hit the road and returned. The dirt bags have stayed behind, keeping the ideological fires burning.'[50]

As former financial officer Steve Peterson told Inc.: 'The last two to three years I was there, I pushed to bring in outside directors,' he says. 'A true board of directors needs people from larger companies.'[51] These meetings started in 1996, at the instigation of new CEO David Olsen. Employees also, according to Setnicka, all have access to the company's books (which, as a privately held company, are full of closely held secrets). Says Setnicka: 'Before '91 things were a bit closed, but now any employee can come and see what's happening with the numbers. We have to, we're expected to know.'

Succession

In an earlier study of high performing companies, the authors found that one consistent feature among them is that they make seamless succession at the top a priority.[52] Wacky companies, by contrast, tend to avoid dealing with succession, even though the issue will soon reach a crisis point for many of them.

When we were researching this book in 1997 and 1998, we were surprised at just how many of our wacky leaders were on the verge of leaving, or of at least trying to leave. These companies were at a key point in their history, just as their founders were expressing a desire to pursue other interests or, as with Chiat/Day, UNBT and

VeriFone, just as their organisations were acquired by larger concerns.

How well these companies cope with the transfer of power – whether it's sudden or gradual – will determine whether wackiness was just a phase they went through during the jurisdiction of one strong-willed leader, or whether they will be able to maintain their wacky energy for the long term.

Most of our wacky leaders seem to be easing out gradually, often with several false attempts, and few appear to have groomed an heir. Paul Hawken, Yvon Chouinard and Ben Cohen, for example, have all responded to a desire to step away from day-to-day management and devote their energies to broader issues.

Most find it hard to let go of the company they founded, and have struck a compromise by designing a kind of elder statesman role for themselves. Herb Kelleher, Anita Roddick and Richard Branson, for example, have stayed on as CEOs or chairs of their respective organisations, but now behave more like roving ambassadors – playing figurehead, lobbying governments, and performing PR stunts.

Branson, for example, spends up to three months each year working from his private island in the Caribbean and allocates a quarter of his time for PR stunts. Anita Roddick has hired others to handle day-to-day management at the Body Shop so she can concentrate on product development and maintenance of the vision and values. Southwest's Herb Kelleher spends much of his time in Washington lobbying against airline regulation.

Ricardo Semler has so empowered his employees he now sees his role primarily as a catalyst to provoke and enable changes within the company. He is free then to spend his time wandering, talking, observing in the factories.

Even control-freak Julian Richer has reached the point where he feels he can afford to let go of the reigns a bit. He now spends only one week in two in the office, only one in three in the summer. He's branched out into consultancy work, starting up his own firm to pass the Richer wisdom on. He has been employed as a consultant by over 20 companies, ranging from a sewage equipment manufacturer to large national retailers.

Though many companies avoid the issue, Richer recognises the importance of grooming a successor: 'It is no good making yourself the lynchpin of the entire company, because when you come to sell it or hand it over to someone else, the business is worthless if it cannot exist without you.'

And, apart from making the business more saleable, he feels leaders have a responsibility 'to ensure that the company does not fall apart if they step under a bus one day'.[53]

At Virgin, the concern is the same, the potential accident more exotic. As the adventurous Richard Branson told Forbes magazine: 'We try to run the organisation so that if my balloon ever went down, the people running their organisations could carry on running.'

However, though these leaders like to say they're not indispensable, they do find it hard to let go.

SOL's Joronen has tried to take a back seat and give other people more responsibility for the day-to-day running of the company. 'My role is not to disturb my people so much, and I find it the most difficult thing – to let them make their own mistakes,' she says.

IKEA's Ingvar Kamprad has the same problem. He has already appointed a successor, but still finds it hard to let go. 'I put my fingers in too much,' he says.

Some wacky leaders remain involved long past retirement age – sometimes out of interest, sometimes out of fear that, without their constant stimulus and goading, their organisations will drift into normality. They fear their ideals will be corrupted, lasting beliefs will be overtaken by temporary fads, and professional management will drain away the creativity and the fun.

Unfortunately, these fears have some foundation. Without a wacky leader to push and prod their followers to stay different, companies do tend to drift toward more conventional behaviour.

This is what happened at the FI Group, a British information technology company founded in the early 1960s as the first European telecommuting business. Considered leading edge in its day, the company hired hundreds of mainly women to work from home on computer software projects. The founder, Steve Shirley (her name is Stephanie but in the early days the name Steve opened more doors), had strong ideals about the kind of workplace she wanted to create based on her own experience of trying to combine demanding domestic responsibilities (including caring for a child with disabilities) and challenging, intellectually fulfilling work. Her company also pioneered employee ownership and involvement in decision making.

Shirley decided eventually that she wanted to wind down her role as executive and cultural leader. The company had reached a size where it was becoming a burden rather than a source of fulfilment. Her first attempt to appoint a successor as CEO was a disaster, however, and she had to take back the reins. She had made the mistake of bringing in a professional manager and expecting that the culture of the company would remain essentially the same.

Her second attempt was more thoughtful and much more successful. She selected a potential successor who shared most of her ideals, but who also brought big-company experience. She worked with the CEO-elect to develop a programme that would gradually transfer power and ownership within the organisation to the employees until Shirley no longer had majority control. This time, when she handed over responsibility, there was a much stronger understanding of how the organisation could exploit its distinctiveness, capitalise on the motivation and momentum generated through employee ownership and sustain strong business performance.

Some followers prefer a drift towards normality. In many interviews, the second tier of management sounded relieved at the idea of their leader's retirement. And who can blame them? Many of these leaders have such forceful personalities and high energy that their subordinates, much as they admire them, find it easier to get on with things when they're not around.

Mitch Curren, for example, expresses a mixture of admiration and relief when she says that her boss, Ben Cohen, 'is no longer a one-man approval or disapproval squad.' As one executive said of Patagonia's Chouinard: 'Yvon is a very creative person, but there are certain things he should have let his professionals run.'[54]

How conventional a company becomes depends, of course, on what sort of professional manager steps in to take the helm. The future of the company depends on the character and drive of the successor, or where he or she fits on the matrix of leadership styles.

If a new leader emerges with a similar style, the company can retain its wackiness. If the new leader is most comfortable in one of the other quadrants, then he or she will gradually undermine the culture, dragging it back to 'normality'.

Ben & Jerry's, for example, appears to be easing towards convention. Ben Cohen and Jerry Greenfield have, gradually and erratically, stepped back from day-to-day management over the years. In early 1997, to much snide press coverage (next flavour, Lock-'n'-Load Rocky Road, quipped *Time*) former gun company executive Perry Odak became CEO. Odak, formerly chief executive at US Repeating Arms Co., the maker of Winchester rifles, seemed an unlikely choice to lead the makers of Peace Pops and supporters of gun control.

According to *Time* magazine, Odak (whose $300,000 salary blew Ben & Jerry's salary ratio to pieces) planned to turn the management team into what he calls 'a well-oiled machine'.[55]

He has, apparently, done just that. Says Mitch Curren: 'Perry Odak has brought some conventional processes to the company that we needed. Since Perry, for example, we've spent more money and time with traditional forms of advertising, like radio advertising. And we do market research now – to figure out what people are screaming for.' And, though it's probably not Odak's fault, parties at Ben & Jerry's aren't, says Curran, 'quite as rambunctious as they used to be'. In the most inspiring cases, though, the rest of the organisation has seized the vision enough that the company's core wackiness can continue and even grow into the second generation of management.

At Southwest Airlines, for example, no one's worried about the future. Kelleher doesn't plan to retire soon, and Southwest's carefully nurtured culture is safe even if he does.

'Herb has three years left in his five-year contract and he's not planning to retire,' said Sartain in a 1998 interview. 'And he's got VPs at several levels who could step in. He is so visible and we love him so much, but he is the third CEO and other people have done the job and done it well.'

When Sam Walton, founder of Wal-Mart, retired in 1984, his ultimate successor, David Glass, was asked about the transition the company would have to go through. He replied: 'There's no transition to make, because the principles and the basic values he [Walton] used in founding this company were so sound and so universally accepted.' Glass had been in the business for eight years, sufficient both to absorb the business philosophy and to influence it before his appointment as president and CEO.

Now in his seventies, IKEA's Kamprad has long been planning his succession. In 1984, he transferred his equity in the company to a charitable foundation in Holland, ostensibly to prevent his three sons – Peter, Jonas and Mathias, all managers with IKEA – from getting their hands on the company. His concern was that family disagreements over the company's future might tear the company apart.

And, instead of a family member, Kamprad chose IKEA manager Anders Moberg as his successor. Moberg joined the company in 1970 and worked his way up from the mail-order department. He was retail manager France when he was selected as president-elect in 1986. He now runs IKEA's day-to-day operations.

While the circumspect Moberg might say that Kamprad is irreplaceable, it would be better for IKEA if he weren't. A lot of people are hoping that the company can continue to thrive without its quirky, innovative and deeply principled leader. IKEA Sweden purchasing manager Sven Kulldorf isn't worried. The succession, he says, 'will mean some changes. But even if you take away the founder, the values are so strong throughout the organisation that if somebody tried to go against those values there would be a revolution which either would remove that person or would result in lots of people leaving.'

Sometimes the founder had such a mark on the personality of the company that his style is retained even after his death. W. L. Gore financial officer Shanti Mehta told the editors of The 100 Best Companies to Work for in America that 'Bill Gore never called me into his office. He always came to my desk. Sat on my desk, and talked to me as if he had all the time in the world. He was a real spring from which love flowed throughout the organisation. And the culture was nourished that way. After his death the responsibility of doing this has fallen squarely on the shoulders of all of us, and it is very important we do that.' Mehta has continued Bill Gore's practice of sitting on associates' desks and chatting with people.

Visa's Dee Hock worked hard to ensure the values resided in the organisation as a whole, not in his leadership alone. When it was suggested that he was indispensable, he responded: 'Utter nonsense.

It's the organisational concepts and ideas that were essential. I merely came to symbolise them. Such organisations should be management-proof.'[56]

In May 1984, at the age of 55, Hock set out to prove it. He resigned from Visa and, three months later, with his successor in place, dropped completely from sight. Six years later, in an acceptance speech as a laureate of the Business Hall of Fame, Hock explained his actions: 'Through the years, I have greatly feared and sought to keep at bay the four beasts that inevitably devour their keeper – Ego, Envy, Avarice, and Ambition. In 1984, I severed all connections with business for a life of isolation and anonymity, convinced I was making a great bargain by trading money for time, position for liberty, and ego for contentment – that the beasts were securely caged.'

Hock now works with Peter Senge, author of The Fifth Discipline and a leader in organisational redesign, at the MIT Center for Organisational Learning, a consortium of 20 companies dedicated to cutting-edge work in corporate adaptability. 'Dee is one of the most original thinkers on the subject of organisation that I've come across,' Senge says.

Others have made similar, if less dramatic, moves away from the nitty-gritty of business to a more philosophical, aesthetic life, where they can spend their time pursuing their theories and ideas, without the daily demands of business. This doesn't prevent them from poking their noses in at the office, but it does free them up to pursue their ideas.

Smith & Hawken founder Paul Hawken, for example, resigned as chairman and CEO in 1991 – when the company was grossing $60 million a year – to devote his energies to speaking and writing on the topic of sustainability. As he told Inc. magazine at the time: 'It's been a wonderful odyssey, but I feel it's time to get back to some of the things I set out to do in the first place.'[57]

Hawken is now something of a fixture on the socially responsible business lecture circuit. He's often found, if not on the same podium, at least mentioned in the same breath, as Ben Cohen, Yvon Chouinard and Anita Roddick as leaders in the environmentally conscious business movement.

Hawken has also written a number of books on alternative

economics, including *The Next Economy*, *The Ecology of Commerce*, *Seven Tomorrows* and *Growing a Business*, and produced a TV series based on *Growing a Business*. He currently serves as chairman of The Natural Step, an educational foundation that teaches business leaders how to mix business with environmental responsibility.

Lars Kolind took over as president of Oticon in 1988, at the age of 50. When we were researching this book, he announced his plans to step down as president in May 1998. As Kolind told us, 'I feel that both the company and I will benefit from a change. There is a whole new generation of young people who are ready to run with the ball and why shouldn't I let them do it?'

Kolind is satisfied that he is leaving Oticon in good shape. 'The company is doing incredibly well in all respects and I expect that to continue. So why stay? Personally I intend to spend more time with my family and to get involved more in social and political work. I want to make a difference in society.'

Hatim Tyabji was finishing up his tenure at VeriFone when we spoke to him. What will he do now? 'I'm on boards, teaching, but I'm too intellectually active to have that satisfy me. I'll create a new industry. I don't know what it is yet, but I can assure you I will not follow somebody else. There's a tremendous amount of pleasure and pride in ploughing your own ground.'

THE BOTTOM LINE

- ▶ Differentiating values are learned outside the business world – and certainly not at business school.

- ▶ The main value of benchmarking against competitors is to learn how *not* to do things.

- ▶ Be a role model for inspiring values – never ask any employee to do anything you're not prepared to do yourself.

- ▶ Letting go is the hardest bit – the true test of how well the values have marinated into the organisation.

NOTES

1. Donna Korchinski, 'Marines Whip Managers into Shape', in *The Globe and Mail*, 17 July 1998.
2. Brenda Marks, 'The Underwear Makes the Man', in *The Waterbury Republican-American*, 10 November 1996.
3. J. Fierman, 'Winning Ideas From Maverick Managers', in *Fortune*, 6 February 1995.
4. J. Kutler, 'VeriFone's Unconventional Chief', in *American Banker*, 20 April 1995.
5. Richard Branson, *Losing My Virginity: The Autobiography* (Virgin Press, 1998).
6. Apple Computers, Applemasters Web site.
7. Cole Morton, 'Cookie Dough Dynamos', in *Independent on Sunday*, 15 February 1998.
8. Darryl K. Taft, 'Top 25 Executives', in *Computer Reseller News*, December 1997.
9. Richard Branson, *Losing my Virginity*, 1998.
10. Aun Koh, 'From Prison to Profits', in *Asia Inc.*, August 1997.
11. Janet Perry, 'Masayoshi Son, CEO of Softbank', in *On the Internet Magazine*, 1997.
12. Bala Pillai, 'Interview with Softbank President Masayoshi Son', in *Space Net Magazine*; http://www.spacer.com/spacenet/text/sb-a.html.
13. Laura Tyson, 'The High Priest of Taiwanese High-tech', *Financial Times*, 18 May 1998.
14. J. Fierman, 'Winning Ideas From Maverick Managers', 1995.
15. Kevin Freiberg and Jackie Freiberg, *Nuts! Southwest Airlines' Crazy Recipe for Business and Personal Success* (Orion Business, 1998).
16. Laura Tyson, 'The High Priest of Taiwanese High-tech', 1998.
17. Michael Marlow, 'Joe Boxer has Plans from Jeans to TV Screens,' in *DNR*, 14 April 1997.
18. MOS company literature.
19. David Sheff, 'Interview with Richard Branson', in *ASAP Forbes*, 24 February 1997.
20. Brian Dumaine, 'Asia's Wealth Creators Confront a New Reality', in *Fortune*, 8 December 1997.
21. Stan Shih, *Me Too is Not My Style*, quoted in Laura Tyson, 'High Priest of High Tech', 1998.
22. Fred Lager, *Ben & Jerry's: The Inside Scoop — How Two Real Guys Built a Business with a Social Conscience and a Sense of Humor* (Crown Publishers, New York, 1994).
23. Fred Lager, *Ben & Jerry's*, 1994.
24. Camilla Cornell and Ian Cruickshank, 'Top 40 Under 40', *Financial Post Magazine*, 19 April 1998.
25. Fred Lager, *Ben & Jerry's*, 1994.
26. Harry Quadracci, President's letter to staff, 1984 (quoted in Levering and Moskowitz, *The 100 Best Companies*, 1993).
27. Elizabeth Conlin, 'Small Business: Second Thoughts on Growth', in *Inc.*, March 1991.

28. Robert Hof, 'Scott McNealy's Rising Sun', in Business Week, 22 January 1996.
29. Darryl K. Taft, 'Top 25 Executives', 1997.
30. Michael Marlow, 'Joe Boxer has Plans', 1997.
31. Robert Hof, 'Scott McNealy's Rising Sun', 1996.
32. Mick Brown, in Daily Telegraph.
33. W. Taylor, 'At VeriFone It's a Dog's Life (And They Love It!)', in Fast Company, November 1995.
34. Darryl K. Taft, 'Top 25 Executives', 1997.
35. David Sheff, 'Interview with Richard Branson', 1997.
36. Edward. O. Welles, 'Lost in Patagonia', in Inc., August 1992.
37. Edward. O. Welles, 'Lost in Patagonia', 1992.
38. Cole Morton, 'Cookie Dough Dynamos', 1998.
39. Robert Hof, 'Scott McNealy's Rising Sun', 1996.
40. Edward. O. Welles, 'Lost in Patagonia', 1992.
41. J. Collins, 'The Foundation for Doing Good', in Inc., December 1997.
42. Ben Cohen and Jerry Greenfield, Ben & Jerry's Double Dip: Lead with Your Values and Make Money Too (Simon & Schuster, New York, 1997).
43. Greg Farrell, 'Chiat's End Game', in Adweek, 12 July 1993.
44. R. Buchanan, 'Brave New Work', in Details, February 1995.
45. David Sheff, 'Interview with Richard Branson', 1997.
46. Roger Trapp, 'Cult of the Boss Fails the Academic Test', in Independent on Sunday, 24 May 1998.
47. Julian Richer, The Richer Way (Emap Business Communications, 1995).
48. Laura Tyson, 'The High Priest of Taiwanese High-tech', 1998.
49. Fred Lager, Ben & Jerry's, 1994.
50. Edward. O. Welles, 'Lost in Patagonia', 1992.
51. Edward. O. Welles, 'Lost in Patagonia', 1992.
52. Walter Goldsmith and David Clutterbuck, The Winning Streak, Mark II (Orion Business Books, 1997).
53. Julian Richer, The Richer Way, 1995.
54. Edward O. Welles, 'Lost in Patagonia', 1992.
55. Various authors, 'High-Caliber Help for Ben & Jerry's', in Time, 13 January 1997.
56. M. Mitchell Waldrop, 'The Trillion-Dollar Vision of Dee Hock', in Fast Company, October/November 1996, p. 75.
57. George Gendron, 'The Changing of the Guard', in Inc., June 1992.

7 Doing it different with pride

'The most compelling point I will make about Patagonia is the pride we take in being a different type of business.' (Patagonia human resources director, Terri Wolfe)

'Our goal is complete global domination of the computer support services market and enslavement of the human race. It's been done before, but never with such style.' (Robert Stephen, chief inspector of the Geek Squad)

Everyone you hire is so important. Often people make mistakes, but you allow for that, too. Praise people – like plants, they must be nurtured – and make it fun. Value them and give them the opportunity to contribute in ways that excite them. Keep it vibrant. Everything comes back to people. Nothing else. You get loyalty, enthusiasm and great service for your customers.' (Richard Branson)[1]

There is something about working for a wacky company that drives people to do things they would not normally do.

BC Ferries' third mate Clive Quigley works ten 12-hour shifts, back to back, and spends his few free hours composing sea shanties to entertain passengers.

Workers at the Finnish cleaning company SOL regularly turn up to weekend events dressed in their bright yellow work uniforms, even though there is no requirement to do so.

Southwest Airlines pilots have the best safety record in the US industry. They also help flight attendants clean the planes. In 1995, they committed to a remarkable ten-year labour contract.

This may be odd behaviour in the workplace, but it's also a sign of dedication and of a willingness to go the extra mile for customers, for colleagues and for the company.

What we've seen again and again in our wacky companies is an uncommon level of mutual respect and trust between employees and employers. People in these companies, at all levels, seem to genuinely value each other. They work exceptionally hard (often for little financial reward), perform outrageous stunts to entertain customers and colleagues, and seem willing to do what it takes to get the job done. And, if you ask them about their jobs, chances are they won't say what they do – they'll tell you who they work for.

This attitude is what helps wacky companies extract extraordinary performance from ordinary people. It's a powerful force in generating commitment, performance, good will, and (as we'll see in the next chapter) innovation. We call it pride.

The origins of pride

This force is not something that can be laid on as an extra; rather, its roots lie deep within the corporate psyche, in a company's values, history, and attitude towards employees.

Pride comes from identification with the company's values

Employees of wacky companies feel proud to work where they do because they identify strongly with the organisation's values.

At Patagonia, for example, employees put in hours and show levels of energy and commitment rarely seen in more conventional environments. And, while it's true that in return they enjoy such goodies as gourmet vegetarian meals and surfing breaks, most Patagoniacs say the reason they go the extra mile for their employer is because the company's values, working style, and passion for the outdoors aligns with their own.

'The most compelling point I will make about Patagonia is the pride we take in being a "different" type of business,' says HR director Terri Wolfe. 'We strive to be a model to other companies world-wide in demonstrating our desire, effort and success at being a responsible corporate citizen of the world.'[2]

Dick Snow, who manages a Ben & Jerry's retail shop, has noticed a similar effect among his workers: 'The social mission motivates my staff. When the line has been out the door for twelve straight hours, I need a staff that's completely convinced they should go the extra mile for me. In another situation, the person might think, "Hey I'm making six bucks an hour. The owner's already made enough money for today. Why am I busting my butt?" but my scoopers know that if the shop makes money, a good chunk of it goes to social projects that they help choose. My philosophy, based on what I've learned as a Ben & Jerry's franchisee, is that the harder you try to blow your money on seemingly unprofitable community projects, the more money you end up making.'[3]

A company's values don't even have to form an exact match with a worker's to generate pride and commitment. A 1990 Ben & Jerry's employee survey found that 88 per cent of employees were proud to work for the company, even though only 61 per cent felt the social mission was in line with their own values. Though by 1992, says info queen Mitch Curren, both figures were over 90 per cent.

Pride comes from being part of a success story

It's natural to feel pride in being a member of a winning team. Chiat/Day, for example, had such a powerful reputation for producing the best creative work in the industry that talented people were willing to work longer hours at lower pay than they would for others just so they could include Chiat/Day work in their portfolios.

Others do less glamorous work, but take no less pride in it. At Cooper Tire in Findlay, Ohio, people are so proud of their product they're prepared to sign it – tire builders each stamp their own name inside every tire they make. The trucking department at another company has taken to enclosing a Polaroid photo of its warehouse team with each bill of lading, and signing it, 'packed with pride'. (They once received a note back from a recipient – signed 'unpacked with pride'.)

Playing the underdog

Pride is even sweeter when the team has won against the odds. There's something about playing the David to a competitor's Goliath that instils a kind of underdog pride in both employees and customers – a pride that lasts even when the company has outgrown its original rivals. Virgin (when it was small enough to be convincing) masterfully played this role against British Airways – so well that, during the eighties, some people would fly Virgin as a political statement. Apple Computer's underdog position had the same effect – to this day Apple users are fiercely loyal to their machines.

It's unlikely anyone will ever feel so strongly about a vacuum cleaner, but if anyone can inspire loyalty to a household appliance, it's British designer James Dyson. Dyson's invention, a bagless vacuum cleaner, is hardly glamorous. It is, after all, just a domestic appliance, and such a funny looking one that industry leaders dismissed it as a niche 'designer' object. Dyson couldn't get an existing manufacturer to take his ideas seriously, so he went into production himself. He struggled for a decade, working alone in the coach house behind his family home, and came close to bankruptcy before launching his first product, the DC01, in 1993.

The DC01 was an immediate success, becoming Britain's best-selling vacuum cleaner in just 23 months, overtaking sales of the manufacturers who refused to take him seriously when they had the chance. The DC02, launched in 1995, achieved similar results.

Though Dyson is now the industry leader, producing 10,000 machines a day, he's still very close to his underdog roots. His operation is strictly anti-corporate and he takes pride in being an inspiration to other one-person bands. 'What we have done, that nobody thought we could do, is to take on the multinationals and beat them in a very short space of time, which I hope gives other people heart,' he says.[4]

Dyson, like any good folk hero, has lent his name to the language. British householders may still 'Hoover' their carpets, but in some quarters, 'doing a Dyson' means to design, engineer, manufacture and market your own invention.

For Southwest Airlines, being the underdog, especially in the early days when its competitors tried to keep it grounded, generated an *esprit de corps* that permeates the organisation to this day. Says vice president, people, Libby Sartain: 'In the early days, we had three planes. All the big airlines did everything they could to ensure we didn't fly. That created a maverick mentality. We all got in and worked together in a team-oriented do-whatever-it-takes environment. Whenever we got going, some other threat would happen. So, we always had this environment.' 'The warrior mentality, the very fight to survive, is what truly created our culture,' adds corporate secretary and executive vice president Colleen Barrett.'[5]

Southwest employees also take pride in the fact that their airline makes flying available to people who couldn't otherwise afford it – customers who no doubt relate to Southwest's underdog image. Once, when Braniff's coach price between Dallas and San Antonio was $62 and Southwest's fare was $15, a shareholder asked Kelleher if he could just raise the price two or three dollars. 'You don't understand,' said Kelleher. 'We're not competing with other airlines, we're competing with ground transportation.'[6]

At Ben & Jerry's, says former CEO Fred Lager: 'One aspect of our culture was a work ethic that could be traced back to the days at the gas station when the business was struggling to survive. It hadn't been unusual for Jerry and Ben to put in seven-day, 100-hour weeks. Though the company's survival was no longer a day-to-day concern, there was still a "whatever it takes" attitude among the staff.'[7]

That little guy image worked for the outside world, too, and was used masterfully during the Pillsbury Doughboy campaign in 1984. Market leader Häagen Dazs, owned by the food conglomerate Pillsbury, had given distributors a hard to refuse, us-or-them, ultimatum, threatening to drop any distributors who carried Ben & Jerry's products.

Says Lager: 'We knew that in the courts, Pillsbury's financial resources and staying power gave them terrific leverage over us. In the media, the advantage was ours. We decided up front to cast ourselves in a fight against Pillsbury, not Häagen Dazs. Häagen Dazs versus Ben & Jerry's was one ice cream company against another. Pillsbury versus Ben & Jerry's was the Fortune 500 against two hippies.'[8]

Jerry Greenfield picketed Pillsbury's Minneapolis headquarters alone with a sign reading 'What's the Doughboy afraid of?' (a reference to the character used in Pillsbury's ads). He also handed out leaflets explaining their case, and letter writing kits for passers by to mail in to Pillsbury. Back in Vermont, a Doughboy Hotline offered more kits to callers.

Cohen and Greenfield knew how to tap the vein of anti-corporate sentiment held by many Americans. A small classified ad in the alternative magazine *Rolling Stone* ran: 'Help two Vermont hippies fight the giant Pillsbury corporation. Send $1 for the facts and a bumper sticker.' Not only were they able to gather national support

for the cost of a classified ad, they could charge their supporters for
the privilege. Showing an inspired knack for PR, Cohen and
Greenfield even hired a plane to drag a banner over a stadium during
a football game. The national news coverage this generated may or
may not have intimidated Pillsbury, but it did garner an immense
amount of almost free publicity for the company.

Häagen Dazs founder Reuben Mattus later told *The New Yorker* that
Ben & Jerry's 'got PR and exposure they couldn't buy for millions.
What they did in a couple of years took me eighteen years to do. I
did it the hard way.'[9]

Pride comes from being part of a bold experiment

'To boldly go' has found a place in the language for a reason.
Though not everyone is brave enough to take the first plunge into a
new industry or a radical new way of working, those who do get all
the benefits of being first, and of the pride this generates. (They also
get all the downsides – it's a risky business!)

VeriFone's Hatim Tyabji, for example, takes great pride in his
company's achievements. 'We had the courage to take risks,' he says.
'For example, today it's fashionable to talk about the Internet. In
1986, nobody had ever heard of it. We created the world's first
virtual company.'

There's nothing like tackling a Mission Impossible to inspire the
troops. On 4 July 1997, the Jet Propulsion Laboratory (JPL) landed a
spacecraft on the surface of Mars. That project was just part of a long
history of successful missions that has created an extraordinary, and
self-perpetuating, sense of pride and accomplishment at JPL.

'The success of the Pathfinder mission is another addition to the
lore that is part of JPL's culture,' writes flight system manager Brian
Muirhead in a book on the project. 'We've done a lot of jobs that at
first seemed near impossible, starting with the first spacecraft ever
launched by the United States. JPL has developed an attitude that is
experience-based, a confidence that comes from seeing what people
can do in the face of seemingly impossible odds.'

This groundbreaking spirit also affected the crew of BC Ferries.
'The ambiance on the vessel is one of the main compliments I get
back,' says customer service manager Marie Graf. 'The crew made

the trip for most of the customers because they were committed and they were enjoying their jobs.'

The work is arguably harder than on other routes. Staff live aboard on ten-day runs and, with multi-tasking and socialising with customers, they're very much on duty for the full period – yet most appear to relish it, and there's no shortage of volunteers.

'It can't help but add to the enjoyment of a trip when you have staff that work ten straight 12-hour shifts, then walk off the ship smiling. We empower our staff, we think they're the greatest, and they feel so of value on this route,' says Graf.

Pride comes from being valued

People mean very different things when they talk about values, or about valuing someone or something. One result has been the development of the values triangle, shown in figure 7.1.

Value can be either a matter of:

- beliefs
- respect ('what I value about your contribution is'), or
- worth, as in added value.

Each interpretation offers an opportunity for alignment or alienation of employees and customers, with those of the company.

Employees who share similar beliefs to those espoused by the company are likely to stay longer, make decisions more in line with the strategic intent and demonstrate greater commitment. And be proud to be part of it. Customers are more likely to trust companies who share their beliefs.

Employees who receive respect from the company and their colleagues – for example, by being listened to – will tend to treat colleagues, customers and suppliers in a similar fashion. Customers, who perceive their needs and feelings to be respected, have greater loyalty.

Employees are also likely to be more motivated to seek to improve the company's financial performance if doing so enhances their own worth, in terms of their financial position, marketability or employ-ability. In customer terms, this means value for money.

This three-fold understanding of values provides a useful means

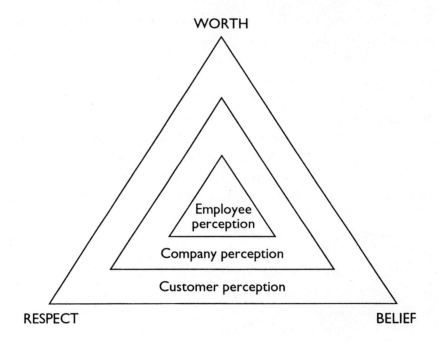

WORTH

Employee
perception

Company perception

Customer perception

RESPECT

BELIEF

Figure 7.1 The values triangle

for establishing how people feel about the way values are and are not applied. The more deeply values are shared, the more confident the company can be in letting loose some of the controls on which it has relied.

In wacky companies, values are deeply shared. This is largely because wacky companies value their employees – at all three points of the values triangle.

And they value their employees, not just because happy, well-motivated employees are good for business, but because they believe it's the right thing to do. Their treatment of employees stems not just from business needs, but from different beliefs about people – what they deserve, what they are capable of, and what's important in life.

What's not important in life, it seems, is money. Wacky companies don't, on the whole, pay exceptionally well. While some offer higher than average salaries to ensure they keep the cream of the crop, others, because of their reputation as great places to work, can get away with paying less (though often with benefits to compensate). Still other wacky companies have little choice, for competitive reasons, but to pay the going basic wage. All three groups have employees proud to work for them, and crowds more wanting to join.

In Finland, for example, a highly developed welfare system means that unemployed cleaners and other low-paid workers are often better off financially if they don't take a job. Not surprisingly, the Finnish cleaning industry has difficulty attracting staff. But that's not been the case at SOL, where people are continually applying for work. In December 1996, new applicants numbered 500, of which 350 were cleaners.

Mirage resorts, a chain of Los Angeles casinos, is known for providing such high standards of service and overall customer experience that its newest hotel is expected to make as much money from non-gambling activities as from gambling. Mirage's new Treasure Island Casino runs at 99.4 per cent occupancy and has generated a return to investors averaging 22 per cent a year. Yet the company's employees are for the most part working for minimum wage. CEO Steve Wynn wins their enthusiasm not by paying them more than competing hoteliers, but by treating them at least as well as the punters dropping thousands at the tables. He spent more per square foot building the employee cafeteria than the hotel's coffee shop, and decorated the back stairs and service corridors to the same plush standard as the guest areas. And if a manager can't explain why he's asking employees to do something, they don't have to do it.[10]

Wacky companies recognise that, for most people, money is not a prime motivator. People want to be paid fairly, of course, and enough to cover their basic needs, but beyond that, financial gain appears relatively unimportant in how people feel about their jobs.

This has, traditionally, been the case at Virgin, where many employees work for less than the going rate because they enjoy the buzz, independence and fast pace at Virgin. In the early days of his business empire, chairman Richard Branson showed an extraordinary knack for getting people to work for little or no financial reward. Branson gave people the sense that their work was somehow for the greater good and that forgoing financial reward could be fun. He knew how to make people feel valued even without a pay cheque.

According to Bob Nelson, author of 1001 *Ways to Motivate Employees*: 'To be competitive, each company needs to obtain extraordinary results from ordinary people. You have to make employees feel valued so they want to do their best work on a daily basis and to consistently act in the best interests of the organisation. You can achieve this enhanced level of energy and initiative by focusing more on how you treat employees rather than how much more you will pay them. For the best results, pay them fairly, but treat them superbly.'[11]

Or, as University Bank's Carl Schmitt, puts it: 'I have to pay people well both monetarily and psychically.'[12] What, then, is psychic pay? What motivates employees and makes them feel proud to be part of the company they work for? It's not rocket science – what they want is what anyone would expect of a community they're with every day:

- ownership
- respect
- responsibility
- trust
- a sense of belonging
- security
- information
- the freedom to be themselves.

Ownership

What makes money motivating is not so much how *much* people are paid, but *how*.

Most wacky companies have some element of employee ownership in their pay packages. While conventional companies do little more than rent employees' time and skills – whether it's with an hourly minimum wage or an executive's salary package – employees of wacky companies usually get a piece of the profits.

Andy Law, the co-founder of London advertising agency St. Luke's, finds the traditional pay system exploitative. He's critical of the way many advertising agencies are run, with senior management taking the lion's share of the profits from the creativity and ideas of younger staff. 'There are a lot of greedy people in the advertising business,' says Law, 'The industry is driven by ego. By and large, it does not respect its employees.' St. Luke's, by contrast, is completely employee owned. Every one of the hundred or so employees – from the creative director to the switchboard operator – receives equal shares in the business.

Entry level salaries for Southwest's bargaining unit (84 per cent of employees are union members) are comparable to those of other airlines, while managerial and administrative staff are, in many cases, passing up better starting salaries in other industries.

Southwest employees, however, own about 10 per cent of the company, and, says vice president, people, Libby Sartain, 'Most people who spend their career with us retire as millionaires.' This is becoming a problem, she adds: 'Many long-term employees are retiring too soon because they have enough money to retire. We're losing them at a time when it's hard to get good people.'

Not surprisingly, Southwest staff take an interest in the company's financial standing. Says pilot Chic Lang: 'It amazes me how you can go talk to a ramper or a flight attendant and they'll tell you what the stock price is that day.'[13]

The minimum wage check-out clerks at Wal-Mart wouldn't find that at all amazing. The closing price of Wal-Mart stock is broadcast daily over their store and warehouse intercoms and employees are kept abreast of their own store's weekly sales and profits. They have reason to care – profit sharing and stock ownership plans based on a stock that, between 1982 and 1992, multiplied in value 45 times. Wal-Mart employees work long hours for scant wages, but some retire with hundreds of thousands of dollars in the bank.

Starbuck's, like Wal-Mart, is a rarity in that it gives stock options to retail employees. Both the employees and the company have reaped benefits. CEO Howard Schultz, who gives every employee options called bean stock (as in jack and the beanstalk) recalls that 'bean stock began to affect people's attitudes and performance immediately. I started hearing comments like "I'm bean-stocking it" when someone figured out a way to save the company money. People started coming up with innovative ideas about how to cut costs, to increase sales, to create value. Most important, they could speak to our customers from the heart, as partners in the business. And that, I think has made all the difference.'[14]

Jim Buckley has noticed a similar effect at W. L. Gore. 'People own part of the company and want it to prosper,' he says. 'We don't talk about expense, we talk about investments. Any money that goes out better work towards our goals.'

But it's not just being a stockholder that gives that feeling of ownership, he adds. It's also having the leeway to make decisions that matter. 'Over 50 per cent of our associates say they are leaders of their plant or company,' says Buckley. 'Their thinking goes something like this: "If there's a decision that impacts me or where I work I can have a say in that decision. Consequently, I'm a leader in my division."'

Respect

Wacky companies give their people the chance to feel like leaders. They invariably have a high opinion of their employees – and of their potential employees (the admiration often extends to people in general).

Something we heard from virtually every company representative was that wacky leaders expect ordinary people to be capable of great things, and they are rarely disappointed.

'Bill's belief in people was very high,' says Jim Buckley about his late boss Bill Gore. 'We believe people can walk, talk and chew gum at the same time, and if people are given good information, they can make good decisions. Family units do it all the time. Bill Gore tried to do everything he could to perpetuate that feeling that people are capable. We believe you give people all the information they need and they'll do a good job. They prefer to do good work.'

'You assume that every switchboard operator will excel and they will,' says Richard Branson. 'The girl who opened what will be the best bridal shop in Europe was flying on the airline as an air hostess. She came to me with an idea and I said, "Go to it." She did. Now it's Virgin Bride. By having the freedom to prove herself, she has excelled.'[15]

'I think our story proves there's absolutely no limit to what plain, ordinary, working people can accomplish if they're given the opportunity and the encouragement to do their best,' wrote Wal-Mart founder Sam Walton in his autobiography.

This sentiment is echoed by Richer Sounds: 'We believe in the worth and value of people; that our colleagues are the most important assets. Respect of the individual is an overriding principle. We believe in positive reinforcement. That is, people being encouraged from mutually high expectations and peer review rather than table pounding managers, that average people should be made to feel winners with the maximum freedom and independence within an outer framework of discipline, responsibility and common sense.'[16]

'People don't set low targets [for themselves]; they always set them very high. People act like that. If it's 100 per cent your target you always over-optimise yourself,' says SOL CEO Liisa Joronen.

Responsibility

Valuing people also means giving them the freedom to fulfil their potential.

The Wisconsin-based Quad/Graphics has more than 5,300 employees, but only 12 executive officers.[17] The printer can operate with such a lean team because it gives its hourly workers extraordinary responsibility. In 1973, for example, when founder and CEO Harry Quadracci brought in new presses, he refused to put anyone in charge of the pressroom. 'Just as each lawyer is a partner and runs his own part of the business, I said each pressman is going to run his own press,' said Quadracci. Other managers objected on the grounds that it would fragment management. 'That sounds like a good idea,' said Quadracci. 'Let's fragment management.'[18]

Daniel M. Kehrer, in his 1989 book *Doing Business Boldly: the Art of Taking Risks*, describes Quad/Graphics' career track: 'Elsewhere it might take someone eight to ten years to become first pressman, the person in charge of the press and the five member crew it takes to run it. Even then, he'd still be an hourly wage earner. Quad has compressed that time to three to five years. Its first pressmen have been as young as 22 years old. They become salaried managers with a say in all areas that affect their press.'

Another principle of Quadracci's has been called management by walking away. When it was decided that the company's delivery drivers should carry loads on their return journey to make the trips more profitable, the drivers asked what they should carry and how they should find it. Quadracci reportedly said: 'How should I know? I don't know anything about driving an 18-wheeler. I'm not going to carry your loads.'[19]

Quadracci trusts his workers enough to take his entire management team off site for two to three days a year for a planning retreat called Quad University, leaving the plant entirely in the hands of the hourly staff.

Much of what we've described as pride – the trust, the responsibility, the value placed on employees – is effectively empowerment – or giving people the power they need to get the job done.

Empowered employees are proven value-adders. A 1996 study by the University of Southern California's Centre for Business Effectiveness found that companies with 'high use of power-sharing programs' had a 10.3 per cent return on sales compared to a 6.3 per cent return among low-use organisations. In addition, in a 1995 *Personnel Journal* reader survey, 81 per cent said they thought an empowered workforce is 'worth the time and energy it takes to create', and 81 per cent said it would be an 'integral part of workplaces in the future'.[20]

As Ricardo Semler, Liisa Joronen, Lars Kolind, and other empowering leaders have discovered, once you have an empowered workforce, a process of continuous change is almost inevitable as workers grow in their confidence to make increasingly radical decisions.

When Ricardo Semler, for example, first formed factory committees to enable employees to participate in management decisions, the committees concerned themselves, predictably, with issues such as money and other factors affecting their own conditions of work. As they grew more confident, however, and as Semler's radical new culture took hold, they began to take bigger and bigger decisions, examining and improving on production methods and processes and, eventually, reinventing the way the company worked.

Trust

Wacky companies can give employees more responsibility than other employers do because they trust their employees more than other employers do.

In virtually all of our wacky companies, managers and employees trust each other to use common sense, to act in the company's best interest, to treat others with respect, to behave like adults, to do the right thing and to get the job done. This frees up enormous resources that would otherwise be consumed in checks and balances – the punch clocks, rule books, supervisors and job descriptions – for use in productivity and innovation.

Management writer Tom Peters, in his book *The Pursuit of Wow!*, relates an experiment in which two groups of executives were given identical information about a difficult policy decision. One group was briefed to expect trusting behaviour from each other; the other group was told to expect untrusting behaviour. Even in such an obviously artificial setting, the trusting group reported significantly better decisions. In addition, trust group members reported being more open with their feelings, experiencing greater clarity about the group's goals and searching for more alternative solutions.

A large part of SOL's success is due to the trust it places in its employees. Armed with portable computers and mobile phones, staff can work wherever they like, at home or in the office, and are trusted to keep a tally of their own hours, provided they meet democratically voted annual performance targets.

'If you trust your people 100 per cent, they will do almost anything for you,' says Joronen – or Liisa as she is known to everyone in the company. 'Happy and satisfied people do better work. Left to their own devices they also set higher targets.'

Trust works both ways in organisations, as Rhino Food CEO Ted Castle reminds us: 'People don't come to work for a company and trust that company right off the bat. It takes a number of years for people to develop trust for their employer.'[21]

A sense of belonging

A great many wacky companies look like one big family: Quad, Hershey and SWA all boast a lot of couples, siblings, children and various relatives among their staff. In some cases this is typical of large employers in small towns (who else are you going to work for in Hershey, Pennsylvania?). In many cases, though, it's a result of choice and personal recommendation.

Southwest Airlines, for example, has 300 married couples on staff, and more than half of Quad/Graphics' employees have relatives working for the company. Semco gives preferential hiring treatment to friends and relations (though not immediate family members) of its employees.

As with families, when people are proud of their company – and vice versa – they show it, with company mementoes and photos for all to see. The reception area at Great Plains Software in Fargo, North Dakota, for example, boasts a showcase with photos of everyone who works for the company, listed by first name. A map hung outside the human resources offices shows each employee's hometown with a pin and a flag with his or her name attached. Great Plains sends a press release to the local newspaper for every new employee.

At Southwest Airline's Dallas HQ, instead of art on walls, there are hundreds of photos of employees at parties – parties that mark both personal and professional milestones.

Also like families, wacky companies make allowances for eccentricities and give people permission to try and fail; they can also be fraught with emotion, intrusiveness and expectations.

Says erstwhile Smith & Hawken employee Meredith Maran: 'I realise that Smith & Hawken's corporate culture is best described by one word: emotion. In this beauty-driven company, love – or its dark side – charges each interaction. Everything – job descriptions, salaries, hirings, and firings – *everything* – is personal. The same brilliant, impulsive man who hired all these wonderful people has built a company as manic as he is. Smith & Hawken weeps, exults, sulks, coos, rages. It puts its arms around me and squeezes tight.'[22]

Southwest, too, is imbued with emotion. 'Love' and 'someone up there loves you' were early marketing themes at Southwest, and the concept has stuck. Now the company's NYSE symbol is LUV, and Southwest management goes to great lengths to make staff and customers feel loved. Everyone of the 23,700 employees gets a birthday card. There are cards, too, when people get married or have babies.

Affection has long been rife at Virgin, too – especially in the early days. The cousin of one employee who worked on Branson's first commercial venture, a student magazine, recalls his initial impressions of the fledgling entrepreneur. On arriving at the magazine's London offices, he was surprised to be greeted by Branson with a kiss. 'I thought, Christ, this is odd, but also what an interesting and exciting place to be – because it was a friendly kiss.'[23]

One British computer company has even quantified the amount of emotion needed to keep things running smoothly. At Happy Computers' London offices, a poster proclaims 'We need hugs. Four a day for survival, eight a day for maintenance and twelve a day for growth.' 'People work best when they feel good about themselves and the role of management is to make them feel good.' Explains managing director Henry Stewart, 'Hugging builds supportive relationships. The hugs are part of a supportive, fun, open atmosphere at the aptly named Happy that includes hiring an adult-sized bouncy castle for each annual general meeting. Employees, like trainer Mat Hirst, seem to like it. 'I could earn a lot more elsewhere but I choose not to because the atmosphere here is so supportive and nurturing,' he says.[24]

While Happy Computers, Virgin and Southwest promote love, Rosenbluth International opts for friendship. 'Our company is built on something that's foreign to most companies,' CEO Hal Rosenbluth told *Fast Company* magazine. 'We're a company built on friendship. When I was in college, I was taught not to work with friends because you can't get productivity out of them, you can't make the tough decisions.' But, he argues, 'it's exactly when things get tough that you want to work with your friends. In fact, if your people are anything less than that during a downswing, you're in trouble.'

If that's the case, the people at Great Plains Software should do well in good times and bad. 'Everybody here is your friend, they're not just your co-worker,' says Kevin Montplaisir, an applications development systems analyst. 'And the projects, they're team efforts, they're not something where, if something goes wrong, you lay the blame on somebody, or point the finger.' Adds Spider Johnck, a creative marketing director: 'There's a real blur between the time that people are working and the time that they're socialising.'[25]

All new hires at Great Plains have lunch with president Doug Burgum. Denise Johnson, who works in marketing, told the editors of The 100 Best Companies to Work for in America, 'I thought it was very unusual for the president of a company to ask questions and actually want to know about me – my hometown and my life. It made me feel like I was really part of the team.'

All this teamwork has helped Great Plains reach second place in terms of revenue from small business accounting packages, and has kept employee turnover down to 7 per cent – extremely low in the software industry.[26]

Not all wacky companies adopt the family model. 'We are not a family at Netscape,' insists CEO Jim Barksdale. 'That would put a lot of pressure on me. It would mean I'm the dad. Think of Netscape as a basketball team,' he suggests, 'opportunistic on offence, tenacious on defence. Then I can be the coach.'[27]

Security

An important part of being valued, and proud, is a sense of security. Because wacky companies do not just rent their employees' hearts and minds, they can't let them go when they face a downturn.

At Southwest, though people have been fired, no employee has ever been laid off (except three released and immediately rehired in 1973). 'We probably fire fewer people than other companies,' says vice president, people, Libby Sartain. 'If we do, it's usually in the first six months, and usually for absences or for not fitting into the culture.'

Consistent growth means Southwest has never had to face lay-offs. Other wacky companies haven't been as fortunate. They have faced downturns, and while they try to be supportive of their employees, they are sometimes forced to cut the payroll. Some have solved this problem as they solve most things – by thinking outside the box.

In 1993, dessert maker Rhino Foods had a temporary overload of ten production jobs, a quarter of its workforce. Ted Castle, president and owner, asked the workers themselves to help determine how to avoid lay-offs. With the help of Marlene Dailey, director of HR, ten volunteer employees found foster jobs in other local companies. 'They said that no one had tried this before and that we as a company would be sticking our neck out,' quality assurance technician Stephen Mayo told *Personnel Journal*. Jobs were guaranteed on return and volunteers kept their seniority and benefits. Rhino even topped up salaries where the foster employer paid less than Rhino. 'People ask me if I'd do it again,' says Mayo. 'In a heartbeat. It's like a vacation: you go somewhere a few months knowing you'll be secure here. You know you're eventually coming home. And it's nice to get back home.'[28]

The system also avoided the morale devastation that's inevitable with big lay-offs. Says Dailey: 'If we got to an area where we'd have to downsize again, we'd absolutely consider that,' she says. 'It was a really effective [initiative] during a potentially devastating time. It turned out to be scary and tense, but it really ended up cementing the team.'

Ben & Jerry's, a customer of Rhino's, tried a similar scheme in 1991 when one production line was closed for three and a half months. Instead of being laid off during that period, about 35 people remained on the payroll to do odd jobs around the plant and in the community, such as painting fire hydrants and winterising homes for elderly people.

Virgin, too, faced this issue. Says Richard Branson: 'It was in the depths of the recession. We had 400 too many people. I went to the staff, explained the situation and asked for advice about what to do. Many letters came back with ideas. Many people – people who could afford it and for whom it worked for other reasons – volunteered to take anywhere from three to six months off as a sort of sabbatical. Six hundred volunteered. As soon as we could, we brought them back in when we were expanding again. When they came back, they were rested, inspired, and very happy to return.'[29]

'If you survey your company – in a secret, confidential survey that won't affect anyone's job – you'd find that 15 or 20 per cent of the people could at times afford it and would love it. More female than male, probably. Certainly many people with young children. But they would never suggest it themselves; they would be frightened that it would look as if they were less committed to the company. The truth is, it could make them more committed. And prove your commitment to them,' says Branson.[30]

Semco, dealing with the dramatic vicissitudes of the Brazilian economy, came up with a system called the Satellite Program to avoid having to make large-scale redundancies. The programme helped employees set up their own businesses by helping them find suitable premises, leasing them machinery at favourable rates, and firing them (they got better government severance pay that way). Though Semco couldn't guarantee these satellites any business, by 1993, half of Semco's manufacturing had been turned over to satellites run by ex-employees. Says Semler: 'The Satellite Program is an extension of our philosophy of empowerment. Our new entrepreneurs have complete control over their workplace − at least the control an owner has. They are almost always even more productive than they were at Semco.'

Springfield Remanufacturing will also help employees launch their own businesses, funding them up to 80 per cent. Many have become suppliers to SRC, but some have become competitors.

And, through Ben & Jerry's Entrepreneurial Fund, half the proceeds from factory tours go to award low-interest loans to people starting new businesses, including employees. To receive funding, the new businesses must have a socially acceptable theme.

Involvement − information

Most wacky leaders believe that the more employees know, the more they can do. They encourage open communication, from open doors to open books.

The method of preference is face-to-face, informal, and immediate; executives are uncommonly accessible too.

Rebecca Jenkins, MD of UK trucking company the Lane Group, briefs the company's drivers about developments in the company, in person. 'At my first drivers' meeting,' she recalls, 'only two drivers turned up. Now we have 90 per cent attendance because they want to know what's going on in the company.'

All Rosenbluth offices post schedules for company meetings, and any associate can attend. Or, if they really want to know what's going on, they can hang out with a top executive for a day. Jeanine Shumaker had been in the company's communications department for just a month when she signed up to shadow CEO Hal Rosenbluth. When he suddenly had to make a trip to Mexico City on that date, Shumaker went along. 'I just sat there with my mouth dropped open and thought, this is too cool,' she told *Fast Company* magazine. 'We were acquiring another travel agency, so I made a role for myself communicating that while I was down there. I was able to contribute.'

Wacky companies take the time to keep employees informed, and make it a priority even when faced with pressing production demands. Rhino Foods, for example, shuts down for half an hour every other week for a two-way, company-wide meeting. 'It really makes a difference – in people getting to know each other, in people knowing what's going on in the company and really feeling connected to it,' says human resources director Marlene Dailey.[31]

There are few walls, real or figurative, in wacky companies. People don't divide into fiefdoms. In some cases this is because everyone does every job anyway. In others, where the business dictates that jobs are arranged functionally, people make a point of trying out each others' jobs. That way, everyone can see what the others up are to, and up against.

When UNBT senior vice president Suzanne Powers saw friction developing between the tellers and the back office people who process the tellers' transactions, she had them switch jobs for a few days. 'They both thought the other group didn't appreciate the challenges of their own job,' Powers told *Inc*. The tension was diffused.

The Lane Group operates a job swap scheme which allows drivers to take a turn in the office and office staff to spend time on the road with the drivers. Senior managers are also expected to muck in. 'Directors will go out and work a night shift or spend the day with a driver,' says CEO Rebecca Jenkins. 'It's not compulsory, but it is part of the way things are done around here, and they know that I expect it.' Does that apply to the managing director? 'I worked the night shift in our Hayes depot three weeks ago,' she says.

IKEA makes sure that managers keep in touch with their co-workers by holding 'anti-bureaucrat weeks'. For one week each year managers abandon their desks to work in stores or warehouses.

At Semco, employees are encouraged to exchange jobs with one another. The onus, however, is on them to find another employee to swap with. They may then spend up to a year planning and training each other before making the move. Semler estimates that less than a third of managers haven't swapped jobs at least once, with about 20–25 per cent changing each year. 'We felt that a minimum of two years and a maximum of five years in a job were ample,' says Semler.

At SOL, employees are expected to spend a proportion of their time away from their normal functions doing other types of work. One reason is to help cover holiday leave, but it also helps employees gain skills in other areas.

Employees at wacky companies also have access to financial and other information that, as former VeriFone CEO Hatim Tyabji, puts it, 'most companies would be *appalled* by'.[32] Let them be appalled. Most working people like to know what's going on. It's a truism that information is power, but it's also useful and motivating.

To many working people, information is more important than money. According to the 1994 National Study of the Changing Workforce, conducted by New York's Families and Work Institute, 'open communication' was ranked highest by respondents asked to list items they had considered to be 'very important' in choosing their current jobs. Salary ranked sixteenth.[33]

All VeriFone's corporate information is available online, world-wide, for immediate access. The company's top 250 people, for example, can track sales down to the last day, even the last hour. Another system posts the travel itineraries of everyone in the company.

Grocery chain Whole Foods provides all its staff with figures on store sales, team sales, profit margins, even salaries – a book in each store lists salaries and bonuses for all employees by name. The company's books are so open that the US Securities and Exchanges Commission has designated all 6,500 employees 'insiders' for stock-trading purposes.[34] CEO John Mackey calls it a 'no-secrets' management philosophy. 'In most companies,' he says, 'management controls information and therefore controls people. By sharing information, we stay aligned to the vision of shared fate.' 'If you're trying to create a high-trust organisation,' he says, 'an organisation where people are all-for-one and one-for-all, you can't have secrets.'[35]

Ricardo Semler, who gives employees access to financial information to help them sort out their own salaries and bonuses, would agree. 'No one,' he says 'can expect the spirit of involvement and partnership to flourish without an abundance of information available even to the most humble employee.'

Of course, most humble employees don't have a degree in financial management. Making the books accessible can take more than simple opening them up.

At Wisconsin Label, for example, manager Terry Fulwiler asked employees to enact the roles of various costs, then handed out play money to dramatise the balance sheet. At Foldcraft Furniture, manager Chuck Mayhew used a cookie recipe as a metaphor for purchasing, production and sales. Ron Eardley, former president of Image National, a sign manufacturer in Boise, Idaho, used a giant dollar to illustrate the company's revenues, which Eardly sliced up as his chief financial officer enumerated costs.[36]

Few companies, though, have gone further than Springfield Remanufacturing, a Missouri-based engine re-fitter that shuts down for half an hour each week so employees can study the latest financial statements and keep up with what their CEO, Jack Stack, calls the 'Great Game of Business'. In 1980, the company was almost suffocated by a 172-day strike at its parent company, International Harvester. Stack, then a plant manager at the parent company, organised a buyout. At 89 per cent debt, it was one of the most leveraged buyouts in history, yet the new company continued to lose money. 'I felt the only way to turn things around was to get people to think like owners,' says Stack. Handing over stock wasn't enough. 'I needed to teach anyone who moved a broom or operated a grinder everything the bank lender knew. That way they could really understand how every nickel saved could make a difference.'[37]

In 1994, Springfield invested $300,000 in financial training, six times what it spent on upgrading production skills for its 800 employees. Now, each week the company cafeteria resonates with talk of margins and costs of goods sold, and of the score in the game – Stack talks about business in terms of a game: one that people will enjoy once they know the rules. Not surprisingly the company is back in the black and distributing big bonuses. It's employee-owned, too.

Finding the right people

A critical part of instilling pride among workers is attracting the right workers in the first place. This is rarely a problem for wacky companies – most are caught in a virtuous circle that makes it easy for them to attract and keep the people they want.

First, of course, are their reputations as good employers and fun places to work. This alone helps wacky employers attract talent even in high-tech and low-wage industries, where recruitment can be tight and competitive.

Second, because each has a clear and different philosophy, these companies find it relatively easy to attract like-minded people – people who instinctively understand and interpret the company's values. There are, after all, a lot more off-beat people looking for jobs than companies willing to let them be themselves at work.

Employees whose own values match those of their employer – especially if those values find little representation elsewhere – are more likely to take pride in their own achievements and in the company's achievements, and will go the extra mile to ensure the enterprise succeeds. They are also more likely to stay working for a company they admire. This can only be good for customer retention, productivity – and profits.

Of course, much as they might want to work for a given wacky company, not all applicants have the right stuff. And that 'right stuff' doesn't necessarily show up on a CV. In fact, it hardly ever does. When wacky companies screen applicants, they're mostly concerned about talent, values and attitude. They're less concerned with formal qualifications, and they care nothing at all for such trivia as gender, race and social class. And, if they have an age preference, it's usually to favour groups that their more narrow-minded competitors have overlooked.

Like the army and the marines, many wacky companies prefer their recruits young, inexperienced and idealistic. At Australian music retailer Sanity, for example, inexperience is definitely an advantage. According to *Australia's Business Review* weekly, the chain prefers to hire store staff who are friendly, knowledgeable about music, ambitious – and untainted by other retailers.

At Toronto TV station Citytv, job-hunting media studies graduates may be disappointed. Newsroom director Stephen Hurlbut started out as a cameraman and one star reporter was originally a maître d' who talked CEO Moses Znaimer into a job when he walked into his restaurant.

British vacuum cleaner designer James Dyson prefers to hire young people right out of university, on the grounds that their minds have yet to be warped by big business and they are still open to new ideas and working methods. The average age of Dyson's employees is 25. His marketing manager was appointed when just 23 years old, the head of engineering at 28, and the head of graphics at 27.

UNBT, California's Un-bank, went the other way, snapping up experienced fifty-somethings who'd been downsized from more narrow-minded banks. These bankers commanded higher salaries, but their judgement and productivity more than compensated.

All of these employers recognise that the right attitudes and fit with the company values are more important, and harder to come by, than the requisite skills and experience. You can always train for skills, they reason, but trying to change attitudes is a losing battle.

At Rosenbluth International, CEO Hal Rosenbluth has never had a secretary who could type, but they have all been friendly. Said one company recruiter: 'Nice is mandatory. We can train people to do anything technical, but we can't make them nice.'[38]

Nice can be a hard thing to judge, and an easy thing to fake for the duration of a job interview. Rosenbluth recruiters have ways of getting round this. Rosenbluth himself likes to interview potential executives while playing basketball with them. 'I like to see who's passing the ball, who's hogging it, who's taking shots they shouldn't,' he says.[39] Other recruiters will put their candidates behind the wheel of a car. The reason: it's tough to put on an act or be someone other than who you really are when you're behind the wheel in city traffic.[40]

At Patagonia, employees are outdoors enthusiasts first, designers and marketers second. In its hiring, Patagonia still seeks out 'dirt bags'. 'These are the passionate outdoor people who are our core customers,' writes Chouinard. 'We believe that it is easier to teach these people business than to turn a businessman into a passionate outdoor person.' As Mike Mesko, a Patagonia buyer and forecaster told *Wired* magazine: 'You don't *have* to climb Mount Everest to work on our team. If you were into, oh, long-distance running at high altitudes, that would be OK.'

Says HR director Terri Wolfe: 'We believe in hiring people, who are our core product users and ecologists. We know that we can teach them about our business, where we may not be able to teach a technical business person to love our products and the environment. Those with a passion for our products can quickly learn a number of jobs at Patagonia, appropriate to what they like to do. This keeps the employee–user–customer continuum alive. Many of our jobs do require technical expertise; we maintain a bias towards hiring outdoor people who have the necessary qualifications. We take a long time to hire the right outside person each time.'[41]

Others disagree. As former Patagonia chief financial officer Galliano Mondin told *Inc.* magazine: 'I could never get at why these people were hired. Some guy would come in. They'd give him a psychological test and say, "Yeah, he's the right person for Patagonia," but that person had no business being there.'[42]

At Southwest, it is more important to fit in with Southwest's caring culture than to demonstrate ruthless efficiency. Says vice president, people, Libby Sartain: 'We've had executives who stepped on lots of toes and left dead bodies in their paths but got their projects in on time, and they didn't understand why we objected. We'd rather people took longer on the job and did it with more sensitivity and teamwork.'

Says British consultant Adrian Simpson, who spent some time studying with Southwest: 'What they have created is freedom in a framework. And it's an explicit deal. You have to buy into the values. It's the Southwest way – if you don't fit, it will eject you very quickly and quite harshly. But it's so explicit so that seems fair to me.'

But is it really fair? It's quite understandable that companies want to screen people to fit with, say, a belief in teamwork, or a positive attitude toward customer service. Many of our wacky companies have, however, taken up activities and philosophies that extend beyond the conventional sphere of business and into such former no-go areas as politics, society, and even family values. Does fitting in require ideological conformity as well? Have some of these employers crossed the line to where they demand that employees conform, not just in their actions, but in their beliefs as well?

No one wants to enforce conformity. There is, however, a bias towards certain social values evident in some company hiring practices. At Ben & Jerry's, says info queen Mitch Curren, values do matter. 'We attract and try to hire the type of people who understand the values-led aspect of our business, what it is to do business with a social mission component, and that it's their responsibility to work those social responsibilities into their day-to-day decision making. We do look for progressive social values in hiring.'

And those values don't always sit right with employees. 'Some people have left the company because they couldn't stay with a company that, for instance, treats gays equally. But they left because of their own convictions,' she says. Most, however, stay. Ben & Jerry's have, according to Curren, a very low staff turnover. As a mid-nineties staff survey indicated, over 90 per cent of Ben & Jerry's employees say they chose to work for the company because of its values.

Patagonia has been accused of what a 1992 *Inc.* article described as a stifling, cult-like atmosphere, and a pervading eco-orthodoxy. Employees were given, wrote Edward Welles, 'not-so-subtle pressure to contribute time and money to Chouinard's causes and to look upon their employment at Patagonia as a calling, not just a job'.[43]

Public affairs director Lu Setnicka has heard it all before. In an unprompted response to accusations of mind control, she says: 'We're not walking around like Stepford Wives. People here are encouraged to challenge the status quo, and to present their points of view, even though they may not always match what the company wants. Once a month we have an open forum for all employees, the objective of which is to share information and get questions and concerns out. It's an open mike, everyone has a chance to speak.'

Hiring for values has created some difficulties for companies like Ben & Jerry's and Patagonia, notably in finding a balance between uniformity and diversity, between people who share the values and people who bring in new ideas and needed skills and experience. Both companies have had problems finding like-minded people at a senior level.

For Starbuck's CEO Howard Schultz, it's precisely at the senior level where he most wants to see values that match with his own. 'Whether I'm hiring a key executive, selecting an investment banker, or assessing a partner in a joint venture, I look for the same kind of qualities most people look for in choosing a spouse: integrity and passion. To me, they're just as important as experience and abilities. I want to work with people who don't leave their values at home but bring them to work, people whose principles match my own. If I see a mismatch or a vacuum where values would be, I prefer to keep looking.'[44]

Joe Boxer's chief underpants officer Nicholas Graham would have to look long and hard to find someone (other than Joe Boxer) whose bizarre world-view matches his own, and it's comforting to know that he's not even looking for clones. For all the company's outrageous antics, you don't have to be crazy to work there. In fact, says Graham 'boring and normal is something I require of the accounting people'. As for the others? 'Joe Boxer is not a particular person. I don't say who is and who isn't a Joe Boxer person.'

Those who do make the mark at wacky companies tend to stay. Rosenbluth International, for example, has a staff turnover of 12 per cent, as opposed to the industry average of 30 to 50 per cent.[45]

At St. Luke's not one member of staff has left to join a competitor since the company was founded. At Ben & Jerry's, staff turnover is only 12 per cent. Not bad, in what is essentially low skilled, manual work.

Odetics employee turnover is about 10 per cent, or half the rate in comparable high-tech companies. Gore's employee turnover is about half to two-thirds of the national average, according to associate Jim Buckley. At Southwest, too, turnover is low, about 6 per cent, with many employees having 25 years or more of service.

Developing people in line with the values

Managers at wacky companies know that the first days in a new job can affect a new employee's morale, learning speed, attitude about the company and acceptance of the culture, so they put as much effort into orientation as they do into recruiting.

Every new recruit at Richer Sounds is assigned a mentor or buddy who shadows them for the first month providing advice and guidance. Often the shadows are junior members of staff themselves. Giving them this responsibility early on in their career is a demonstration of the trust Richer has in its employees.

At W. L. Gore, according to associate Jim Buckley, 'We spend a week with new associates to help them understand our culture, values and philosophy – this is full time, they don't go to work until they've had this training.'

At MEMC Electronic Materials in St Peters, Missouri, operations manager Mike Benton assigns new hires to write a research paper. New supervisory and management level employees spend their first four weeks researching and writing a report about part of the manufacturing process. They then tag along with a company veteran for several weeks before taking on any management responsibility. The recruits also receive a workbook filled with hundreds of questions about every part of the company. This forces them to talk to a wide variety of co-workers – people they might not otherwise meet. 'It's designed to get people outside their department,' says Don Otto, director of employee relations.[46]

Rosenbluth International employees are inculcated in that company's culture from day one. Everyone, no matter where they are hired, or for what job, comes to Philadelphia for a two-day orientation at the firm's training centre. They learn about the Rosenbluth philosophy through role-playing, skits, even finger painting. Day one ends with a high-tea service on white linen, often hosted by CEO Hal Rosenbluth. Says Rosenbluth executive Frank Hoffman: 'The main purpose is for them to experience service that's a cut above,' he says. 'The product means nothing – in this case it's water and tea bags – but the way you do it is everything.'[47]

The Rosenbluth orientation includes a 'goodies bag' to welcome new arrivals on their first day, including lunch coupons, 'cheat-sheets' that introduce co-workers, office supplies, and gag gifts like balloons.

'When people start a new job, they start with a very positive attitude. We want them to maintain it,' says Keami Lewis, Rosenbluth International's manager, culture development. 'If they're happy, they'll contribute more, they'll make better decisions, serve clients better, and be better to work with and better to work for. This is a way to say "Welcome to the team," to continue that good feeling. When you put together a new team, or change the dynamics of a team, you have to address trust, involvement and friendship so they'll immediately start to feel part of the team.'[48]

Training

Employees, new and long-standing, also have plenty of opportunity for training and development at wacky companies – not surprising really, if you hire for attitude that you need to train for skill.

Staff at Quad/Graphics, for example, train each other, in their own unpaid time, on topics ranging from press operations to improving interview skills.

James Duffy, manager of employee development at Applied Materials Inc., in Santa Clara, California, took a Quad factory tour. 'I was impressed with how they integrate new employees into the teams that operate the presses. All the training is done in unpaid time. Instructors aren't paid. I asked, "What's the cost per student?" and the education teacher said, "A buck and a half." It's amazing. The people are highly invested in the company emotionally. Their training curriculum is pretty heavily operations and technology oriented. That makes sense when you see how capital intensive the [printing] business is. They do a good job hammering home what they expect of the employee.'[49]

At IKEA, training concentrates on both skill development and personal development. 'A company that doesn't train and develop people,' says IKEA Sweden purchasing manager Sven Kulldorf, 'is no good.'

At SOL, CEO Liisa Joronen uses training to give employees a view of the bigger picture – how the business works and what part they play within it. Joronen trains staff not just in their own jobs, but also to see how the business works and what part they play within it. Staff take, and are tested on, seven, four-month-long training modules covering subjects such as budgeting, people skills and time-management, which are far beyond the scope of their own jobs.

The emphasis the Lane Group, a British transport company, places on training is borne out by its training budget, which is almost double the national average.

The costs of pride

Sometimes, being a good employer can backfire in unexpected ways.

Starbuck's, the American coffee house chain, broke new ground by paying its counter staff more than minimum wage, offering health benefits and stock options even to part-timers, referring to staff as partners rather than employees, and generally treating them with respect. As a result, the company attracted a higher than average standard of fast food worker – so many university students, part-time novelists and starving artists took jobs behind the counter at Starbuck's that the company gained a reputation as a hot bed of wanna-be intellectuals.

What happened? Instead of following the normal fast food career path of working their way through school, then moving on to more substantial careers after graduation, employees, especially in areas (like Canada) that offered relatively few employment alternatives, began to see work at Starbuck's as a permanent career.

These employees noticed that in a single month (April 1997) Starbuck's had produced revenues of almost $70 million – 35 per cent more than the same period in 1996. They also noticed that Starbuck's was expanding at the rate of millfoil weed in a warm lake, with new outlets popping up at the rate of one per day, and had even raised the price of its products – all without, in their view, passing any benefits on to employees. Some hourly staff began to agitate for even better pay and conditions and, in a few locations, unionised, worked to rule, and even walked off the job.

Though employees at wacky companies rarely express their disappointment quite so stridently, wacky employers do often face – and occasionally fail to live up to – high employee expectations. This can be a real problem at some socially responsible organisations, where employees join hoping to contribute to social change and find there's still a lot of hard, boring work to be done. 'There's always the tension between doing employee-backed social ventures and getting the job done,' says Ben & Jerry's Mitch Curren. 'Somebody's got to make the ice cream. How do you get the ice cream made yet find ways to get people off the line?'

'One of the problems at Smith & Hawken, says former editorial director Meredith Maran, 'was that you had a bunch of people walking around with this non-profit mentality, acting like they were working for Greenpeace instead of a direct mail business.'

Says Craig Cox, editor of *Business Ethics* magazine: 'Employee expectations are often so high, they're impossible to manage. If you come to work for a socially responsible company, you expect to have more flexibility, more informal relations with supervisors, the autonomy to fashion the job the way you choose. It can be quite a shock to find out that the visionary founder is not an attentive manager or that there's still a hierarchy and still some lousy grunt work that somebody is going to tell you to get done.'[50]

THE BOTTOM LINE

▶ Pride is what makes employees go the extra mile.

▶ Pride comes from feeling valued.

▶ Pride comes from *sharing* values – when the company, the employees, and the customers all espouse the same beliefs about what counts.

▶ Track record is less important in hiring decisions than values fit.

NOTES

1. David Sheff, 'Interview with Richard Branson', in *ASAP Forbes*, 24 February 1997.
2. Terri Wolfe, in a speech to the American Apparel Manufacturer's Association, October 1996. Patagonia Web site: www.patagonia.com.
3. Ben Cohen and Jerry Greenfield, *Ben & Jerry's Double Dip: Lead with Your Values and Make Money Too* (Simon & Schuster, New York, 1997).
4. 'Long Road to a Big Clean-up', in *The Times*, 30 July 1998.
5. Kevin Freiberg and Jackie Freiberg, *Nuts! Southwest Airlines' Crazy Recipe for Business and Personal Success* (Orion Business, 1998).
6. Kevin Freiberg and Jackie Freiberg, *Nuts!*, 1998.
7. Fred Lager, *Ben & Jerry's: The Inside Scoop — How Two Real Guys Built a Business with a Social Conscience and a Sense of Humor* (Crown Publishers, New York, 1994).
8. Fred Lager, *Ben & Jerry's*, 1994.
9. Calvin Trillin, 'Competitors', in *The New Yorker*, quoted in Lager, the *Inside Scoop*, 1994.
10. B. O'Reilly, 'The Secrets of America's Most Admired Corporations: New Ideas, New Products', in *Fortune*, 3 March 1997.
11. Bob Nelson, 'Dump the Cash, Load on the Praise', in *Personnel Journal*, July 1996.
12. Elizabeth Conlin, 'Small Business: Second Thoughts on Growth' in *Inc.*, March 1991.
13. Kevin Freiberg and Jackie Freiberg, *Nuts!*, 1998.
14. Howard Schultz and Dori Jones Yang, *Pour Your Heart Into It* (Hyperion, 1997).
15. David Sheff, in *ASAP Forbes Online*, 24 February 1997.
16. Richer Sounds' Web site.
17. Robert Levering and Milton Moskowitz, *The 100 Best Companies to Work for in America* (Doubleday, New York, 1993).
18. Daniel M. Kehrer, *Doing Business Boldly: The Art of Taking Risks* (Random House, 1989).
19. Robert Levering and Milton Moskowitz, *The 100 Best Companies*, 1993.
20. Gillian Flynn, 'Why Rhino Won't Wait 'Til Tomorrow', in *Personnel Journal*, July 1996.
21. Gillian Flynn, 'Why Rhino Won't Wait 'Til Tomorrow', 1996.
22. Meredith Maran, *What It's Like to Live Now* (Bantam Books, 1995).
23. Mick Brown, *Richard Branson, The Authorised Biography* (Headline, April 1998).
24. Benady, Alex, 'How to be a Happy Company', *Real Business*, June 1997.
25. Robert Levering and Milton Moskowitz, *The 100 Best Companies*, 1993.
26. Robert Levering and Milton Moskowitz, *The 100 Best Companies*, 1993.
27. Bill Birchard, 'Hire Great People Fast', in *Fast Company*, August/September 1997.
28. Gillian Flynn, 'Why Rhino Won't Wait 'Til Tomorrow', 1996.
29. David Sheff, 'Interview with Richard Branson', 1997.
30. David Sheff, 'Interview with Richard Branson', 1997.

31. Gillian Flynn, 'Why Rhino Won't Wait 'Til Tomorrow', 1996.
32. W. Taylor, 'At VeriFone It's a Dog's Life (And They Love It!)', in *Fast Company*, November 1995.
33. Bob Nelson, 'Dump the Cash', 1996.
34. Charles Fishman, 'Whole Foods is All Teams', in *Fast Company*, April/May 1996.
35. Charles Fishman, 'Whole Foods is All Teams', 1996.
36. No author, 'You Gotta Get a Gimmick', in *Inc.*, November 1994.
37. J. Fierman, 'Winning Ideas From Maverick Managers', in *Fortune*, 6 February 1995.
38. Robert Levering and Milton Moskowitz, *The 100 Best Companies*, 1993.
39. *Inc.* magazine, quoted in Robert Levering and Milton Moskowitz, *The 100 Best Companies*, 1993.
40. Tom Peters, *The Pursuit of Wow! Every Person's Guide to Topsy-Turvy Times* (Vintage, 1994).
41. Terri Wolfe, in a speech to the American Apparel Manufacturer's Association, October 1996.
42. Edward O. Welles, 'Lost in Patagonia', in *Inc.*, August 1992.
43. Edward O. Welles, 'Lost in Patagonia', 1992.
44. Howard Schultz and Dori Jones Yang, *Pour Your Heart Into It* (Hyperion, 1997).
45. Robert Levering and Milton Moskowitz, *The 100 Best Companies*, 1993.
46. Bill Birchard, 'Hire Great People Fast', in *Fast Company*, August/September 1997.
47. Rob Walker, 'Back to the Farm', in *Fast Company*, February/March 1997.
48. Rob Walker, 'Back to the Farm', 1997.
49. Teri Lammers, 'Inc's Guide to Great Company Tours', in *Inc.*, July 1990.
50. Anne Murphy 'The Seven (Almost) Deadly Sins of High-Minded Entrepreneurs, in *Inc.*, July 1994.

8 Walking around corners backwards

'Above all else, innovation requires a willingness to embrace
chaos. It means giving rein to people who are opinionated, wilful
and delight in challenging the rules.' (Tim Brown, European
director of IDEO)

'Creative people always take two steps into the darkness. It's not
the two steps that's the important bit, it's the "always".' (?What if!
founder, Dave Allan)

Wacky companies take risks and steps into the unknown that more
conventional management teams wouldn't dream of or wouldn't
consider without so much time-consuming analysis that they miss
the opportunity. We call this 'walking round corners backwards',
because it demands a mixture of confidence, optimism and courage
rarely seen in business.

Wacky companies are usually the first in with new products, new
marketing concepts and, sometimes, whole new industries. Softbank's CEO Masayoshi Son, for example, made and designed a new
computer product while still in college; James Dyson's bagless
cleaner was the first major innovation in that humble appliance for
decades; the Body Shop has forever changed the way cosmetics are
marketed; and Virgin's new financial services arm looks set to
change the way that industry operates.

Wacky companies are also the first to try radically new working
practices. When Liisa Joronen founded SOL, her radical ideas on
worker participation were largely untested – as were Gore's and
Semler's, each arising independently in different corners of the
world. Joronen admits that when she decided to let workers set their
own performance targets, it was a step into the unknown. Many
outsiders were sceptical, but her belief, that 'people work better
when they manage themselves', has been vindicated. Today,
experimentation is a central feature of the company's philosophy

and Joronen regards it as a competitive weapon in the conservative business of industrial cleaning.

Visionary companies like SOL, and like Gore with its lattice organisation, VeriFone with its disregard for time and space, and Chiat/Day with its virtual office, have all changed the how, when, and where of business. Social responsibility-focused entrepreneurs, like Smith & Hawken, Ben & Jerry's and Patagonia, have each in their own way, redefined the why.

These companies repeatedly and consistently accomplish the impossible, often against great odds, inexperience and a shortage of cash. Sometimes it seems they operate on sheer nerve. Guts come into it, too, as does a certain amount of beginners' luck.

As Karson Druckamiller, one of Southwest Airline's original maintenance crew, says of the upstart airline's early days: 'Some things we did because we didn't know it couldn't be done.' Scott Johnson, a flight despatch specialist, relates a typical early flight crew conversation: 'No, I don't think there's a regulation against that. You're doing what?! No, I don't think that's illegal.'[1]

Inexperience, like tight time and cost constraints or difficult market conditions, faces every company at some point, usually early on. These conditions force companies to innovate or die. Wacky companies, invariably, choose to innovate.

Somehow, though, they always seem to do more than that. Where a conventional company may be able to *overcome* a financial squeeze or competitive challenge, wacky companies somehow twist these awkward situations right round to turn them to their advantage.

Richard Branson, for example, when he first launched Virgin Airlines, had to compete with British Airways, without a BA-sized marketing budget. His solution: turn himself into a walking, talking advertisement for the Virgin brand name.

Ben Cohen and Jerry Greenfield started their business short of ready cash and unencumbered by experience. So they made do, collecting rock ice straight from a frozen lake, offering suppliers payment in ice cream, and promoting the shop with carnival acts (starring themselves) rather than print advertising.

The two never hired a marketing think tank to create the irreverent, down home image that's been such a great part of their success. The hand-lettered packages; the flavours they invented themselves and the off-beat PR stunts that later became their trademark, were simply all they could afford at the time. But it worked, and they parlayed their funky, unpretentious image into a multi-million dollar company. Says former CEO Chico Lager, 'Ben & Jerry's had, more by accident and necessity than by design, perfectly positioned the company with a unique identity in the suddenly overcrowded superpremium market.'[2]

Later, when Ben & Jerry's faced what could have been a serious internal and image problem – the stepping down of the founder – they turned it into a public relations event. They ran a contest, called 'Yo! I Wanna Be CEO', inviting applicants to explain, in 100 words or less on a package top, why they wanted the top job at Ben & Jerry's. The contest wasn't a serious recruitment drive (they quietly visited a headhunter as well), but it did serve to turn a potentially negative situation into a media coup. Of the 22,000 applicants, many may have been aiming for the second prize: a lifetime supply of ice cream.

Wacky entrepreneurs don't have any advantage over the rest of us – most start out just as broke and inexperienced as the next entrepreneur. What makes them different in their attitude about risk, about possibilities, and about their own abilities?

The adventure grid

Wacky leaders have the confidence to walk around corners backwards because they combine two critical qualities: optimistic curiosity and self-belief. Optimistic curiosity is an almost childlike attribute – an insatiable interest in what would happen if; an ability to think the unthinkable and wonder how to make it work. Optimistic curiosity also involves an expectation that, even if this experiment doesn't work, it will lead to another that does, and impatience with those who prefer a more cautious approach.

Self-belief is what helps wacky entrepreneurs succeed against the odds. It consists of four key aspects:

- I'm right: I have a deep and clear belief in my own basic assumptions about the business, even if the details are not always as clear-cut.

- I *can*: I have the ability to make this happen, in spite of what others might say.
- *Other people will follow me*: if I show it can be done, if I have enough enthusiasm, then I will gather around me people who will help make it happen.
- *It's worth the risk*: trying and failing is always better than not trying at all.

Virgin's Richard Branson, probably more than any other leader, exemplifies these attributes. The travel mogul once told *Forbes* magazine that his next step is out to space. Virgin Space. 'I believe that there are enough people willing to pay large sums of money to be passengers on these flights to make it feasible in my lifetime. Eventually, Virgin Express will shuttle around space like we do in Europe. Mars ain't that far off. Who knows? It's virgin territory.'

Such a statement is typical of Branson. It shows his almost childlike desire to explore new horizons, and his unquestioning belief that new horizons can always be reached.

The matrix in figure 8.1 shows how powerful this combination of personality traits can be.

People and organisations that are low on both self-belief and optimistic curiosity ask 'Why change?' as a defence against doing things radically different. To them, creative ideas, challenging questions and steps into the unknown are unnecessary risks.

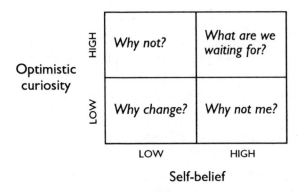

Figure 8.1 Combinations of personality traits

People and organisations with high optimistic curiosity and low self-belief are happy to talk about new ideas and concepts, but constrained about genuinely putting them into practice. They may pioneer, but rarely have the tenacity to capitalise on their leadership position. Typical of these are inventors whose ideas are marketed by larger firms.

Those with high self-belief and low optimistic curiosity have few radical ideas of their own, but are adept at making ideas work when they have been proven by others. Typically, these people market the inventions of the above inventors.

Wacky companies and their leaders are high in both attributes. They have the enthusiastic innocence to wonder what lies around the corner and the confidence to find out and to make the most of their discoveries. 'What are we waiting for?' is a common phrase, both in their board rooms and at operational levels.

That, or something equivalent in Swedish, is probably what IKEA CEO Ingvar Kamprad said after a group of his managers spent about two weeks in Shanghai and Beijing. For Kamprad, it was all he needed to launch IKEA products into the vast Chinese market. 'We don't ask so many questions before we start up things,' says Jan Kjellman, head of IKEA's Swedish division where the international design team is located. 'We launched the Swedish Cottage range without any market research, but the customer liked it very much.'

Kamprad's philosophy is that no amount of marketing analysis could ever ascertain what customers want as well as his executives can from observation, from visiting stores and understanding customers.

His gut feelings aren't always bang on – business started off slowly in North America before IKEA adjusted its designs to match larger new world living spaces, but overall the method (or lack thereof) has worked, helping the IKEA empire expand ten-fold in two decades.

This 'go for it' approach is common among wacky leaders. So sure are they of their philosophy, their values and their intuitive understanding of their customers that they'll happily take leaps into new situations that other companies would analyse to death.

Ben Cohen, for example, has always trusted his taste buds – even though they are, strictly speaking, kind of faulty. A sinus problem means he can't taste and smell very well. Says former Ben & Jerry's CEO Fred Lager, 'He had great instincts about what would and wouldn't work, and we relied almost exclusively on them. We never did any demographic studies or test marketing of a product before we rolled it out. If Ben thought it was a good idea and I didn't raise any insurmountable financial or operational objections, we'd do it. And he never let concerns about costs of goods sold distract him during the creative process. If it tasted great, Ben figured we'd make money on it.'[3]

Joe Boxer's Nicholas Graham has sold millions of dollars worth of clothing over the last ten years, but he doesn't do any market research. Instead, he says, he designs what he wants. And a good thing, too. Research – and common sense – would have killed Joe Boxer's first underwear design, a pair of tartan boxer shorts with a (removable) racoon tail, but Macy's Department Store sold out in two days. Graham knows who his customers are and he gives them what they want: 'Our customers are fun seekers; they like to have fun,' he says.

Australian entrepreneur Brett Blundy launched a whole retail chain based on a street corner conversation. Leaving a sportswear trade show in the US, Blundy was, he recalls, 'mobbed' by four fashion-conscious teenage girls who wanted passes to the industry-only show. 'These girls were the epitome of streetwear fashion,' he says. 'I told them they could have our passes if they talked to us for twenty minutes. So we sat in the gutter outside the trade show, talking about fashion, brands, music and so on.'[4] Based on that information, he went on to launch Australia's most successful music retail chain.

Blundy and leaders like him have the curiosity and self-belief necessary to drive such leaps into the unknown. What makes these leaps possible, however, is the company's culture and systems. Wacky companies have both a willingness to try the new and untested, and a solid framework of values. The two elements are shown in figure 8.2.

The spirit of adventure is a measure of how much freedom and leeway a company allows its people to experiment and innovate – as

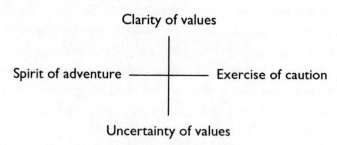

Figure 8.2 How wacky companies make leaps into the unknown

evidenced by its flexibility and attitude to mistakes. The clarity of values is a measure of how clearly, widely understood and accepted the company's values are.

Most of our wacky companies operate in the top left quadrant, where people are both willing to take risks and are firm in their understanding about which risks are worth taking. The two elements work together: a high level of consensus between leaders and employees about the company's basic purpose and direction enables the company to try out new ideas quickly – and drop them just as rapidly if they don't work.

The freedom to make mistakes

The key to encouraging innovation and to moving into the adventurous side of the graph is to create an environment where employees feel they are free to make mistakes, but not such big ones that they risk the company.

If the approach sounds a little too soft, suitable for, say, advertising agencies or gift shops but not serious projects where safety or large investments are involved, think again.

Even the ultimate tough guys, working in situations where not just profits, but lives, are at stake, use this model. As US Marines Corps Major-General Michael Williams explained to a group from Computing Devices Canada, a supplier to the US military, when it comes to decision making, there's not a great deal of difference between marines under fire and managers in fast-paced businesses.

Both must learn to think and act quickly under pressure, in dangerous situations, with incomplete information.

In both situations, communication with bosses is often 'tenuous or non-existent,' says Williams. People can't always phone back to the office for direction. Sometimes the lowest ranking person is forced into a life-and-death decision.

The leadership model for the Marines is to teach people to make the right choice at the right time. Since even Marines are human, they do make mistakes, so an important part of the training is to allow soldiers to make honest errors and learn by them. When there is no room for mistakes in an organisation, says General Williams, 'that's poison. The idea that one mistake is fatal is just terrible because it breeds an adverseness to risk. It stifles innovation; it leads to micro-management . . . If every decision that you make offers you the least amount of risk, it also offers you the least gain.'[5]

Mark Brown, managing director of Innovation Centre Europe, a UK-based training consultancy, agrees: 'Mistakes must be allowed, otherwise, people tend to do what is easy, obvious and safe, and will not produce work that is innovative, ingenious, exciting or brilliant.'[6]

At VeriFone, says former CEO Hatim Tyabji, 'Mistakes have to be allowed for because the one who makes the most mistakes is me. The mistake is evaluated upon whether it was stupidity, in which case I get very upset, or whether it was a genuine mistake. Someone can do something that has huge ramifications for the company, but it will look different than if someone was careless.'

At W. L. Gore, employees have a great deal of freedom to take risks. How much of a risk to take is, says associate Jim Buckley, determined by the concept of 'Waterline Decisions'. 'If [the risk] will affect the security of the company, then seek knowledgeable help. People get to understand quickly when they should be asking for help,' he says. 'We don't like to make mistakes, but we also try not to chastise. You can't make a mistake with safety, but we are a new product development company, so we're going to have failures. Those aren't viewed as mistakes. We learn from failures.'

Gore's lattice structure works automatically to put the brakes on excessive risk taking. An individual's history of risk taking and errors will affect his or her ability to put together teams for future projects.

Some people will avoid leaders with a history of screw-ups; others will be drawn to projects involving a level of risk.

At Gore, people reminisce about the late Bill Gore, the company's founder. As associate Joe Tanner told The 100 Best Companies to Work for in America, 'Gore would let people make mistakes because he knew they'd grow from them. Besides, Gore reasoned, "Maybe it's not a mistake, maybe it's an invention."'

In fact, Goretex, the company's leading product, was discovered partly by accident. In 1969, Bob Gore, now president, was fiddling with the insulating material PTFE (the material his father had had such faith in a decade earlier), heating up rods to see if they would stretch like other plastics. They wouldn't. After days of gently tugging the rods, only to have them break, a frustrated Gore violently yanked one. To his surprise, it stretched. Further lab testing (and a road-testing winter camping trip) determined that the material was both waterproof and breathable. Gore, by trial and error, had stumbled onto an unheard of and long-sought combination – Goretex, the holy grail of technical fabric.[7]

Southwest Airlines employees also tend to be willing to take risks on the company's behalf because they know they are free to use their own judgement. 'We would rarely fire someone for just making a big mistake,' says Southwest's vice president, people, Libby Sartain. 'Though we do have a problem when people lie, cheat, steal, or don't show up for work.'

Gary Youngblood, an executive at Alagasco, an Alabama natural gas company, as part of an empowerment drive, made up a bunch of business cards and handed them out to employees saying, 'This is your "Get Out of Jail Free Card". If you try something and it fails, then you turn in this card and you're forgiven. And you see me and get another one.' Profits tripled at Alagasco in the six years after new CEO Warren encouraged greater risk taking and less of the 'utility mindset'.[8]

Richard Zimmerman, CEO at Hershey Foods since 1985, is trying to change the company's slow moving conservative culture by introducing an award called the Exalted Order of the Extended Neck. He explained: 'I wanted to reward people who were willing to buck the system – a little entrepreneurship, a little willingness to stand the heat for an idea they really believe in.'[9]

The free flow of ideas

Wacky companies seek out ideas from elsewhere – from other companies, but also from places most conventional companies wouldn't think to look.

Richard Semler, for example, had already experimented beyond the bounds of any other Brazilian company, so, for fresh ideas, he sent an employee on a world-wide fact-finding mission. He wanted to find out what other companies were doing to break through the kind of functional systems that were stifling his company's innovation.

?What If!'s consultants – called inventors – need constant stimulus if they are to avoid becoming stale. To keep them fresh, the company sends them on paid visits to other companies with a reputation for original thinking. Two inventors, for example, spent several days at the Dallas headquarters of Southwest Airlines learning from the US masters of madness. The company has also started organising conferences that bring together some of the most inventive minds around, but not necessarily business minds. Speakers so far have included Richard Noble of NASA who led the Thrust Super Sonic Car team that broke the world land speed record, and Steve Carver, who worked with Richard Branson on his original attempt to cross the Atlantic in a hot air balloon.

Patagonia employees can gain fresh insights into ecological issues by spending, on the company payroll, anything up to two months doing environmental work anywhere in the world. 'Rather than sending a cheque, we send a human being,' says public affairs director Lu Setnicka. 'The environmental group benefits and we benefit from having an employee learn more about their work.'

Ben & Jerry's employees also have the opportunity to do volunteer work in the community and be paid their normal salary for this work. Interested employees are invited to design their own community volunteer programme. Normally the programme is limited to a total of five employees performing 50 hours of community service each year, but it has been expanded in special cases.

Wacky companies also find innovative ways to keep ideas flowing within the company. Whole Foods, a teamwork-based US grocery chain, uses competition to encourage employees to seek out ideas from elsewhere in the company. Staff there have created what president Peter Roy calls 'a culture of incremental progress'. The system is based on empowered teams, intense inter-team competition and complete access to information.[10]

Empowered employees have the power and freedom to come up with improvements in their own store operations. Staff in each store are motivated, largely by competition, to learn what they can from other stores. Detailed sales and financial data, available to all staff, make this possible. Thus, ideas and innovations spread naturally through the chain.

Store manager Ron Megahan routinely examines printouts of the top-selling products in other stores and regions to find out what he can learn. 'This isn't rocket science,' he says. 'I want to see the products that are moving in another region.' CEO John Mackey puts it another way: 'If you don't cross-pollinate, you become a hick.'

At the Dyson factory, everything including engineering, design, production and servicing is done under one roof – an arrangement that CEO James Dyson believes encourages the cross-fertilisation of ideas.

Dyson, like many other innovative leaders, recognises how valuable it is to have staff, especially creative staff, actually talking to one another; that ideas arise and flow in conversations in a way they just don't in e-mails, memos or phone calls. He's also recognised that some of the best inspirations come from chance encounters.

They've always known this at W. L. Gore & Associates. Says associate Jim Buckley: 'We're a culture of one-on-one communications. Our network is very fast. Associates talk about things.'

Pathfinder's Brian Muirhead noticed this too: 'We used all forms of electronic information exchange, especially e-mail and voicemail. It all helped, but something special happens with face-to-face communication. Chance encounters while just walking down the halls often resulted in valuable insights. I'd ask how things were going, and someone would launch into a story about a potential problem I hadn't heard about yet. There were a lot of times when an encounter would turn into a problem-solving session and we'd make a decision right there in the hall. Too often people hold issues or information until the next staff meeting or until they can get on the decision-maker's calendar. But when you see the boss right outside your office, it's a great opportunity to make something happen immediately.

'Just by seeing each other every day, you learn people's names, you go and have lunch, and opportunities for creativity and enhanced productivity just happen. Also, if everybody is pretty much interconnected, then problems don't get a chance to get very big without somebody else knowing about it.'[11]

Create a stimulating physical environment

Many wacky companies, especially those whose businesses depend on a rapid flow of ideas, arrange their workspaces to make chance encounters happen.

Michael Bloomberg runs an international news service as well as radio and TV networks in New York. He likes pandemonium, but with a purpose. 'It may seem like chaos, but every single thing that goes on here is carefully planned. Like an explosion,' he told *Fast Company*.[12] What looks eccentric and chaotic to the casual observer has actually been carefully designed to create the best possible environment for staff interaction, face-to-face communication, and the quick flow of ideas.

First, the elevators only open on one of the office's six floors – that ensures everybody has to come in and out of work the same way, and are thus bound to see and talk to each other and to share information – the lifeblood of the media business. Staff members reach the other five floors via a spiral staircase, where they are, again, bound to bump into each other. Everyone, even Bloomberg, wears a nametag with the first name writ large. There's free food and coffee in the food court, too. It's a nice perk, but Bloomberg's main motivation (as is IKEA's with their in-store restaurants) is to make sure people don't leave; that they keep their ideas circulating within the building. Staff are also given purposely crammed workspaces, averaging four square feet each. 'I like to see people brimming over with ideas, all over the guy next to them,' Bloomberg says.

An extreme use of the chance encounter principle is the innovation campus or compound, where people don't just work together, they also live, play and study in the same space. This is what Acer CEO Stan Shih has in mind with his $8 billion project called Aspire Park – a futuristic technology park under construction in Taiwan. Once it is completed in 2010, about 10,000 employees will work, learn, play, and live there, and – Shih hopes – create an Asian software industry. The idea, according to *Fortune* magazine, is to let creative sparks fly, to let people work in an environment like Silicon Valley, where kindred souls can inspire each other and create great software.[13]

Besides designing workspaces that keep people moving and talking to each other, many wacky companies go out of their way to create environments that are conducive to relaxed, creative work. Others look as if they're trying to generate chaos; still others look as if someone let a toddler get at the design plans. But, whether it's to spark ideas or just to keep people happy, they're all designed with a purpose. In every case, the philosophy of the company permeates the physical design of the workspace.

Geraldine Laybourne, CEO of children's TV network Nickelodeon, thrives on ideas. And she knows how to keep them coming. Since 1980, Laybourne has turned a business employing five people into one with 300 staff, over $300 million in revenues and access to 60 million American living rooms.

Laybourne designed her New York office building as an ideas factory. She got rid of the corner office, but she also got rid of most of the right angles – creating a mix of oblong, oval and pinwheel shaped rooms, some with tilted walls. There's a pyramid reaching three stories through the middle of the building. Corridors have chalk and cork boards, so staff can write ideas down wherever they may strike.

'I'm a spatial dyslexic. I'm always taking detours, which probably makes me a good producer of children's television,' she maintains. It's a good thing her staff agree. Says vice president Anne Kreamer: 'When things operate on planes and grids, invention is squelched.'[14]

Doug Hall runs RSI, or Richard Saunders International, a creativity consultancy near Cincinnati, Ohio. His headquarters, a three-storey Victorian country place called the Eureka! Mansion, is something of a creativity play pen.[15]

Client groups, including reps of such marketing giants as PepsiCo and Nike, pay five times the standard consultants' rate to come here for intensive multi-day brainstorming sessions, and for the RSI guarantee: Hall promises they'll come up with 30 commercially viable ideas in three days at the mansion. He does come through – according to *Inc.*, the average American home has 18 products or services that Hall helped develop. He's so confident of this that, with one client, Celestial Seasonings, he waived his fee in return for a share of the gross profits resulting from the ideas.

Hall's method is based on structured brainstorming exercises, a playful atmosphere, and a lots of sensory stimuli. For play, the mansion is equipped with water guns, teddy bears, helium balloons, arcade games, jukeboxes playing up-beat rock 'n' roll, and nurf bazookas (so clients can bombard each other with foamy balls).

Upstairs, a storage room called the stimulus library is stocked with every imaginable brainstorming bit of stuff: toys, fasteners, odd looking products, things with bizarre textures, things to pick up, look at, play with, smell and compare. These sensory stimuli, Hall finds, are invaluable in triggering ideas.

Hall's brainstorming sessions cover all the senses. The food, for example, is deliberately a cut above most corporate catering. 'If corporations would double their food budget, they'd get more than double their return on investment,' says Hall.[16] Eating is inspiring, as is wandering around, having fun or doing just about anything but sitting at one's desk.

During Doug Hall's ten years at American consumer goods giant Procter & Gamble, he found he got better ideas wandering about the neighbourhood than he did sitting in a conference room.

?What If!'s Dave Allan and Matt Kingdon had much the same experience. When they left consumer goods conglomerate Unilever to start their own innovation consultancy, Allen and Kingdon realised that their best ideas came to them when they were away from the office, often at home. So, in designing the ?What If! offices, they set things up so they could feel more at home in the office. They created a climate for innovation by banishing standard office furniture and instead decorated their North London office with armchairs, rugs and fun touches like a foosball table.

The top floor, called the thinking zone, is the least office-like part of the building, and is meant to be the most inspiring. It's a light, peaceful and uncluttered space and a computer and phone free area, where the only concession to technology is a TV and video concealed behind an antique lectern.

Helsinki cleaning company SOL also designed its offices to be homey but, in this case, the setting is more that of a town than a house. SOL's headquarters, in a renovated film studio in Helsinki's industrial area, are known as SOL City. The central design, arrived at after extensive consultation between Joronen, her staff and the architect, is based on a cityscape. The walls are painted a vivid red, white and yellow – some in the style of building facades. The open plan area, with a lofty ceiling decorated as a starlit sky, conveys a sense of being outdoors in a city plaza. The building is divided up into themed 'neighbourhoods'. One area looks like a tree house, another like a marketplace with a small fountain. There are also areas that loosely correspond to a dining room, a living room, a kitchen, and a patio, decorated with comfortable sofas or outdoor furniture, as appropriate. The result is a bright, expansive interior that looks, and feels, a lot like a home, or a hometown.

Into the heart of wackiness

IDEO is the largest industrial product design firm in the world. Its teams of designers, psychologists and eccentrics create about 90 new products a year, and are widely regarded as among the most innovative wackos operating today.

With a client list that includes Xerox, Motorola, British Airways, Black & Decker, Hewlett Packard, Nike and Shell, IDEO people have been involved in such diverse projects as helping create the very first Apple Computer mouse and the design of the 25-foot mechanical whale in the 'Free Willy' films.

Founded in 1991, the company has a turnover of around $50 million, and 350 employees and nine offices around the world. We spent a day at their London offices to see what the ultimate innovative workplace really looks like.

European director Tim Brown, one of 45 staff based in Camden Town, London, has some unsettling news for those who like their workspaces tidy. 'Above all else,' he insists, 'innovation requires a willingness to embrace chaos. It means giving rein to people who are opinionated, wilful and delight in challenging the rules.'

'It demands a loose management structure that does not isolate people in departments or on the rungs of a ladder. It needs flexible workspaces that encourage a cross-fertilisation of ideas. And it requires risk-taking.'

Despite intense pressure and tight deadlines, the company maintains an air of creative anarchy, which it believes is the ultimate environment for innovation. Staff are encouraged to play at work, and if there are any rules at all, they're there to be broken.

Along with the last word in computer imaging, IDEO offices are literally strewn with cardboard, foam, wood and plastic prototypes. Staff work wherever they happen to be and scribbled notes are scattered all around. To the untrained eye, it may look like a chaotic mess. But David Kelley, the company's 46-year-old founder and front man, describes the firm as 'a living laboratory of the workplace'. 'The company is in a state of perpetual experimentation,' he said. 'We're constantly trying new ideas in our projects, our work space, even our culture.'

The company epitomises the chemical soup organisation described in Chapter 3 (Dismantling the Organisation). All work is done by project teams which form and disband in a matter of weeks or months. There are no permanent job assignments or job titles.

'If a client wants to know what someone's job title is, we'll give them a job title. But people change their roles so often and wear so many different hats that job titles are fairly meaningless,' explains Rosemary Lees, an employee in the London office.

IDEO management also believe that designers, in particular, benefit from seeing the work and cultures in other offices for themselves. Staff go on six-month secondments to other offices – and are also free to transfer themselves to another location if they can find a colleague prepared to switch.

But it is the company's special approach to brainstorming which has attracted the attention of other firms. These sessions have been elevated almost to the status of a science. Typically, project leaders call a brainstorming session at the start of a new assignment. People are invited to attend, and most sessions involve a multidisciplinary group of around eight participants. (Attendance is voluntary, but refusal to take part is frowned upon.)

Once the brainstorming starts, participants can doodle or scribble on almost anything – there are whiteboards on the walls, and conference tables are covered in white paper. Low tech is accompanied by high-tech in the form of multimedia presentations using video and computer projections.

To ensure the best results, the firm's five principles of brainstorming are displayed on the walls:

- Stay focused on the topic.
- Encourage wild ideas.
- Defer judgement.
- Build on the ideas of others.
- One conversation at a time.

The aim is to create a whirl-wind of activity and ideas. Speed is essential to the process, with the most promising ideas being developed and worked up into prototypes in just a few days. To make brainstorming more effective, the company has also developed a special type of camera copier which photographs whatever drawing and scribblings emerge from the sessions.

But even the firm's brainstorming rules need challenging. According to Tim Brown, there is a danger in formalising any aspect of the innovative process. 'Having a process is useful,' he says, 'but it's a delicate balance between process and innovation. You have to be very careful that you don't end up with a system that squeezes out the innovation. It's no good if you crank the handle and you know exactly what is going to come out the other end. You also have to be prepared to fail a lot. The great thing about a prototype culture like ours is that we have lots of spectacular failures. We celebrate that.'

THE BOTTOM LINE _____

▶ Many of the most useful innovations occur because people didn't know it couldn't be done.

▶ Different principles stimulate different approaches.

▶ A spirit of adventure, combined with clarity of values is what stimulates original solutions.

▶ Who can innovate in an unstimulating environment?

Notes

1. Kevin Freiberg and Jackie Freiberg, Nuts! *Southwest Airlines' Crazy Recipe for Business and Personal Success* (Orion Business, 1998).
2. Fred Lager, *Ben & Jerry's: The Inside Scoop — How Two Real Guys Built a Business with a Social Conscience and a Sense of Humor* (Crown Publishers, New York, 1994).
3. Fred Lager, *Ben & Jerry's*, 1994.
4. Neil Shoebridge, 'Sanity's Cool-for-Kids Drives the Competition Crazy', *Australia's Business Review Weekly*, 25 May 1998.
5. Donna Korchinski, 'Marines Whip Managers into Shape', in *The Globe and Mail*, 17 July 1998.
6. Margaret Coles, 'Crazy Ideas Can Solve Problems', in *The Times*, 28 April 1998.
7. No author, 'Present at the Creation: Gore-Tex', in *Outside*, October 1997.
8. Robert Levering and Milton Moskowitz, *The 100 Best Companies to Work for in America* (Doubleday, New York, 1993).
9. Robert Levering and Milton Moskowitz, *The 100 Best Companies*, 1993.
10. Charles Fishman, 'Whole Foods is All Teams', in *Fast Company*, April/May 1996.
11. Brian Muirhead and Price Pritchett, *The Mars Pathfinder Approach to Faster-Better-Cheaper* (Pritchett and Associates, 1997) (www.pritchettonline.coml).
12. Nancy Hass, 'The House That Bloomberg Built', in *Fast Company*, November 1995.
13. Brian Dumaine, 'Asia's Wealth Creators Confront a New Reality', in *Fortune*, 8 December 1997.
14. J. Fierman, 'Winning Ideas from Maverick Managers', in *Fortune*, 6 February 1995.
15. John Grossmann, 'Jump Start Your Business,' in *Inc.*, May 1997.
16. John Grossmann, 'Jump Start Your Business', 1997.

9 Staying different

'Keeping it crazy is going to be a challenge, but we've been all right so far.' (Joe Boxer CEO, Nicholas Graham)

'Being different has always been the cornerstone of our success. Being ourselves catapulted us into the spotlight. If the more we grow the more we become like everyone else, we'll have lost a big edge.' (Mitch Curren, Ben & Jerry's info queen)

'The number one threat is us! We must not let success breed complacency, cockiness, greediness, laziness, indifference, preoccupation with nonessentials, bureaucracy, hierarchy, quarrelsomeness, or obliviousness to threats posed by the outside world.' (Southwest CEO, Herb Kelleher, in a letter to employees)[1]

In late 1995, seven years after he had completely dis-organised his company into a state of productive chaos, Oticon CEO Lars Kolind sensed something was not right. The business, a Danish hearing-aid manufacturer, was dangerously close to being organised again. So much of the employees' time had been devoted to the development of one new product line that the temporary teams had assumed an air of permanency; the ever-shifting spaghetti organisation was gridlocked.

Kolind, who is also known in the company as the king of chaos, fixed this by exploding the organisation in a different direction. He re-arranged projects geographically in the building based on their deadlines. Under the new system, technology and support functions were moved to the first floor. The second floor became the new home for teams involved in product development and other medium and long-term projects. Short-term projects moved in upstairs. The result, Kolind reports happily, was 'total chaos'.

Organisation, bureaucracy, convention and normality are ever-present threats to wacky companies. Just as water finds its own level, the natural tendency for organisations is to become more bureaucratic and conventional with time. Without care, attention and regular shake-ups, they risk becoming gridlocked, and losing their essential wacky flair.

The treats to valuable difference arise in many ways but particularly from growth, new management, international expansion and imitation. Perhaps the biggest of these is a wacky company's own success. Many companies find it difficult to maintain their small company character when they get big enough to need an organisational chart.

Too big, too fast

So many wacky companies become, quite literally, the victims of their success. Those that rely on an underdog or little-guy image to appeal to customers and employees have the most to lose when they join the ranks of the big guys.

Starbuck's, a US coffee shop chain, is a case in point. It began in the mid-1970s with a few Seattle area outlets offering the kind of neighbourly feel and European coffeehouse atmosphere that was, until then, missing in American cities. Starbuck's set itself up as a good employer too, and a good customer – trying to do its best for everyone from plantation workers to counter staff. So cosy, so personal, so *nice* was Starbuck's that it quickly became one of the fastest growing companies in the world, at one point opening a store every day somewhere in North America.

Unfortunately, it's hard to like a big company, and even harder to be a likeable big company – especially one still resting on its counter-culture laurels. So, even though Starbuck's practices haven't changed significantly, its sheer size has made it unpopular in some quarters. Some community groups have resisted the opening of new shops, complaining the big chain pushes out more characterful local cafés, and some employees, like shift supervisor Lori Bonang, feel they've been left behind. 'They really believe they are one of the best employers around. The company was built on very strong principles, but somehow they have grown too fast and have forgotten us.'[2]

A similar sentiment is felt acutely at Ben & Jerry's, where managers and employees have long struggled with the conflict between setting up the systems needed to cope with the company's rapid growth, and maintaining the culture and values that fuelled that growth in the first place.

'It is more difficult to stay weird as we grow. I'm not sure its a good thing or a bad thing, but we're not as out there as we used to be,' says info queen Mitch Curren. Curren, who joined the company in 1988, has seen the changes. 'Most of us know the old days were not necessarily good, but a lot of us feel the loss of some of the community we had when we were smaller. You see people in the hallway and you don't know who they are. It's uncomfortable. Some people feel we're getting too big. That we might be losing our values focus.'

It may be hard to maintain a small company culture in a big business, but it's not impossible. The trick is to create the necessary systems without losing sight of one's core values, and to make a concerted effort to preserve the essential parts of the company's original culture.

Ben & Jerry's main cultural defence weapon is communications. 'In the early days, you'd just yell,' says Curren. Now the company tries to maintain its sense of community through a company newspaper, The Rolling Cone, and video display terminals in the break rooms flashing company news throughout the day. The company also shuts down production every six to eight weeks for two-hour, all hands meetings. Much of the information disseminated at these meetings is one-way, with managers (often Ben and Jerry themselves) letting people know what's going on in the company. Much is two-way as well, with employees having a chance to give feedback.

'We actually can talk to Ben and Jerry, and they tell us what's going on. They're very informative and help us know what's happening,' says production line worker Julie Labor. At other organisations, she says, she didn't even know the company leaders' names. 'They probably were just sitting at home collecting a paycheque. I don't know. I never saw them.'[3]

Former CEO Fred Lager describes these meetings as 'a means through which we preserved and passed on the company's culture, values and operating philosophy'. An important part of the culture that management sought to pass on, says Lager, 'was an irreverent attitude that questioned traditional assumptions about how things had to be done'.[4]

This may go part of the way toward explaining how some meetings ended with top management performing belly bouncing contests, or why board meetings were often held without an agenda, while board members floated in Ben Cohen's swimming pool.

Some companies, rather than struggling to stay wacky in the face of growth, choose to limit, or even reduce their growth. Patagonia's Yvon Chouinard, for example, never wanted his company to grow as big as it did. During the late 1980s, however, his designs became fashionable. Patagonia clothing (called Patagucci in some circles) became as much a fashion statement for the environmentally appearance-conscious as necessary equipment for those actually venturing into the outdoors. 'We outgrew our loyal customer base and increasingly were selling to yuppies, posers, and wanna-bes,' he complained. 'These people don't need this shit to get in their Jeep Cherokees and drive to Connecticut for the weekend.'[5]

By 1991, Patagonia sales had reached $100 million. At that rate, Chouinard calculated that the company would reach a billion dollars in sales by 2002. He didn't want that to happen. Not for the reasons apparent to his accountants – that the company's runaway growth, excessive hiring and indifference to fiscal reality were financially unsupportable – but for reasons apparent to Chouinard. He agreed that such rapid growth wasn't good for the company (fast growth and longevity don't, as a rule, mix in the clothing industry) but more importantly, he believed that it was not good for the planet.

He writes: 'We were growing the business by traditional textbook ways: increasing the number of products, adding retail stores, opening more dealers, and developing new foreign markets . . . and we were in serious danger of outgrowing our britches. We had nearly outgrown our natural niche, the speciality outdoor market. Our products were carried in most of the outdoor stores we wanted to be in. To become larger, we would have to begin selling to general clothing and department stores. But this endangered our philosophy. Can a company that wants to make the best quality clothing in the world become the size of Nike? Can a three-star French restaurant with ten tables retain its three stars and add fifty tables? Can you have it all? I don't think so.

Although I'd tried in the past to limit this runaway growth, I'd always failed. So now I was faced with the prospect of owning a billion-dollar company, with thousands of employees making outdoor clothing for posers. I needed to do some soul searching so I could reconnect to my original philosophy of simplicity and quality.'[6]

Things didn't get simple right away. By 1991, a recession in the US meant that sales fell flat, inventories built up and profits fell dangerously. So, in the summer of 1991, just shy of its 20th anniversary, Chouinard threw Patagonia into hard reverse, laying-off 20 per cent of the workforce and cutting 30 per cent of its product line.

'Going back to a simpler life based on living by sufficiency rather than excess is not a step backward; rather, returning to a simpler way allows us to regain our dignity, puts us in touch with the land, and makes us value human contact again. Technocrats tell us we can't go backward and that a company must keep growing otherwise it will die. If this is all true, then we are doomed,' says Chouinard.[7]

Patagonia's was a hard, even painful, way to protect a company's values from the dangers of growth. Others choose instead to maintain their wackiness by controlling growth from day one – either by keeping their units small or by finding ways to help the culture grow with the company.

Some opt for the amoeba approach. As described in Chapter 3 (Dismantling the Organisation), these companies, notably Virgin and Semco Brazil, keep their culture safe from big company bureaucracy by breaking up large units whenever they grow beyond a certain size.

Others preserve their culture by growing in a planned, controlled way that prevents dilution. Southwest Airlines is strict about this, valuing its culture above all else. The airline expands (with some exceptions) into just one or two cities a year so that it can devote the necessary time and attention to transplanting the culture in each new location.

Maintaining the culture is a priority for CEO Herb Kelleher: 'The bigger you get, the harder you must continually fight back the bureaucracy and preserve the entrepreneurial spirit. Sure, you need more disciplines and more systems, but they're adjuncts. They are not masters; they are servants. You've got to keep the entrepreneurial spirit alive within the company, no matter how big it gets.'[8]

Vice president, people, Libby Sartain admits it's not always easy, especially in a company where a quarter of all employees joined in the last two years. 'It was really easy when we started, because everybody knew each other, but we've grown very quickly in the last few years so we have to work very hard to keep the culture and environment the way we want it to be,' she says.

In 1990, Kelleher instituted a culture committee, one of the company's few long-standing committees; it involves about 120 people from all levels of the company and is charged with keeping the culture alive.

Some of the culture committee's sub-groups include the freedom team, whose job it is to keep people informed about the freedoms they enjoy as Southwest employees, from the freedom to wear casual clothes and fly home free, to the concept of empowerment and the freedom of knowing their jobs are secure. 'We're so busy loading and unloading planes every 20 minutes we have to be reminded of these things,' says Sartain.

The seven-year itch committee looks at causes, and possible cures, for employee burnout. 'It does happen,' says Sartain. 'It's not Nirvana here. You can't work as hard as we do and not get tired. That's where the fun, freedom and feeling appreciated for what you do comes in – it helps relieve the burnout.'

Though the company works hard to maintain its style, no one wants to preserve every detail, she adds. 'The culture has changed and evolved over time. It's an evolutionary process. We don't, for example, have flight attendants wear hot pants anymore – it's just not politically correct these days. And we don't always jump out of overhead bins. Most of our flights are too full now. As we move on and adapt, the culture evolves. But it's the same at heart.'

Management at US grocery store chain Whole Foods, who have plans to grow the chain from 43 stores to 100 by the year 2000, maintain their unique culture the same way they make yogurt or sourdough bread: start each new batch with a dab of the old.

When Whole Foods opens a new store, it assigns veteran employees to key roles at the new location; staffing each new store with about 30 per cent existing employees.

Says president Peter Roy: 'It's not the size of the company that creates the feeling. It's the core values. You can't dilute it too quickly.'

International expansion: the perils of other cultures

Dilution is even more of a risk when companies attempt to recreate their culture outside their home turf. Sometimes wackiness just doesn't travel well.

Ben & Jerry's international expansion has been lacklustre – though to be fair, their out of country scoop shops have been up against everything from the collapse of the Soviet Empire to the vagaries of the Canadian Milk Marketing Board. In Britain, despite coining the national catch phrase of the decade (note to Tony Blair: 'Cool Britannia' started life as a Ben & Jerry's flavour), Ben & Jerry's has yet to make much of an impact. Both Taiwan's Acer and the UK-based Body Shop suffered losses when they tried to enter the US market.

Other wacky ideas have been exported with relative ease. Gore's lattice structure, for example, appears to have worked as well abroad as it did in the US. 'Bill [Gore's] second and third plants were overseas. He was organising joint ventures in Japan when "made in Japan" was synonymous with tacky,' says W. L. Gore associate Jim Buckley.

The VeriFone virtual formula has also skipped easily round the globe – perhaps because it so rarely touches down. VeriFone people seem to be as at home with the virtual workplace in Bangalore as they are in Brisbane or San Francisco.

And nothing, one would think, could be more culturally specific than household furnishings, yet IKEA has become a global phenomenon, selling the same Billy bookcases to families in Oslo, Toronto and Taipei. With only a momentary blip from a misunderstanding of Americans' furniture buying needs (big, big, bigger), the expansion rolls on.

Why the difference? Ben & Jerry's wackiness lies in its politics, which don't travel well. Its popularity in America is rooted in its history as an upstart, rebellious, hippy company, famous for supporting causes, like gun control and voter registration, that are radical in America but mainstream, or even irrelevant, elsewhere.

The same goes for its working practices: benefits, like maternity leave and medical insurance, that seem generous in America are commonplace elsewhere. All Ben & Jerry's really had to export, besides its off-beat marketing, was its conventional new self and a product that, while good, isn't inimitable. The Body Shop's North American experience was almost a mirror image of Ben & Jerry's European escapades – the cosmetics company's fame as a pioneering environmental crusader was strictly home grown. Overseas, the Body Shop was just another natural cosmetics store.

The wackiness at Gore and VeriFone, by contrast, lies in their structure and working practices, and that's something that can, with care, be exported. IKEA's lies in its product design, its prices, and the shopping experience it offers customers. Most significantly, all three of these companies had no parallel even at home, so they weren't attempting to impose their national style on others.

Imitation: what happens when others catch up?

Wacky companies are pioneers. They forge ahead, take new risks, and are often dismissed or ridiculed by more cautious business people. Inevitably, though, others copy their successes and, in time, what was once outrageous becomes mainstream.

'Our model of business is becoming the norm,' says VeriFone's Hatim Tyabji. 'And people who laughed at us are now following. People thought we were a bunch of loonies, that it was some kind of social experiment, but now they see our track record and they're following us.'

VeriFone is still out front. Other formerly wacky companies have, however, lost their wacky edge. Not because they've changed their behaviour, but because others have caught up.

San Francisco-based garment maker Levi Strauss, for example, pioneered casual dress at work and many other management practices which were considered wacky at the time, but have now become commonplace. The company, though it hasn't changed its practices, even lost its position in the book The 100 Best Companies to Work for in America as the factors that once made it an outstanding employer have became ordinary, and other companies are doing more exceptional things.

Most wacky companies, though, make an effort continually to push the boundaries of the way they work and by extension, the way everyone works.

Nor are they too worried about being copied. In fact, many are quite happy to pass their knowledge on. Ricardo Semler is inundated with managers from all over the world visiting Semco Brazil on fact-finding field trips; Paul Hawken is a major feature on the college and business lecture circuit; and Ben & Jerry's factory is the biggest tourist attraction in Vermont. SOL's Liisa Joronen says her first order of business when she launched her company was to explain to the business community what she was trying to do: 'I spent that spring speaking very much. I was like a religious priest explaining the SOL philosophies,' she says.

Patagonia has even encouraged others to copy its product innovations. In 1993, the company, working with its suppliers, developed a fabric called PCR Synchilla made from recycled plastic bottles. 'We could have patented it,' says spokesperson Lu Setnicka, 'but we chose not to. Instead we marketed the heck out of it, hoping to encourage other companies to use it.' Patagonia is also encouraging others to use organic cotton. Management would rather have more manufacturers using organic products than have the marketing edge to themselves.

Not everyone is quite so generous. Ben & Jerry's, for one, have to work hard to keep ahead of imitative competitors eager to keep up with their new flavour concoctions. 'There are new knock-offs of our flavours constantly, so we have to innovate all the time,' says info queen Mitch Curren. 'Once people started to notice us, they started to copy us. Now, the minute we do something new, it's not long before it's copied.'

If Ben & Jerry's are concerned that someone may steal a march on their Jalepeno Nut Crunch, they're not at all troubled by others nicking space on their moral high ground. Like other companies that focus on social responsibility, they're pleased to see competitors supporting social causes, however self-serving their motives may be.

'One of our goals is to spread the idea that you can run a business responsibly and make money at the same time. We hope one day businesses will be judged not just by their financial return, but also by their social return. We hope they don't copy. We hope they take that info and tweak it to fit their own organisation,' says Curren.

The idea is spreading. Socially responsible business practices – or at least the use of social responsibility as a differentiating factor – is becoming more common on both sides of the Atlantic.

The concept, sometimes called 'Cause Marketing', was, by 1997, the fastest-growing segment in the US advertising industry. That year, about 800 companies belonged to a San Francisco-based group called Business for Social Responsibility, and American companies spent about $500 million for the rights to sponsor various social programmes, from research on AIDS to support for local fire departments.[9]

It appears there's gold in those good intentions. A 1997 survey by Cone Communications and the Roper Group found that 76 per cent of consumers said they would switch to a corporate brand or product that supports worthy causes, provided the price and quality were on a par with other goods. That's up from 66 per cent in a 1993 study.[10]

Pioneering socially responsible companies, like the Body Shop and Ben & Jerry's, may see some of their competitive advantage reduced as more companies join them on moral high ground, but most don't mind. If anything, they're glad to have some company on the firing line.

Having stuck their heads above the parapet, these trailblazing companies have become easy targets for critics. The Body Shop, for example, was pilloried in the press for, inadvertently, failing to follow some of its own animal testing policies. In 1993, Ben & Jerry's were accused by competitors of pursuing the same restrictive practices they had so charmingly campaigned against in the doughboy campaign years earlier. 'People have it ingrained in their heads that if they buy Ben & Jerry's all the monkeys in the rain forest will have trees,' says Chuck Schiffer, a retailer who sued after the company cut off his supply of ice cream. 'Corporately, they're absolutely vicious.'[11]

Says Craig Cox, editor of *Business Ethics* magazine: 'Once you raise the bar and urge business as a whole to raise its standards, you paint a bull's-eye on your back. The press will watch closely for signs of hypocrisy.'[12]

Body Shop's Anita Roddick has experienced this personally. 'You create a legend or a myth around the business. But the press ultimately grows bored with you and starts looking around for deficiencies. You have to expect you'll be held up for rigorous examination. This is not for the chicken-hearted.'[13]

New management – values at risk

Besides time, growth and imitation, a major threat to a wacky company's character is a change of management. As we saw in Chapter 6 (Wacky Companies Need Wacky Leaders), the loss of a leader can mean the loss of a company's vital eccentricity. Even with a carefully chosen successor and continuity of ownership, a change at the top can, and usually does, irrevocably change a company's style and spirit.

With a change of ownership a change in culture is almost inevitable. This is why we were saddened to see so many of our original sample attract the attention of acquisitive conglomerates: Chiat/Day merged with TBWA and was acquired by agency holding company Omnicom in 1995; VeriFone was acquired by Hewlett Packard in 1997, and University National Bank and Trust, the wacky little Un-bank described in Chapter 1, was acquired by Comerica Bank-California in 1996. In each case the CEO chose not to stay on.

Sometimes an acquisition happens with no warning – as with the software company whose spokesperson said in mid-interview, 'Sorry, gotta go now, we've just been acquired.'

It's too early to tell what will happen to the more recently acquired companies. Mehta Mehling, a spokesperson for VeriFone, assured us that the new Hewlett Packard-appointed CEO Robin Abrams 'is going to keep a lot of Hatim's [Tyabji's] philosophy and style'. Though how much of Tyabji's raw energy will stay with the company remains to be seen.

Comerica spokesperson (and former UNBT employee) Roberta Washburn was also reassuring, claiming that, since the bank's strategy was to grow by acquiring small community banks, 'we have tried very hard to maintain the best practices of each of those acquisitions'.

Best practice doesn't mean the same to everyone though, and it seems that any wackiness still at UNBT is largely cosmetic. 'Some of University Bank's off-the-wall habits are still there. They still have the Walla Walla Onions, and the alien stayed,' says Washburn. (Among its many eccentricities, UNBT sent a bag of sweet onions to every customer each year, and had a mural of an alien space ship on its outside wall.)

What has changed, though, are the more fundamental aspects of founder Carl Schmitt's philosophy, particularly his insistence on limiting growth and his slavish attention to customer service. During his tenure, Schmitt took great pride in getting his customers' statements out promptly, even if that meant a long night of envelope stuffing for staff members. 'We don't do that anymore. Departments do it during working hours,' says a clearly relieved Washburn. 'Carl was very much an innovative thinker,' she concedes. 'But, with innovations in the banking industry he realised he had to make some changes, and to think what was best for the bank, customers, and employees.' Schmitt, who retired after the acquisition to grow onions in Walla Walla, Washington, had little say in the new owners' policy changes.

The FI Group's Steve Shirley, by contrast, was able to pass her philosophy, if not her original working practices, on to the new management team.

During the 1970s, Steve Shirley created the first European telecommuting business, with hundreds of mainly women working from home on computer software projects. Shirley's ideals were strong and based on her own experience of trying to combine demanding domestic responsibilities and challenging, intellectually fulfilling work. Her company, FI Group, also pioneered employee ownership and involvement in decision making.

When the company reached a size where it was becoming a burden rather than a source of fulfilment, Shirley decided to appoint a successor. But she brought in a professional manager and found that the culture of the company was not going to stay the same. So she took back the reins, and her second attempt at finding a successor was more cautious, more thoughtful and much more successful. She selected someone who shared most of her ideals, but also brought big company experience. She worked with the CEO elect to develop a programme that would gradually transfer power and ownership within the organisation to the employees. When she finally handed over responsibility, there was a much stronger understanding of how the organisation would need to evolve.

The toughest part was recognising that some of the characteristics that had made FI so different would eventually have to disappear. For example, it was no longer tenable to have the majority of employees working from home. However, Shirley felt she could focus FI's ideals of liberating people in other ways – most significantly through increased employee ownership and involvement. The more ownership Shirley passed to employees, the more those ideals came to be seen in practice, with employees at all levels learning to question top management about its behaviour and how their money was being spent.

FI today is a substantial, high performing niche player in the computer outsourcing market and has retained its independence. The price it has paid has been the acceptance of a higher degree of normality. The workforce is no longer mostly female, virtually no one works permanently from home, and majority ownership by the employees has given way to the capital demands a large company inevitably creates for itself. Yet, because Steve Shirley made such an effort to keep the company's original values alive, FI retains a unique culture. Its success today is due to a considerable degree to the comfort client companies feel in entrusting their people to an organisation with such a strong track record for looking after its own employees.

Sadly, it seems everyone must eventually change with the times. Morgan Cars, the British auto maker which resolutely refused to adopt production line methods and continues to this day to build its cars one at a time, largely by hand, is finally having to change its century-old methods to gain more access to the US market.

Morgan, whose sports cars are much loved by collectors, knew a thing or two about the value of scarcity. According to *Car & Driver* magazine, 'Morgan made sure that production was always a few steps behind. Indeed, in the UK today, the company takes a bloke's order with a modest deposit and expects him to wait for as long as six years before the company gets around to building the car. Few companies can get away with that – and Morgan recognises that it cannot do business in America that way.

'But (whisper this) – a gentle revolution has now begun. Annual production has already increased, from 430 cars five years ago to 470 in 1997. The ancient factory – more like a 1930s' roadside garage – has been reorganised with a kind of flow line. It used to take 37 days to make a car; it now takes 24.'[14]

Many collectors would find this change more tragic than progressive, but every company, wacky or otherwise, must adapt to change at some point in its life. Like Morgan Cars and the FI Group, each must determine how to adapt its character to cope with the new environment.

Broderbund Software faced a similar challenge. Founded in 1980 by brothers Douglas and Gary Carlston and based in Novato, California, this maker of educational and games software enjoyed market leadership and 80 per cent margins throughout the eighties.

Broderbund's reputation as a hot bed of creativity and its track record as a leader in developing innovative games enabled it to attract the best and brightest talent and keep that reputation intact. In the gaming industry, you are only as good as the talent you can attract and keep.

In the early nineties, however, a flood of competition cut both market share and margins and, in 1996, new CEO Joseph P. Durrett introduced tight new cost controls. Now employees were under pressure to meet deadlines, and every creative decision was held up to the financial light. As Harry Wilker, senior vice president for product development, said at the time, 'Now every creative device has an economic question. Can you sell this? Can it be merchandised?'[15]

Broderbund management had to find a way to keep the company's essential creative flair alive while running a much tighter ship. Fortunately, management discovered that the techniques they'd used to foster creativity in the past – such as recruiting the best talent, trusting them to do good work, encouraging communication, and recognising that good ideas can come from anywhere if you let them – function just as well in cost-conscious environments as they do in free and easy ones.

The company continued to operate that way, valuing their creative people and giving them a fair degree of leeway. However, Broderbund's competitive situation meant that managers were also charged with applying some new control mechanisms, such as ensuring every project had a blueprint, setting and checking on each project at specific stages in its development, and being prepared to shake up or, where necessary, kill stalled projects.

One veteran software engineer was surprised to find that creativity, if anything, improved under the new constraints: 'People have to do more with less. It makes you *more* creative because, for instance, you have to improvise. By pitching in, we learn more about what each other does. I learned on one product, for example, how bad the off-the-shelf digital video tools were and I only learned that because I pitched in to help. Once I learned that I was able to write better, customised ones.'

And, like other wacky companies, Broderbund recognises that money − beyond a fair wage − does little to motivate creative workers. Broderbund staff are paid competitive salaries, but most enjoy the work so much they've done it at some point in their lives for free. 'Most of the people in this industry, outside of the few stars, are not primarily driven by economics,' says Wilker. 'Making good money is important to them and they are well paid, but that is not what drives them.'

'It's not really work when you watch cartoons and play with things instead of doing boring accounts receivable all day,' says one software engineer. The best thing about working at Broderbund, or any wacky company for that matter, he says, 'is that you never really have to grow up'.

Like Broderbund, most IT companies face such a skills shortage that they find they are competing with each other not so much for customers as for new recruits. This has made for some fascinating changes in management practices. Every IT manager already knows that to keep their business alive they must attract good people. Now they're discovering that to attract good people, they must behave more like a wacky company.

We knew this was an established trend when we revisited the most rigidly controlling business leader we had ever come across. Ross Perot, the far right failed US presidential candidate, ran his company EDS like a military academy until he sold it to General Motors.

His new company, Perot Systems, shows little trace of the boot camp style. In fact it looks much like any other IT company. What happened? Perot had no choice but to lighten up. The young university graduates needed to run the company aren't the sort of people who normally warm to Perot's neoconservative, xenophobic policies, so the company has been forced to change its spots to attract the workforce it needs.

An article by Jim Champy, chairman of Perot Systems Consulting Practice, even advises IT companies to 'loosen up', and to do just what wacky leaders have been doing all along.[16] In fact, his advice, suggesting that employers

- jettison overly controlling practices regarding dress, travel, hours and office recreation
- understand young grads' concern for social issues
- provide the freedom to let them experiment with independent projects
- create a highly collaborative environment
- give them a financial stake in the business, and, above all
- value their contribution and tell them so,

reads just like a blueprint for a wacky company. What does this prove? Wacky will out. Eventually, even the most rigid organisations will see the value of doing it different.

THE BOTTOM LINE _____

▶ Professional managers always want to 'cure' the wacky company – they recognise no sanity but their own.

▶ Rapid growth attracts professional managers – so develop barriers to keep them out.

▶ Society, and the business community, will catch up eventually. Accept the inevitable gracefully and be flattered by it.

▶ Remember that it's easier for competitors to catch up if you allow your principles to be diluted. Wacky company leaders spend most of their time fighting 'normalisation'.

NOTES

1. Kevin Freiberg and Jackie Freiberg, Nuts! Southwest Airlines' Crazy Recipe for Business and Personal Success (Orion Business, 1998).
2. Lee Moriwaki, '"Unstrike" at Starbuck's', in The Seattle Times, 25 May 1997.
3. Jennifer J. Laabs, 'Ben & Jerry's Caring Capitalism', in Personnel Journal, November 1992.
4. Fred Lager, Ben & Jerry's: The Inside Scoop — How Two Real Guys Built a Business with a Social Conscience and a Sense of Humor (Crown Publishers, New York, 1994).
5. Edward. O. Welles, 'Lost in Patagonia', in Inc., August 1992.
6. Patagonia Web site, http://www.patagonia.com.
7. Patagonia Web site.
8. Kevin Freiberg and Jackie Freiberg, Nuts!, 1998.
9. Daniel Kadlec, 'The New World of Giving', in Time, 5 May 1997.
10. Daniel Kadlec, 'The New World of Giving', 1997.
11. Carolyn Friday, 'Cookies, Cream 'N Controversy,' in Newsweek, 5 July 1993.
12. Anne Murphy, 'The Seven (Almost) Deadly Sins of High-Minded Entrepreneurs, in Inc., July 1994.
13. Anne Murphy, 'The Seven (Almost) Deadly Sins of High-Minded Entrepreneurs, 1994.
14. Ray Hutton, 'Morgan makes a serious comeback', Car & Driver, April 1998.
15. G. Rifkin, 'Competing Through Innovation, The Case of Broderbund', in Strategy and Business, Second Quarter, 1998.
16. James Champy, 'Seven Ways to Court Computing's Hottest Grads', Computerworld, 11 June 1998.

10 How to drive your company insane

So here you are. You want to set up your own decidedly wacky company from scratch; or you want to convert an existing, hidebound, traditional organisation – company, division, department, even work cubicle – into one with genuine character. Where on earth do you start? After all, since every wacky company is by definition unique, there aren't any well-trodden paths to pursue. The advice that follows isn't meant to be prescriptive (if you truly have what it takes to become a wacky leader, you'll want to develop a set of ground rules all of your own). Rather, this chapter aims to set your mind to work on some of the critical questions you'll need to ask yourself along the way.

On balance, it will usually be a lot easier to start anew, putting your ideas into practice in a virgin enterprise, than to attempt to convert an existing one, say wacky leaders like Gore's Jim Buckley. 'Don't try to change an existing company,' he advises. 'It's a hard thing to do, unless it's small and everybody has bought in. Some have tried, but when the going gets tough they've reverted to the command and control mode that they are familiar with.' Certainly, very few of the wacky companies we have found have evolved out of long-established traditional organisations. Even SOL, which was originally part of a long-lived family business, only developed its sense of character when it was relaunched as an independent new venture.

There are notable exceptions, however. BC Ferries' Route 40 is a remarkable example of a purposefully wacky department within a conventional organisation; Birse Construction introduced wackiness into an established company in a highly conservative industry; and young Ricardo Semler brought radical change to his formerly bureaucratic family business.

Radical changes in culture are possible, with the right leadership and an acceptance that:

- many – perhaps most – of the people who have served the organisation faithfully for years will leave, voluntarily or otherwise. You may make new friends, but you'll make a lot of enemies on the way
- to the burden of developing new ways of doing things, you will also have to add the task of undoing all the old systems and attitudes. And you'll expend a great deal of energy preventing people from backsliding
- while the owner-entrepreneur can forgive his or her mistakes and expect employees to forgive him or her, too, the corporate innovator must always keep one eye on the wolves outside the door. It is not uncommon for a holding company to see temporary setbacks as evidence of failure and an opportunity to remove an irritating anomaly. The business will only absorb your personality if you are around long enough to make it happen.

If, like Route 40, the wacky venture can survive all these minefields, it has the capacity to influence the entire organisation. Customer service manager Marie Graf reports: 'Yes you can have a wacky company within a more conventional company, but it's infectious. We've already got a hit on our hands and it is starting to filter through to other routes.' In 1998, BC Ferries hired native artists to give on-board craft demonstrations on another route, and executives met with community liaison committees along the coast, listening to their needs. It remains to be seen, however, how much of the substance and philosophy of Route 40 can be transferred with these behaviours.

So, don't give up if you are determined to buck the odds and take on the challenge of converting a conventional organisation into a wacky one. It can be done.

If you still think you could become a wacky company leader, then consider these questions:

Question 1: Do I care enough?

To build a really different enterprise demands passion and commitment. Most people complain about things they don't like in the companies they work for – things they regard as silly, petty, short-sighted, wrong-valued or commercially obtuse. Some go so far as to make suggestions about how things could be done differently. A few have the intrapreneurial guts and skill to work within the organisation to bring about changes they care enough about. But it is a rare bird indeed who is prepared to put their own money where their mouth is, alongside most of their time and mental energy. Wacky leaders know that is what they want to do and they sink everything into making it happen. They are more likely to be self-financed too – it's difficult to get conventional backers on board with a wacky idea, and most wacky leaders aren't prepared to make the sort of compromises that are called for when using other people's money.

Doing it differently invariably means swimming against the tide. You need the commitment to explain what you mean over and over again, to people who never seem fully to understand; the thickness of skin to ignore criticism and not get bored with the sound of your own voice; an absolute conviction that you are right; and the stamina that keeps you goading and pushing in pursuit of your vision when most people would have packed it in long ago. You need, in short, to be just a little bit mad.

In ordinary companies, you often see signs on the wall reading 'You don't have to be insane to work here, but it helps'. At wacky companies, it is almost a condition of employment that you do have to be insane, because you can guarantee that other people – competitors, bank managers, investment houses, even the guys who clean the windows – will ridicule what you do.

Even when you are successful, they will still seek to dismiss your achievements as fluky. You have to care sufficiently strongly about the way you think the business should be run that you take no notice. Once self-doubt or compromise set in, the game is lost.

Question 2: What do I care enough about?

What exactly is it that you care about to put yourself and others through such heartache and to pursue with such zeal? How would you describe to the unconvinced exactly what the difference is in the way you would do things? Why should they care? You don't get passionate about something and keep your thoughts to yourself. So use discussions with other people to refine and define what the difference in your business will be. Their reaction will tell you a lot, especially if you consider where their responses are coming from. An enthusiastic response from someone whose values you respect is worth more than one from someone whose values you distrust. A thoroughly negative response from someone steeped in traditional ways is probably a good indicator that you are on the right lines.

Some other, related questions you might consider are:

- Am I driven primarily by the idea, or by the opportunity to make money?
- How do my beliefs about business fit with my broader beliefs about people and society?

If what really turns you on is cash at the bottom of the balance sheet, then now is the time to admit it to yourself. We haven't found a wacky company yet where the leader was obsessed by money. Their obsessions are built around issues of people and products. Money alone just doesn't have the driving force of a powerful personal philosophy or a desire to change the world. If money is your motivator, you'll likely stop when you've made enough, far short of the heights aimed at by most wacky leaders.

To really care about a business philosophy, to devote yourself entirely to it, requires more than an intellectual commitment. It also requires that you have strong, emotional commitments to a number of personal values, outside the world of work. These might, for example, be in the way people should behave towards each other, in the responsibility we have to the environment, or in how society should be more effective in including people on its margins. If you see the business as a vehicle for demonstrating and advancing these values, you are already half way to becoming a wacky leader. If you feel that this isn't the role of a business, you will never achieve more than superficial differences against the competition.

Question 3: Is there a real difference here?

Remember here that differences have to be big enough and deep enough to create a long-lasting character difference between your venture and its competitors. So you might further consider:

- Is what I propose a deep-seated philosophical difference, or simply a difference of style?
- Will the difference be expressed in many, many ways or just a few?
- Is my product or service so fundamentally different from my competitors' that I won't need a big marketing budget to emphasise the difference? That is, am I selling something genuinely, and obviously, different?
- How easy would it be for competitors to copy the substance and spirit as well as the packaging of what I am trying to do?

If it's only a shallow, marketing difference, go back to the drawing board or accept that this will only provide a temporary, short-lived competitive advantage. A genuine wacky company is built around a philosophy that affects everything – from product packaging to the appearance of premises; from the way decisions are made, to the kind of things people say. That's what makes the formula so difficult for others to copy. And the product differences are so obvious to consumers that big marketing budgets won't be necessary. Consumers will find it for themselves.

Question 4: Where will I find my fan club?

Given that wacky companies all reflect the character and beliefs of their founders, it is critical to build around you a group of people – directors, employees, customers, shareholders, and so on – who like you and your ideas. Seek out people who understand what you are trying to say and who empathise with what you are trying to do, but don't look for clones of yourself. You'll need people who have the skills and experience you lack and who are willing to speak their minds and tell you where you've gone wrong. Demonstrate to them in small ways that your methods work, gradually building their commitment and loyalty. Recognise and reward their contribution (in your own unique way).

The fan club is important for many reasons. It provides support when self-doubt looms. It builds into the fabric of the organisation sufficient people who think along the same lines as you do, to take the decisions you would have taken and to monitor what other people do, keeping it in line with the philosophy. With few exceptions, wacky companies have evolved with a partnership at the top – long-lasting friendships between two or more co-entrepreneurs, or between a single figurehead and a circle of trusted executives. If there is one most common reason why potential wacky companies do not achieve their potential, it is because the founder fails to infect an inner circle with sufficient enthusiasm and shared belief.

Question 5: How will I sustain the difference?

Deliciously wacky as the organisation may start out, as it gets bigger, it is very likely to lose the difference. For example, the unique restaurant, with its quirky chef, usually translates poorly into a large chain. Wacky companies find they have to exert constant vigilance against creeping corporatism – the pressure to emulate large companies by creating structures and departments to deal with issues that arise out of size.

The more you allow the company to absorb structures, systems and practices found in conventional companies, the greater the pressure to modify crucial characteristics that make your organisation truly different. If you begin to lose the visible signs of difference, in time the values and philosophy begin to fade as well because they are not being expressed and practised.

If you care enough, you will find ways to sustain the difference – for example, by keeping operations small or by sticking to controlled, sustainable growth by constantly checking that the values are being applied, by hiring only people you can trust to behave in accordance with the values. Because you care, you will innovate here as well, constantly looking for ways to reinforce the way the business and its people behave. You will, in particular, stop to think through what you are in business for, and compare what you see in the business against your conclusions, much more frequently than the conventional CEO might do.

Question 6: How will I sustain the fun?

The simple answer is 'take fun seriously; take it personally'. It's too important to delegate to anyone else. After all, if you aren't enjoying yourself, how do expect other people to? (At one New York firm we know, employees scrupulously avoid the lifts that went to the directors' floor at the top of the building, because who wants to start the morning with a ride with someone in authority who looks so darned miserable? People thought 'What could be going so badly that he looks so glum?', and it affected their whole day!)

So, if you agree that fun is a crucial part of your business philosophy – even if your business is funeral parlours – maybe the following advice will help:

- Hire fun people. As Southwest Airline's vice president, people, Libby Sartain advises, 'Make sure you only hire people who share the vision. As soon as you have someone who doesn't share that, who doesn't care about fun, you're going to lose it.'
- Don't ever take yourself too seriously. Resist the temptation, as you become more successful, to become more dignified. Anything that sets you apart from your co-workers makes it more difficult for them to align with your values.
- Make site visits an excuse for people to let their hair down.
- Be prepared to admit your mistakes and laugh about them.
- Be prepared to help others admit their mistakes and laugh with them.
- Legitimise fun; give it a budget and make that the last budget to be cut in hard times. (Conventional companies make fun the first thing to cut, but hard times are when you need fun most.)
- Don't take yourself too seriously. (Yes, we just said that, but it's important.)

Question 7: When can I start?

You probably already have. Wacky leaders think about their business philosophy and values, consciously and unconsciously, for a long time, before they really understand what they need to do. The commercial opportunity is simply a chance to put those ideas into practice.

Many people have the capacity to become entrepreneurs. Far fewer have the desire or ability to build businesses with unique character. If you are one of the latter, you didn't need to ask this question anyway.

*   *   *

Having read this book, and the advice in this chapter, the greatest compliment you can pay the authors is to ignore the lot! Go out and create a business in your own, utterly personal, obstinate way. Throw away the manuals and rule books. Ignore conventional wisdom. Do it your way. Do it different.

Index